ON THE
ROOF OF
THE WORLD

Tower Face at Laddow Rocks in the Derbyshire Peak District, 1920s

ON THE ROOF OF THE WORLD

EDITED BY RICHARD NELSSON

guardianbooks

Published by Guardian Books 2009

2 4 6 8 10 9 7 5 3 1

Photo credits

Frontispiece: Tower Face at Laddow Rocks: by permission of Rooke Corbett/Rucksack Club; p. vii
Pumori: by permission of John Beatty; p. 1 Charles Pickstone with Joseph Gentinetta: by permission of
S.L.Pearce/Rucksack Club Archive; p. 7 The cave at Laddow Rocks: by permission of Rucksack Club
Archive; p. 19 Geoff Pigott and friends: by permission of Eric Byrom/Rucksack Club Archive; p. 31
Mount Everest and Nuptse: by permission of John Beatty; p. 47 Harry Kelly climbing on Laddow Rocks:
by permission of Rucksack Club Archive; p. 63 Hayfield mass trespass on Kinder Scout: Manchester
Evening News; p. 69 Peter Harding: by permission of Ernest Phillips/Rucksack Club Archive; p. 89 The
Stonnis Club: by permission of Jim Perrin; p. 103 John Menlove Edwards: by permission of Jim Perrin;
p. 107 Trekkers in Nepal: by permission of John Beatty; p. 119 Tenzing Norgay and Edmund Hillary ©
RGS; p. 135 Stanage Edge: by permission of John Beatty; p. 151 Derek Walker and the Towers of Paine:
Guardian News and Media; p. 165 Chugima La above the Gokyo Lakes: by permission of John Beatty;
p. 179 Chris Bonington by Don McPhee: The Guardian; p. 191 Ron Fawcett: by permission of John
Beatty; p. 197 Joe Brown & Jim Perrin: by permission of Jim Perrin; p. 223 The Old Man of Hoy:
by permission of John Beatty; p. 253 Lynn Hill: by permission of Greg Epperson

'Mecca of Climbers' and 'Ten Years After Everest'
by permission of A P Watt on behalf of James Morris

First published by Guardian Books in 2007 under the title
The Guardian Book of Mountains

Guardian Books
Kings Place, 90 York Way
London N1 9GU

www.guardianbooks.co.uk

A CIP catalogue record for this book is available from the British Library

ISBN 978-0-85265-120-9

Designed and set by seagulls.net

Printed and bound in Great Britain by CPI Bookmarque, Croydon, Surrey

CONTENTS

PREFACE

Perhaps it's the shared northern roots that have played a crucial role here – Manchester's great liberal newspaper, and the centrality of that city to the story of British climbing? Whatever the reason, both in its previous incarnation and under the present, less specific title, the *Guardian* has managed, over a century and more, to maintain a close and informed relationship with a mountaineering community notoriously (and often justifiably) suspicious of the mindset and misapprehensions of the press. In consequence, its tradition of accurate and balanced reportage of mountain matters and personalities is unparalleled in British journalism.

If you seek to understand why this remarkable association between a sporting interest and a newspaper has developed, you don't need to ponder long. From CE Montague by way of Patrick Monkhouse, Alastair Hetherington and Roger Alton to Ed Douglas – the paper's current mountaineering correspondent and surely the finest young mountain writer of the present time – *Guardian* essayists, reporters and obituarists have themselves been passionately involved in mountain activity. I remember Roger Alton at the end of my rope on a fierce little climb in Snowdonia roaring and pleading for pity and strength and knowledge as he hesitated to launch into a crucial move. And then, suddenly, having made the move, he found himself calm, in balance, curiously happy. I like to think there's the image of a proper approach to writing about mountains in that. The ones who know nothing fuss and yell; those who have moved into position, who have given themselves to the experience, can reflect upon it calmly.

There are plenty of anthologies of mountaineering literature, stuffed with subjectivity, beset with all the fractious and internal perspectives that bedevil every sport. None of them manages to do what this little book achieves, which is to combine both a celebration of a century in the sport's history with an educated and objective record of the public's perception of it through that time. It starts with a few scrambles on those delectable outcrops of millstone grit that rise from the Staffordshire moorlands at the southern extremity of the Peak District; it ends with an ascent of the marvellous Orkney sea-stack, the Old Man of Hoy. In between, you'll encounter characters, controversies, ascents of the world's great peaks, ethical shifts, media outdoor extravaganzas, fond old reminiscences, reviews of the defining literature of climbing, the advancing extremities of performance on British rock, and more tragedies, surely, than accrue to any other sport. Through all of which, for a hundred years, the *Guardian* writers have maintained their scrupulous, mediating and insightful gaze.

Jim Perrin

INTRODUCTION

Tucked away in the basement of the *Guardian*'s Farringdon Road office, amid discarded filing cabinets and broken air-conditioning units, is the paper's old cuttings collection; shelves full of manila folders bursting with press articles, some many decades old. In the pre-online days, this was the *Guardian*'s archive and it was the librarians' job to maintain it. As a young recruit to the department, I would look for excuses to go down into this dusty world and then head straight for the Climbing and Mountaineering file. Here, I would linger over dramatic accounts of first ascents, profiles and obituaries of extraordinary climbing personalities and reports of controversies dogging the sport.

The history of British rock climbing is usually thought to have begun in 1802 when Samuel Taylor Coleridge, leading light of the Romantic movement, made the first recorded rock climb having descended Broad Stand on Scafell in the Lake District. It was during the mid 19th century, however, that the idea of climbing mountains for pleasure became widely accepted, with groups of wealthy British climbers and their local guides scaling all the major Alpine peaks. This golden age of Alpine climbing culminated in the first ascent of the most dramatic peak, the Matterhorn, a 4,478m rock pyramid in Switzerland, by a party led by Edward Whymper in 1865. After an accident on the descent, in which four climbers died, Alpine exploration went quiet for a while. It was revived by books such as Leslie Stephen's 1870 mountaineering classic, *The Playground of Europe*, a series of essays on the author's fearsome climbs in the Alps that was to influence generations of climbers.

British Lakeland crags were generally viewed as mere preparation for the Alps. However, in 1886, Walter Parry Haskett Smith climbed Napes Needle, a 21m-high rock pinnacle on the side of Great Gable in the Lake District. This was a climb simply for its own sake rather as part of an ascent, and by the late 19th century the concept of climbing on small outcrops of rock purely for pleasure began to gain in popularity. Traditionally, routes up rock faces had followed lines of least resistance, usually big cracks known as chimneys and gullies. Now people began to venture onto the rock walls and slabs between the cracks – much more technically challenging.

The social makeup of climbing began to change too. While the golden age of Alpinism had been driven by moneyed professionals and the leisured upper class, the 1890s were to see the emergence of a domestic climbing scene, populated by members of the burgeoning middle classes. This new type of climber might have aspired to grand tours in the Swiss Alps, but they were more likely to practise their sport on weekend trips to the Lake District or an afternoon on one of the gritstone edges of Derbyshire. Climbing clubs were formed, with wider social profiles than the existing Alpine Club which, having been established in 1857, was still an archetypically mid-Victorian institution: it described the new breed of climbers as 'chimney sweeps'. In Manchester, for example, the Rucksack Club was formed in 1902, mainly for business and professional men to 'facilitate walking tours and mountaineering expeditions'. While ladies, as they were always referred to, had been climbing since the middle of the 19th century, most clubs were all-male affairs. The Fell

& Rock Climbing Club did have a mixed membership but it wasn't until 1921 that the Pinnacle Club, an all-female group, was formed.

Against a background of domestic growth in rock climbing, exploration of the world's highest peaks continued. In 1852, Radhanath Sikhdar, who worked for the Grand Trigonometrical Survey of India, discovered what he thought was the highest mountain in the world. Five years later this was confirmed and, despite it already being called Chomolungma by the Tibetans and Sagarmatha by the Nepalese, the British decided to name this mountain Everest after Colonel George Everest, head of the survey (who was rather embarrassed by the honour). Once discovered, it was inevitable that climbers would want to reach the top of what Whymper would in 1894 proclaim 'the third pole'.

Unfortunately, the two countries surrounding it, Tibet and Nepal, were closed to foreigners. However, in 1913, John Noel, a British army officer, disguised himself and made a clandestine trip into Tibet. He got to within 40 miles of Everest, the closest a westerner had ever been. His thrilling accounts on his return to Britain aroused interest in sending an expedition but the events of 1914 intervened. After the first world war, three expeditions headed to Tibet, with two attempts at the peak. The final one, in 1924, perhaps the most famous expedition to the mountain, resulted in the disappearance of George Mallory and Andrew Irvine and left the still-unanswered question of whether they were the first people to make it to the top.

Edmund Hillary and Tenzing Norgay's success in 1953 as part of a British expedition was undisputed. Following this, large expeditions with scores of porters to transport equipment and Sherpa guides began to conquer all of the world's highest peaks. But by the mid-1970s, mountaineers started to reject this way of climbing, opting instead for lightweight, 'Alpine-style' expeditions, where they carried everything themselves. A decade later commercial expeditions appeared, offering the chance for anyone fit and wealthy enough to climb the world's highest peaks.

Back on the crags of Britain, rock climbing had begun to change in the 1930s, and working class climbers began to appear in the

3

postwar years. Climbers such as Joe Brown and Don Whillans took climbing standards to new heights with bold, technically difficult routes. Over the following decades more and more people from all backgrounds began to climb and, with technological advances in safety equipment, standards kept on rising.

Throughout its history, the press had covered mountaineering with relish. The sport offered drama and tragedy, along with great pictures and larger-than-life characters. Following the Matterhorn disaster in 1865, the *Times*, while giving it plenty of coverage, queried the whole point of such a pastime, asking 'Is it life? Is it duty? Is it common sense? Is it allowable? Is it not wrong?' and publications such as the *Illustrated London News* and the *Sphere* regularly published dramatic mountaineering pictures. Jan Morris (then writing as James) accompanied the 1953 Everest expedition as a reporter for the *Times*, and in the 1990s most of Fleet Street devoted pages to the death of Alison Hargreaves on K2.

Naturally the *Guardian* covered most of major climbing events and landmarks, but from the 1890s onwards it also offered a much deeper and more intimate type of climbing reportage, something that became apparent as I began to unearth articles using the paper's mighty indexing system. This venerable enterprise, dating back to Victorian times, involved every reference to a subject being indexed in copperplate writing in dozens of leather-bound volumes, although thankfully it was changed to index cards in the 1930s.

The *Guardian*'s connection with the sport started around the beginning of the 20th century, when the paper was something of a clearing house for all the latest rock climbing developments. News of new routes on the crags of Manchester's Pennine hinterland, the Lake District and North Wales were first reported on the pages of the paper, often before making their way into published guidebooks. Leading articles, the editorial column where the opinion of the paper was expressed, were full of advice about climbing technique and areas to go, as well as comment and criticism about the climbing matters of the day. No other newspaper was providing quite the same coverage at the time and this respect for the mountains has continued right up to the present day.

4

The fact that the paper was based in Manchester, and so close to the birth and development of British climbing, was crucial to this reporting. The *Manchester Guardian* had been founded by John Edward Taylor in 1821 as a weekly paper in the liberal interest, becoming a daily in 1855. CP Scott became editor in 1872 and under his direction the provincial paper achieved national and international recognition. 'Manchester' was dropped from the title in 1959 and, a few years later, most of the editorial departments moved to London.

However, the physical location of the title counts for little without the influence of editorial staff who actually decided what went into the paper. Throughout its history, the *Guardian* has had on its staff keen climbers and mountain-lovers. CE Montague, a leader writer and essayist on the paper from 1890 until 1925, was a keen alpinist, and two of Scott's sons, Laurence and John, both climbed. Patrick Monkhouse, later to become deputy editor, chronicled Peak District climbs and walks during the 1930s and Alastair Hetherington, editor from 1956 to 1975, was a dedicated fell-walker. In recent years, the then arts and features editor Roger Alton played a part in promoting all aspects of the sport into different sections of the paper. Finally, running through the pages for over a century like a well-used, but trusted old rope, has been the Country Diary, a space of around 300 or so words dedicated to the outdoors. In particular A Harry Griffin, and latterly Tony Greenbank, ensured a regular climbing presence on the paper's pages from 1951.

This fine climbing pedigree has resulted in the paper having a rich, and at times idiosyncratic, archive of mountain-related journalism. In selecting these pieces, I've aimed to cover key climbing and mountaineering events as well as trace developments in standards and social changes within the sport. The book is arranged in chronological order, from 1897 to the present day, with the extracts in each chapter concerning mountain activity from a particular decade.

However, this collection is by no means a definitive history of British mountaineering. Reflecting the paper's regional roots, there is a heavy emphasis, at least until the 1960s, on climbing in the north of England and in particular the Lake District, with less material on North Wales and Scotland. Beyond this, the vagaries of the newspaper business means that sometimes mountain triumphs have been, at best, relegated to a short paragraph, while there are no mentions of climbing notables such as Colin Kirkus or Ron Fawcett.

It is worth remembering that these pieces have been written by journalists whose skill is in making complicated subjects accessible and above all, interesting for the general reader. With this in mind I've chosen articles that approach the subject from different angles, rather than being purely about the actual act of ascending rock or ice. Thus, Tony Greenbank's account of lowering a Morris 1000 van down a steep, ice-covered road or Peter Lennon's tale of a Hungarian house painter scaling the Eiffel Tower sit side by side with reports of the latest exploits in the Himalaya.

I would like to thank Lisa Darnell and Helen Brooks of Guardian Books, Jim Perrin for writing the preface and the book's copy editor, Amelia Hodsdon. Thanks also to Roger Alton, Ed Douglas, Tony Greenbank, Jim Markwick, Jeannette Page, David Rose, Martin Wainwright and Robert White for their help and suggestions.

In researching this book the following librarians and archivists have been extremely helpful: Yvonne Sibbald at the Alpine Club; Dr James Peters at the John Rylands University library; Mariam Yamin, Nicole Schulz and Gavin McGuffie (formerly) at the Guardian's Newsroom archive; Dr Jonathan Westaway at the University of Central Lancashire; the Pinnacle Club's Margaret Clennett; the Rucksack Club's Gordon Adshead; and last, but certainly not least, Guardian News & Media's brilliant research & information department.

I must thank Jonathan Wilkinson, Tim Wilkinson and Philip Nelsson, who over the years have dragged me up things; and finally, Fiona Strang for her patience and support.

CHAPTER ONE

A TUSSLE WITH GLOVES ON

High on the western flank of Black Hill in the northern Peak District is Laddow Rocks, an exposed outcrop of rough gritstone. Few visit here now but 100 years ago it was one of the main arenas for those at the cutting edge of the nascent sport of rock climbing.

One of the first to start exploring, and excavating, these cliffs was a certain Dr EA Baker, a librarian at Derby's Midland Institute who was to later write a 10-volume history of the English novel. At the beginning of the 20th century, Baker was a regular contributor to the *Manchester Guardian*, writing up accounts of climbs not just in the Peak, but in places as far apart as Arran and Wales. Writing about his excursion to Laddow, he described the place as being 'in a pristine state of dirt and disrepair' and his articles gave a unique glimpse into what it must have been like to put up routes on virgin rock. In 1903 he produced the classic guidebook *Moors, Crags and Caves of the High Peak*.

Other climbers, such as JW Puttrell, wrote about new routes in Wales and there were also reports from Sondmore in Norway, the Alps and expeditions to the Himalaya. The *Guardian* prided itself on being a newspaper for like-minded people and an indication that these pieces were more than just vanity projects is illustrated by the story of the writer and climber GT Ewen. On a trip to Laddow Rocks he came across J Anton Stoop, a Swiss climber working in a Manchester shipping office, stuck in a crack halfway up a route, clutching a *Guardian* article and 'trying to find out whether he was on the route described'.

That a newspaper could dedicate so much space to what was a minority sport was down in part to the presence of CE Montague, the paper's chief leader writer under the editor CP Scott. A keen mountaineer and alpinist, Montague urged his readers to get out into the northern hills; he promoted the benefits of holidays in the outdoors and celebrated Alpine mountaineering – while at the same time deflating the pretensions of its grandees. His writing had a strong regional theme, often drawing parallels between Manchester's 'suburban mountain range' and the Alps.

Charles Edward Montague was born in Ealing in 1867 and after attending the City of London school he gained an exhibition to Balliol College, Oxford. Here he was exposed to mountaineering by the educational theorist Richard Lewis Nettleship and by attending the classics reading week held each Easter at the famous Wasdale Head Hotel in the Lake District. He did his first major climb in 1891 and from then on climbed whenever he could, as, according to his biographer, Oliver Elton, 'More than anything except war, climbing satisfied his thirst for adventure.'

Montague joined the *Manchester Guardian* at the age of 23 in 1890, the first of a new wave of editorial appointments made by Scott. Five years later, Scott became a Liberal MP and Montague was promoted to chief leader writer. In effect he was acting editor and wrote many of the leaders, including those during the Boer war.

Montague's life was to become further linked with Scott when in 1898 he married the editor's only daughter, Madeline. She was a climber too and the high point of their year was a month-long holiday in the Alps or Italian Dolomites.

There were other climbers in the Scott clan. John, Scott's second son, climbed in the Lakes and his one identified contribution to the paper was a Letter to the Editor on a climbing accident. A true romantic, one of his wedding presents to his wife was a pair of climbing boots. The eldest son, Laurence, who had joined the paper in 1902, was an indefatigable mountaineer and a member of the Rucksack Club. It was not unknown for Laurence, after working all day on the paper, to catch the midnight train to the Lake District and then cycle through the night to a crag so as to be able to start climbing early the next morning. That evening he would be back on the Manchester train in order to be ready for work the next day.

Laurence also took a keen interest in recent climbing developments so when the *Rucksack Club Journal* printed a photograph of someone attempting one of the hardest climbing problems of the day, the ferocious cave crack at Laddow, he had to go and see it for himself. Unfortunately the picture was a fake, but when he discovered the truth, Scott was keener than ever to do it as the honour and integrity of the club was at stake. Alas, he failed and it wasn't conquered until 1916.

Scrambling on the Roaches

❊ JANUARY 15 1903 ❊

There is nothing in Derbyshire so closely resembling a miniature range of mountains as the Roaches, the lofty gritstone ridge that dominates the borders of smoky Staffordshire and supports a group of rocky peaks within full view of the chimney-stalks and dingy warehouses of Leek. We have here a bit of real highland scenery – cliffy hill-tops and heathery braes, with woods of pine underneath, and a solitude that is all the more delectable because we are only a few miles from a dense manufacturing population. In configuration this strip of country belongs by nature to the Peak; the gritstone whimsicalities of such spots as Robin Hood Stride, the Black Rocks, and Froggat Edge are reproduced here in almost exaggerated form. Geologists say that the rock is Chatsworth or escarpment grit. The traveller on the once-important coach road from Buxton sees glowering above him, on Ramshaw Edge, a grotesque succession of ghoulish faces, bovine and porcine heads, and half-finished monsters springing from the parent rock. And beyond, where Hen Cloud extends its array of pinnacles, he sees still more impossible shapes set in stone, outlines that the camera may prove to be less vertical or only slightly overhanging, but to the eye appear like curving horns, their points overweighted with threatening tons of rock.

On Hen Cloud is to be found the pick of the climbing. It is as shapely and dignified as summit as any 3,000ft sgurr in the Western Highlands; its long ridge bristles with sharp teeth, and the noble cliff fronting it is as imposing in contour, as seen against the clouds, as if its extreme height of 150ft or so were magnified fourfold. We will tackle the most prominent of this handsome set of teeth as a first trial of what the Staffordshire sgurr can offer in the way of problems. It is not a considerable climb – quite the reverse – yet not too easy. Let us call it a tussle with gloves on. For if, as is likely, the stony giant knocks you backwards, there is a thick pad of heather to fall on, with deep cushions of peat below. We get up by means of a winding fissure, which allows the hands a good grip at the bottom, and, when the corner gets too rounded for that, permits the arm to be thrust in to secure a friction-hold. This sort of thing makes careful balancing a necessity. As we transfer our weight so as to get a pull sideways, we suddenly find we have lost what grip we had and tumble back into the heather. Jumping up for a second round, we attack again with more science, and, puffing and blowing, we get a higher grip, and bestride the giant's shoulders right underneath his colossal head. The descent on the other side is quite easy.

Then we cross to Roach End, another peak of strange shape that appears to be a loose accumulation of boulders of all sizes and the most extravagant forms, gnarled, rifted, fantastically weathered, and often perched in situations that seem to defy the laws of mechanics. One enormous mass projects like a natural roof over the artificial roof of Rock Hall, a cottage built in the cliff, with a front of ashlar, and rooms partly hewn out and partly formed by nature in the rock. Until recently, one acquired the freedom of the whole wild domain of the Roaches for a summer's day on disbursing the sum of twopence sterling at Rock Hall. But a fit of insanity indulged in by some trippers who set a spinney on fire has forced the proprietor to impose great restrictions on the public. So the many are fined for the silly exploits of the few.

EA Baker

Conquest of the Matterhorn

❄ SEPTEMBER 8 1897 ❄

The *Guide to Zermatt and the Matterhorn* that Mr Edward Whymper has just published through Mr Murray is the best guide of its kind that we know, and the best chapters in it are those in which he describes again his own long siege of the Matterhorn. What was really most interesting in the ascent of the Matterhorn has always had little notice paid to it, people's attention being much absorbed by the sensational accident that took place while Mr Whymper's party were coming down the mountain after the first ascent. The conquest of the Matterhorn was a triumph of intelligent observation. For years before the top was reached, mountaineers had convinced themselves that the ascent must be made by the south-west ridge on the Italian side. Looked at as a whole, it presented a decidedly easier slope than any ridge or rock face on the Swiss side. Between 1861 and 1865 Tyndall, Hawkins, and other expert climbers devoted themselves exclusively to the Italian side, dismissing the Swiss side as impracticable. After many unsuccessful efforts, Mr Whymper began to observe and reflect on the structure of the mountain. It was composed of a series of stratified beds, like a pyramid formed of books placed flat on top of each other, each smaller than the one next beneath it. But there was more than that to take into account. De Saussure and Forbes had both noticed that the strata rose towards the north-east. It was as if some unyielding object had been placed under one end of the book at the bottom of the pile, so that each book above would in its turn be tilted up at that end. Mr Whymper made again for himself the observations made by De Saussure and Forbes, and then proceeded to think out their bearings. Clearly, a very steep slope on the north-east side would be more easily scaled than a much gentler slope on the south-west side. For, on the former side the breaking off of the strata ascending outwards would leave something like a steep staircase with each step sloping inwards, and thus giving a fine hold, while on the south-west side there would be a staircase much less steep, but made with each step sloping outwards. On the one side one would go up and down as on a ladder, on the other one would be always, as it were, on a whale's back, and apt to slip off its sloping sides. Mr Whymper acted upon these reflections, gave up the Italian for the Swiss side of the Matterhorn, and climbed it without much difficulty.

It is like a parable of the encouragement of technical education. The early attacks on the Matterhorn were like the efforts of certain British industries to overcome all competition, relying solely on rule of thumb and personal strength, vigour, and determination. Mr Whymper did what those industries could do if the employment of the available personal qualities were directed by trained and alert intelligence.

Leader

A good climb near Manchester Laddow Rocks

❄ SEPTEMBER 24 1903 ❄

Although it is not many years since the Peak and its neighbourhood became known to scramblers as an excellent practice-ground, most parts of the district have been ransacked so thoroughly that new climbs are seldom heard of. There is, nevertheless, at Crowden, between Manchester and Penistone, a series of climbs known as yet to only three or four brethren of the sport, and not yet fully explored. When, about a year ago, in a walk up Crowden Great Brook and across the wild and trackless moors to Holmfirth, I came across Laddow Rocks for the first time, there was not a nail-mark nor a cleaned-out hand-hold visible to prove that a cragsman had ever been there; and on a second visit recently, with two companions, one the well-known author of *Crag and Hound in Lakeland*, the other a photographer in quest of sensational snapshots, we found no additions to my own nail-marks and other memoranda of last year's scramble, and the stone man built on a handsome and conspicuous pinnacle remained undisturbed and defiant.

Laddow Rocks are near the boundaries of four counties – Yorkshire, Lancashire, Derbyshire and Cheshire. By nature and by position they and their surroundings of high, bare moors, precipitous edges, and savage cloughs should belong to Yorkshire or the Peak, albeit by some ancient topographical freak they have been put in Cheshire. At a height of 1,500ft above tide level the rocks surmount an abrupt edge overlooking the deep dale or clough of Crowden Great Brook.

From Crowden our crags look merely a blank wall upon the skyline. As we approach, they break up into pinnacles and projecting buttresses, with deep fissures and gullies between. An easy but not altogether safe gully was found about the middle of the crags. Some

13

greasy holds enabled us to drop onto a bridge formed by a large splinter, and a cluster of big spikes steadied us over a shattered wall, full of loose stones. Then came a water-torn section with a few holds, and a vertical pitch at the bottom. Unlike the better-known climbs of the district, which are continually being swept and garnished by parties of scramblers, the Laddow Rocks are in a pristine state of dirt and disrepair. My companions thought that a fully equipped leader should carry a trowel and besom. The loose stones are a continual source of danger, and once at least we had a very narrow escape.

Our next business was to see if a way could be made up the outside edge of Laddow Pinnacle, which I had climbed previously from the narrow neck joining it to the cliff. My friend made a good start up the narrow crack at the bottom of the cliff right under the summit, but after unavailing attempts to push and shoulder each other over the ledgeless faces, we abandoned the direct attack as a failure and took to the gully. By traversing out on the topmost ledge and looking down I could see what made the climb quite impracticable. What looked like shelves and sharp-cut edges were really rounded furrows and ridges, too shallow to afford any grip. Even the ledge I stood on was not safe. The rock was in state of rapid decay, flaking away and breaking off in lumps; one felt as if one were standing on ice. And just as I was about to clear away some of the more objectionable debris I glanced down the cliff, and there, 80ft below, and right in the line of fire, was my friend with the camera. It would hardly have given me a worse shock if I had tumbled on the rope.

One of the most striking characteristics of Laddow Rocks is the abundance of vertical joints. In many places the surface of the cliff has an air-space behind and is to all appearance on the verge of peeling away. Sometimes it has actually peeled off and left square-cut gutters, or chimneys, running straight from top to bottom. In an ill-advised attempt to climb one of the most formidable of these gutters, I found myself pounded on a rickety mass of earth and heather, and utterly unable to advance or retire without help. My friends, with great politeness and self-denial, offered me their heads and shoulders to climb down upon, but it was eventually decided that I should have a rope sent down and explore the rest of the climb. Meanwhile it began to rain. The camera was in danger; and so for 20 minutes I stood on my quivering lump of vegetation and waited for a voice from above. A shout came, and a coil of rope appeared high aloft, with a big stone whirling straight for my head. I ducked under the rock, the stone whizzed past, and then the rope-end tumbled into my hands. But the climb was an impossibility; protruding rocks cut me off on all sides, and the upshot was I had to be slung down on the rope over the last 30ft.

EA Baker

Suburban mountain range

❄ DECEMBER 26 1903 ❄

Of all the four bank holidays in the year, today is the one we towns-men have least learnt to use. At Easter, Whitsuntide, and the beginning of August, everyone now goes out of doors to kiss his mother earth and be strong again. At Christmas there still lurks undispelled in us the dread of early man for his still unbaffled adversaries, cold and rain. We stick by the fire as if in the first fruit of our forefathers' joy at learning to light one; we make as prime an aim of keeping dry as if we had only just caulked the roof of the cave. Affection and repletion reinforce primitive instinct; of all bank holidays it is the one on which most friends are seen again, and on the eve of which the truths enforced by Mr Barrie have been least regarded. Still there are some, and every year there are more, who take to the open for their Boxing Day even though there be no ice to skate on, no snow to toboggan, and no road shallow enough in mud for a bicycle to wade.

They lift up their eyes to the hills; they make, if they can, for the mountains of Wales or the Lakes; if not, they turn due east if they be Manchester men, and at the end of a morning's walk from a suburban station – Glossop, Crowden, Greenfield, or any one of half-a-dozen others – they eat their sandwiches on the tip of the ridge of the Pennine, sitting on the central spine of all England, and seeing the whole country fall away below their feet, eastwards and westwards towards the sea, and southwards to the great central English plain where our northern and western crust of stone, with all its incidents of stone-walled fields, grey cottages, and black pit-heads, dips down under the broad level sea of sands and clays that bear the wheat and hedges and brickfields.

Standing on Stanedge or Langsett Moor, you can almost see with your eyes how Cobden came to be; walking from Oldham to Holmfirth on a soft day, you may suddenly find all the separate industrial history of Lancashire and Yorkshire conveyed to you compactly in a slackening of the rain as you work past Dead Head Moss and leave behind the steep, drenched western slopes on which the ruling wind has dropped most of its taking from the Atlantic, to enter on the drier, brighter eastern slant. On these heights to which a Manchester cyclist can ride after luncheon and be back for tea, there stick out the raw ends of half the forces that have shaped England's life. You get your country's history poured in at your five senses, not merely read of in a book, but seen in the contrast of two landscapes viewed at once, or heard in the several qualities of the sound of moorland streams, or perhaps felt in the goodness or badness of the holds on a wayside rock that you stop to climb, or in the changing intervals between the drops that fall from a soaked cap to your nose as you cross a wide upland.

Of course the Pennine is no Alps. Still it is genuine mountain. South of Whernside, Ingleborough, and Pen-y-Ghent it does not achieve 2,200ft, and the Peak, its last dying effort to be high, rises but little over 2,000ft. Still it has a flora that runs to the Arctic circle; when

Manchester was under ice the Pennine rose superior to the general misfortune; it stood out and kept its ancient grit and limestone unreddened by the rising tide of geological modernisms all the time that a continuous sea was washing over Cheshire and all the southern English plain, making a strait at the gap where the London to Holyhead railway picks its way between the Peak and the Welsh Hills, and laying down the red sand from which Chester Cathedral was to be made and Fallowfield Station in the fullness of time to be scooped.

Of course, to draw these joys from our suburban mountain range you must exercise a little historic imagination. But even the most literal man can get from it authentic mountain thrill. If you put out of your head everything but what you actually see and hear, it feels very much the same to have lost your way in a big snowstorm on top of Kinder Scout and on the Grand Plateau of Mont Blanc. The Downfall, well curtained with ice, yields quite as engaging a 'pitch' as the glassed garden wall of rude construction over which you get at the peak of the Zermatt Rothhorn. The Alport Stone, the Black Rocks Crack, and the Boulder climb at Robin Hood Stride give short climbs that the wise compare seriously with at least the Gable Needle and some of the hard ways up the Pillar Rock and Scafell Pinnacle. The climber who would rather climb the other way about and in the dark as the great masters play chess, can climb down apparently delectable deep holds, by which you 'visit', like Lycidas, 'the bottom of the monstrous world'.

Leader

Satires amongst the Seracs

❄ DECEMBER 16 1911 ❄

If we may judge from the exhibition of Alpine painting and drawings now being shown at the gallery of the Alpine Club, the difficulties encountered in climbing mountains are trivial compared with the difficulties met with in painting them. In the bulk of the pictures, grim and yawning gaps are evident between the obvious intention and the result achieved. The painter in most cases 'encounters snow', and knowing not enough of the craft (of painting as applied to mountains), and being unattended by the necessary guides (the very few being engaged elsewhere), ought by all the canons of the game to turn back. But painters with insufficient experience when they attack snow are very like climbers in the same position. They are out not to be beaten. So they hack (figuratively speaking) a few ill-shapen steps, ascend by great pains ever such a little way, and then proudly build a cairn or a snowman or some other trophy. Like the inexperienced climber, they little know the danger they have been in. The members of the Alpine Club, if they encountered trophies of this kind in pursuit of their own dangerous craft, might comment caustically, but perhaps, it is as well that the hard standards of mountaineering are not brought to bear on mere exhibitions of pictures. Otherwise the practical mind of the alpinist might declare the delicate impression of Mr Pennell's *Weisshorn piercing through the mist* as decidedly dangerous, and Mr ET Compton's *Grandes Jorasses from the Grand Charmorz* as rotten – in both cases in the mountaineering sense, of course. That would be a pity, because these, with Mr Nelson Dawson's drawing of the Tourbillon at Sion and a *Woman with pails of Segantini* (here is the old hand not venturing recklessly among the peak-gobblers), are worth a waist-deep scramble over an appalling expanse of soft wet snow. For their sake, one willingly risks a symphony in the Bavarian textile style or a sonnet from the Japanese – mere crevasses, and all in the day's work.

Geoff Pigott and friends climbing Crack and Corner at The Roaches Rocks, Staffordshire

Lost in the mountains

❄ SEPTEMBER 10 1907 ❄

Mr Bernard Shaw, who has been staying at Llanbedr, Merionethshire, on Sunday went for a walk in the direction of the Rhinog-fawr, by way of Cwm Bychan and the Roman Steps. Before starting he had arranged to leave a note giving particulars of his whereabouts on a certain part of the Steps for the benefit of his friends, who intended following him. Mr Shaw, having arrived at this spot, left a card pinned on a tree: 'Gone on; please follow.' He, however, missed the right turning and wandered in the Trawsfynydd direction. The country thereabouts is most rocky and difficult to traverse. Eventually, after walking a long distance, he arrived at Tynygroes, where he put up at the village inn for the night. As he did not arrive home by 10pm Mrs Shaw became naturally uneasy and reported his absence to the villagers. Search parties were soon organised, lamps were procured, and the whole country in the vicinity was thoroughly scoured, and several men did not return from their all-night search till four o'clock yesterday afternoon. Mrs Shaw, however, received a telegram at 10 yesterday morning from her husband, who was at Dolgellau, saying he would return by the next train. When Mr Shaw arrived at Llanbedr he did not appear any the worse for his adventure. It is estimated that over 300 persons joined in the search. When acquainted with this fact on his arrival at Dyffryn station, Mr Shaw laughingly remarked 'It will do them good.'

The moral beauty of mountaineers

❄ AUGUST 1 1904 ❄

Mr G Winthrop Young gives 'Modern Climbing' a dreadful dressing-down in the August *Independent Review*. The vulgarity of his fellow-climbers oppresses him. He seems to have climbed the

Weisshorn and found on the top a 'hard-featured' lady who found fault with his manners. Anyhow, why was she there? He had wanted, we gather, 'to find wisps of the old fascination drifting on snow slope and solitary ridge'. Why was she there, marring his solitude? Or he hers, the poor hard-featured lady might say?

On these familiar occasions we are each in our own eyes the choice, fit, soul, whose pasture the others contaminate. We get our railway tickets from Mr Cook and use 'Cook's tourists' as terms of abuse; we sigh to 'get off the beaten track', and then we go to the Riffel Alp; we pine for 'the old fascination drifting on snow slope and solitary ridge', and to find it we climb the Weisshorn, or even the Matterhorn.

It strikes us that there is current a good deal of sentimental delusion about the superior moral beauty of the early mountaineers. At any rate we have no Albert Smith now to make a kind of music-hall entertainment out of Mont Blanc. Mr Young's Olympian wrath falls on the modern climber for his occasional notes, in accounts of climbs, that 'a slip here would inevitably,' etc. But what about the 'perpendicular walls' that the fathers of mountaineering were always meeting? How often did those sainted men write: 'Our situation was now critical' and 'To return was impossible'? In one sense it is fair to remember, the whole basis of their glory was shaky, compared with that of the eponymous hero of 'Binks's stomach traverse', on whom this hard and austere Mr Young pours his scorn. The world will never know precisely the shares of relative credit due, for many early Alpine first ascents, to the amateurs whose names are always associated with them and to the Swiss peasants who were their guides and who did not subsequently write books. Binks, however slangy he may be, however indisposed for general conversation, however attached to 'the one loved name' of Binks, has generally wriggled across his stomach traverse for himself. Rock climbing at home is a very genuine sport, at which you cannot buy distinction by employing large quantities of skilled labour.

And as to the annoyance caused to Mr Young and others by the minuteness of its technical details, this is surely no affair of vulgarity of ostentation or any other moral failure, but merely the necessary consequences of a decrease in the scale of operations as compared with the climbing of snow mountains. Such details as Mr Owen Jones's instructions for climbing the Gable Needle or Kern Knotts Chimney correspond fairly to the early Alpine climbers' hints for climbing snow-peaks. In the Lake mountains the whole game is in miniature; the passage of an awkward three feet in a gully corresponds to the passage of the shoulder on the Matterhorn or the ice wall on the Grand Combin. There is nothing immoral in a reduction of scale. And when Mr Young says that the modern type of the rock-climbers 'regard our beautiful English hills as so many targets whose sole interest is the size of the score we can make on them, so many bicycle tracks for record breaking,' it sounds like belated echo of the 'solemn strictures issued from the editorial mouth' which he truly says that the first mountaineers had to endure 50 years ago. Climbers in their little nests should agree. It used to be said of the founders of Alpine climbing that they regarded the Alps as so many greasy poles; now Mr Young says pretty much the same of the founders of rock climbing in England, and we fancy it is about equally untrue of both these bodies of excellent sportsmen.

Leader

A new playground for the rock-climber

❈ OCTOBER 26 1904 ❈

Whilst there are within easy reach of Manchester several good 'practice grounds' for the rock climbing enthusiast, and climbs whose degrees of difficulty have been carefully annotated, the discovery of a new field for the quest of the 'only sport that is free from vice' is not altogether a work of supererogation, especially when, as in the present instance, the vagaries of the railway can be ignored and one's 'quarry' can be reached in 10 minutes from a spot that is within easy cycling range of the city.

Bosley Cloud doubtless is well known to the ubiquitous tripper from Macclesfield, Congleton, and other industrial centres further afield. His initials are profuse and his sandwich papers not unknown upon its heather-clad sides. The Cloud is a picturesquely situated eminence rising about 500ft out of the park-like lands of Cheshire and Staffordshire. The Macclesfield–Congleton road skirts its base, and a byroad to Rudyard forms, for about a mile in length, a pleasantly situated terrace along the lower slope of its north-eastern face.

There was no record of a previous descent of the rock climber upon the place. Probably the comparative insignificance of the rocks, both in extent and height, has spared them serious attention. But none the less Bosley Cloud offers sport of no mean quality, though the quantity is limited. Several of the problems are not to be lightly regarded. Some few we solved; others completely baffled us, although we tried a little engineering and concerted action upon them. One little problem gave us good sport for the space of an hour. This, a sort of Kern Knotts Crack on a reduced scale, was a vertical slit some 30ft in height and varying from six to 18 inches wide. The start was difficult, for no sound foothold offered until one could draw one's body up some seven or eight feet from the cliff base and wedge a boot in the lower part of the crack. Beyond this the difficulties are slight until a small chock stone barring the exit is reached, but as a nerve test the climb is distinctly 'interesting', the slope of the cliff face being towards the climber and the exit entailing careful wriggling over a few small blocks that do not seem over-secure.

Two or three neat things in the shape of 'face climbs' and a short, wide chimney with a large chock stone forming a fairly difficult obstacle, occupied another hour or so. One gully, some 50ft in height, proved, even with a rope from the top, quite unworkable without moving a mass of loose rocks and taking risks that would border on foolhardiness. We concluded a satisfactory afternoon's work with a series of three traverses across the face of a huge unbroken block. The ledges, which were narrow, ran at an oblique angle, and were covered with a slimy epidermis – pretty to look upon but treacherous to the feet. Their negotiation required some care, for, whilst they are sound and afford excellent holds, there are not absent one or two sensational features.

As we adjourned to a cottage hard by to remove the grime from our persons and take a much-needed cup of tea – with accessories – we agreed that Bosley Cloud as an additional bit of practice ground for the rock climber was certainly not to be despised.

JHH

The intrepid Victorians
Advice to the woman climber

❄ FEBRUARY 12 1923 ❄

The advent of Murray's earliest handbook, published in 1838, is one of the first testimonies to the existence of the woman climber. To be sure, she appears in the guise of 'the fair traveller' and must have possessed means, for even on the mildest excursions 'when the travelling party includes ladies a guide is required to attend each'. The early-morning start of a well-equipped mountaineering party must have been a sight for the gods, for apart from feminine eccentricities, Murray, for some reason, insists on the male tourist wearing over his ordinary garb 'a blouse made like a smock-frock, and to be bought ready-made in any German town'.

By the 50s, women climbers had progressed from 'fair travellers' to 'the ladies', and about this time the market was flooded with books of travel written by women, concerned mainly with sentimental descriptive passages and feminine equipment. These are easily distinguished by their titles, which are incorrigibly romantic: *Light*

Leaves Gathered in 1859 and 1860, or, rather more definite, *A Lady's Tour Round Monte Rosa*. This was the era of the 'lady's face-mask', with which every woman was advised to protect herself.

All these books abound in advice of the 'No lady should do this' or 'No lady should attempt that' variety, and indeed it is rarely considered advisable for a woman to use her legs, judging from the number of times she is consigned 'to mule-back by easy stages'. Imagine the emotions of a modern damsel faced by this: 'It [a very easy day's ramble] would be more than a lady could attempt; but I am satisfied that it might be done by a first-rate walker.' Or this intimation about the inn on the Monte Moro Pass: 'No lady ought to complain of the inn merely on account of the roughness of its deal furniture, or the primitive character of its cookery; for without this sleeping place it would be scarcely possible for her unless she incurred dreadful fatigue to cross Moro at all.'

No pains were spared in giving the most minute details as to the complete climbing gown, and the following dress prescription was universally approved as combining usefulness and propriety. 'Small rings should be sewn inside the seams of the skirt and a cord passed through them, the ends of which should be knotted together in such a way that the whole dress may be drawn up at moment's notice to the requisite height.' Taken in conjunction with a face-mask and a warm spring day, one is inclined to sympathise with those women who considered mountaineering a doubtful form of amusement.

Wilson and the knickerbockers

❄ NOVEMBER 15 1966 ❄

My aunt and I spent the summer of 1893 at San Martino di Castrozza in what was then the Austrian Tyrol. It was there that I met and made friends with Wilson, Elizabeth Barrett's maid who took her to church and witnessed her marriage to Robert Browning.

Countless people will have seen Wilson on the stage and on the screen in *The Barretts of Wimpole Street*, but there cannot be many who knew the real Wilson as I had the good fortune to do.

Of one thing I am quite certain, no one else went climbing in the Dolomites in knickerbockers made by Wilson's own hands with the help of a pair of Pen Browning's plus fours as a pattern. The fact that Mr Browning was rather short for a man and decidedly broad, while I was rather tall for a girl and decidedly slim, made that affair very tricky.

In those days San Martino was very quiet. Only one hotel and the inn. People from Vienna stayed at the hotel. That summer Pen Browning, his American wife, and Wilson as well as the Neruda brothers, the sons of Madam Norman Neruda, the violinists, gave the hotel an almost international appearance. We had the only tiled guest room in the inn.

Every afternoon my aunt rested and I went up the valley. It was on these walks that I met Wilson. We exchanged our English newspapers, her *Times* for my *Manchester Guardian*, and though I never asked questions she talked about her past.

But the Dolomites had bewitched me – if only I could climb up among those browns and yellow, red and white rocky peaks and see them at close quarters. At last Aunt Caroline asked the chief guide, Giuseppe, if he would take me for a short walk as far as the first rocks. He gave me a long look: 'Well, with such long legs and arms the young lady should be able to climb, but I will only take her if she wears proper knickerbockers and takes off her skirt when we come to the rocks.' How on earth was I to come by knickerbockers? Lucia, the innkeeper's wife, suggested that the carrier would bring up a roll of good strong 'Loden' when he went down to town next day. And the very next day there it was, but the problem remained. Wilson solved it. 'I'll come down tomorrow with all the necessaries,' she promised.

Early next day Wilson appeared armed with pins and needles, cotton, inch tape, and a mysterious parcel. It contained a pair of Mr Browning's voluminous plus fours. We pinned them on to a length of the Loden and Wilson began pinning and measuring what she called the 'garment' and what I called my knickerbockers. At last the cutting-out began and, as if by a miracle, the front and back were ready to be tacked together. Very gingerly I put on the result of Wilson's work. 'Now,' she said, 'stand on one foot and plant the other on the table.' 'Why?' I asked. 'Because we must see whether the garment will take the strain.' It did. So all was well. Wilson went back to the hotel promising to return next day. And there she was at teatime with the finished 'garment' over one arm. No first-class tailor could have done the job better.

Take off your skirt

At three o'clock next morning, Giuseppe and I started walking up the valley with long strides. Giuseppe carried a coil of rope on one shoulder, an ice axe in one hand and a rucksack on his back. At last we were over the foothills and stopped before a large black boulder. 'Now,' said Giuseppe, 'go behind, take off your skirt, weigh it down with a stone, then we'll start climbing.' I came back feeling rather naked but quite unashamed and ready for anything.

The going was easy until we came to a large hole in a wall of rock. It looked like the entrance to Dante's inferno. While tying me to the rope, Giuseppe explained that this was 'the chimney', that at this time of the day the sides were covered with a thick layer of ice and that he would go ahead and chip hand and footholds for me. 'If you're frightened give the rope a jerk,' he ended. I clenched my teeth and made up my mind not to jerk the rope. But I was more than glad when I scrambled out at the top and sat down beside Giuseppe. 'Now,' he said, 'don't look down, keep your eyes on my feet, we'll soon be at the top.'

And there we were at the top of the world with green valleys on one side and blue lake far down on the other. Suddenly I felt ravenously hungry and tucked into the home-baked bread, the home-made salami sausage, butter, and cheese that Giuseppe unpacked from his rucksack. Close behind us there rose the stately Cimone della Pala that stands guard over the San Martino Dolomites. 'If your lady aunt will allow us another climb, I will take you up the Cimone on Saturday,' remarked Giuseppe quite casually. 'There's a way up on the other side.' All I could say was 'Oh, really.'

Next afternoon, after a picnic tea, I was carrying the tea basket home when a large jagged stone came hurtling down and hit my left arm smartly. Aunt Caroline cut away my sleeve and hurried off to the hotel to ask the Viennese surgeon who was staying there to look at my arm. 'Not broken,' he decided, 'but the bone is badly bruised.' He put on a bandage and a sling. It hurt badly, but the realisation that I should not be able to climb the Cimone hurt quite as much.

Clara Hahn

A famous Snowdon guide
Ruskin and Snowdon weather

❄ FEBRUARY 25 1911 ❄

Tom Ward, an old Snowdon guide, is about to leave the Carnarvon Union Infirmary, after resting there a few weeks to recover from the effects of a slight accident. During the 40-odd years in which he has followed the calling of guide he has, he estimates, ascended Snowdon some 4,000 times along the five recognised routes. Occasionally he struck up a friendship with several notable persons whose visits and conversations he recalls with relish. Lord Avebury he has taken up more than once, and he once had a discussion with him as to the probable age of the mountain. Ward's modest calculation did not go beyond 6,000 years. The late Lord Tennyson was another distinguished visitor whom he knew. He arrived with Lady Tennyson on a bitterly cold day, and for that reason they did not make the ascent. Tennyson, returning from a short walk around, found his lady sitting comfortably with her feet being kept warm on the prostrate form of the guide. The poet was highly amused with the idea of 'the guide's ribs being made into a footstool'. Ruskin was, however, the man who most deeply impressed Ward, who by the way, strongly shares Ruskin's contempt for all methods of loco-motion that tend to produce a 'legless' race. On the day Ruskin paid his visit, the guide, being asked his opinion of the weather prospects, said, 'Bad weather today,' whereupon Ruskin remarked, 'There is no bad weather on Snowdon; only variations of good.' In spite of his 70-odd years, Ward looks not more than 50, and his present inten-tion is to start on Monday on a walking tour of Milford.

The 'Snowdon guide', and Tennyson

❄ MARCH 2 1911 ❄

Mr E Ffoulkes writes from Llanberis: – 'Tom Ward has apparently been entertaining some visitor with his personal recollections of certain eminent men. But I believe Tennyson did not visit the Snowdon district during the period of my friend Ward's residence here. That was my impression when I read the paragraph in last Saturday's *Manchester Guardian*, and on referring to the poet's *Life* by his son, the present Lord Tennyson, I find that his last visit to Llanberis was in August, 1871 – many years before Ward's sojourn here. On that occasion the poet's wife had remained at home at Aldworth, Haslemere, and his companion on his journey in North Wales was his son, Hallam. Mrs Tennyson wrote in her diary: "Aug. 11th. A letter, English hexameters, from the travellers. They had arrived at Llanberis; a jovial party apparently in the room above theirs, in the Hotel Victoria –

Dancing above was heard, heavy feet to the sound of light air,
Light were the feet, no doubt, but floors were misrepresenting."'

THE THIRD POLE

The first world war saw a whole generation of young climbers lose their lives. In June 1924 a war memorial to commemorate members of the Fell & Rock Climbing Club was unveiled on Great Gable in the Lake District, but in time this came to represent all climbers who had died between 1914 and 1918.

The war had also stalled exploration of Everest, but in the 1920s the quest for the 'third pole' began in earnest. Not long after the cessation of hostilities the Alpine Club and the Royal Geographical Society formed a joint Mount Everest committee to plan an attack on the mountain. Despite certain differences in outlook – the climbers were keen to get up the mountain while the geographers were more interested in conducting surveys – they planned a reconnaissance trip in 1921 and an attempt on the summit the following year.

The prospect of filling in one of the few remaining blank spaces on the map caused great excitement, with the *Guardian* stating, 'It is no childish vanity to wish to make sure that British eyes are the first to look down from this supreme white watch-tower over British India.' Although the 1921 expedition was called a reconnaissance, some dreamed of reaching the summit. One of its number, an ex-Charterhouse teacher called George Mallory, complained about the weakness of the climbing team. However, they did succeed in finding a passable route up the mountain and new areas were explored and mapped.

The 1922 expedition had a much stronger team and they reached a record height of 27,200ft in the face of terrible weather. The expedition was marred, however, by the death of seven Sherpas in an avalanche on the North Col. Two years later and probably the most famous expedition to the mountain resulted in the disappearance of George Mallory and Sandy Irvine. But had they made it to the summit first? The geologist Noel Odell had seen them on the summit ridge shortly before they were enveloped in cloud and vanished.

The Everest expeditions were all-male affairs, but that is not to say that female mountaineers didn't exist. One, Emily 'Pat' Kelly, felt 'As in other walks of life, women wanted to find their own feet … and climb some things as well as a man climber.' Instead of always having to be second on the rope, ambitious women wanted to be out in front, leading. As most climbing clubs at the time were for men only, the need for an all-female club became apparent.

Kelly, wife of the eminent climber HM Kelly, put the idea to Eleanor Winthrop Young, wife of the mountaineer Geoffrey, in the summer of 1920 at the Sun Hotel, Coniston. In April 1921 they sent a letter to the *Manchester Guardian*, announcing the formation of the Pinnacle Club – the world's first true national women's club. The letter was printed and, much to their surprise, CE Montague wrote a supportive leader about it. The club was an instant success and is still going strong. The charismatic Pat Kelly died on Tryfan, North Wales, the following year, but her husband later recalled, 'It was remarkable to have the backing of a paper of such prestige, and it was gratifying to have sympathetic approval of male climbers. Most important though was the response from women.'

Aside from supporting all-female ropes, Harry Mills Kelly (always referred to as HM Kelly) was a leading climber in the 1920s, putting up a number of hard routes including the Moss Ghyll Grooves on Scafell. He also pioneered the use of rubber-soled plimsolls to climb in, rather than the traditional hobnailed boots.

The *Guardian* would always find room to report news of the new routes going up – and give space to correcting inaccuracies. There were also quirky dispatches about what to eat when out in the hills, outdoor clothes for women (a daily Women's Page started in May 1922), eerie experiences in the Cairngorms and the joys of rambling.

Actually getting onto the British hills was a major problem in the 1920s, with many fells and moors closed to the general public. The decade saw the access to mountains movement gaining in strength, with the paper giving it plenty of supportive coverage.

Working class rambling clubs had started in Sheffield in 1900 and by the 1920s, tens of thousands of workers spent their Sundays walking. This was a nationwide phenomenon, but in the north it was most pronounced. Attempts to introduce the access to mountains and moorland bill in parliament failed and in June 1927 a mass trespass took place on the Winnats Pass, Castleton. The *Manchester Guardian* pointed out that 30,000 people wanting to walk on the hills of Manchester and Sheffield were more important than the 30 who wanted to shoot five times a year.

Mountaineering and war

❄ APRIL 14 1919 ❄

Many mountain climbers found out during the war that their mountaineering had been the best possible training for soldiering. What most new infantrymen find the hardest part of their work – the making of longish marches with anything up to 80lb strapped on their persons and carried in the hand – comes easily to the guideless climber, because it is what he has been doing for fun on all his holidays. The pack in the small of the back, the highly constricted belt, the cut of the straps into the shoulder, the dour, unlovable boots, the rifle, which there is no one perfect way of carrying for ever – all these, in but slightly different forms, have been the playthings of his leisure, and if the walking be duller on Salisbury Plain it is rougher on the Zmutt Glacier.

On active service, too, the possibility of dismaying a mountaineer with any lack of amenity in his quarters is especially limited, the airiest billet or dampest dug-out being no more than a formidable rival to the Roththal hut and the old ruined Stockje hut as the least eligible residences in Europe. No wonder that the French, the Italian, and the Swiss Alpine Corps are each the pick of its country's whole army. We have no Alpine Corp, but British mountaineers, as a body, found their way so naturally into soldiering that for years the sport has been dormant to a degree perhaps unattained by any other. On the eve of peace there reaches us the latest number of the *Journal of the Fell & Rock Climbing Club of the English Lake District*, and it covers a period of two years, a substantial interval for any periodical. And now that it comes it is full of a kind of ghosts, like the *Alpine Journal* of the war years, the pages of which have been haunted somewhat spectrally by exhumed accounts of old happy far-off climbs and expeditions long ago. In the Rock & Fell *Journal*, too, we find a joyous camping holiday of 1885 described in the letters of a man dead long before the war, and even the intensely living president's 'Nights Out' on the hills were enjoyed in that good time, when everybody was alive. The Rock & Fell Club has suffered, as a fellowship of young men and climbers was certain to do. SW Herford, vividly remembered among mountaineers as the most perfect rock climber of any time or country, was killed early in the war. SF Jeffcoat and Edmund Hartley, his companions in some of his most famous achievements, were killed in 1917 and last year HL Slingsby, Claude S Worthington, and JH Whitworth are a few among the many losses of the club. Of course it, and all mountaineering, will go on and prosper. Apart from all its fine physical uses, the world does not grow to need any the less the mental health and discipline to which it can contribute, nor is the spacious and austere cleanness of mountains any the less thrilling and inspiriting after the life of cities and the racket and dust of affairs. Behind our western front during the war there were several inestimable establishments plainly labelled 'Delousing Station'. When people have long been crawled upon by mordant worries there is no delousing station so good as a great mountain.

Leader

An attempt to scale Mount Everest
British expedition in preparation
Reconnaissance this year

❄ JANUARY 11 1921 ❄

The Alpine Club and the Royal Geographical Society are to organise an expedition of exploration to attempt the ascent of Mount Everest (29,000ft), the highest mountain in the world. The announcement was made last night by Sir Francis Younghusband, who said that now that the secretary for India's permission had been received, the political obstacles in the way of the preparations had been removed. A reconnaissance party is to go out this year, to be followed next year by the climbing party.

An expert opinion
In a letter which we received recently on the subject of an expedition to Mount Everest, one of the greatest authorities on climbing in the Himalaya wrote to us:

'Mount Everest is at present an unknown quantity, so far as any knowledge of its structure is concerned. No one has been sufficiently near it to be able to form any estimate of the configuration of its massif or of the difficulties it may present the mountaineer. As yet only its height is known, and opinion as to the chances of attaining its summit will probably be centred upon the question whether it is possible for mountaineers to withstand altitude conditions sufficiently long to be able to reach the summit.

'Many other possible unfavourable conditions must or should be taken into account in forming an estimate of the chances of success, such as difficulties offered by surface formation or by adverse conditions of its snow and ice covering, and a meteorological nature, which, in the case of unknown Himalayan peaks, are likely to interfere with or wholly prevent the execution of the most carefully prepared plans.'

A great adventure

In his announcement last night, the president of the Royal Geographical Society said:

'An expedition, which would have as its object the ascent of the highest mountain in the world, the approaches of which were as yet unknown to Europeans, must be essentially a great adventure. High risks would have to be run and severe hardships endured – risks from icy slopes and rocky precipices, and such avalanches as buried Mummery's party on Nanga Parbat 26 years ago, and hardships from intense cold, terrific winds, and blinding snowstorms.

'In addition, there would be the unknown factor of the capacity of a human being to stand great exertion at a height more than 4,000ft higher than man had as yet ascended any mountain. The journey would be in the highest degree scientific. It might be taken as certain that the summit of Mount Everest would never be reached unless all the approaches had been first explored with greatest care. The geography of the mountain must be complete. In the present year the Alpine Club and the Society proposed to organise a reconnaissance party to acquire that geographical knowledge, and next year they would send to Tibet a climbing party to apply it in a great effort to reach the summit.'

A porter on the ascent of Mount Everest
What is the object?

❊ MARCH 8 1921 ❊

'What is the object in climbing Mount Everest? What shall we do when we get to the top?' These, said Colonel Sir Francis Younghusband, in a paper read before the Royal Geographical Society last night, were some of the questions that he was being asked as president of the expedition committee. He had even been asked on the telephone by an enterprising journalist to tell him, for the benefit of his paper, 'what good there would be to the general mass of humanity in the ascent of Mount Everest'. Now it was important, Sir Francis observed, that people should have no doubt or misgivings in their minds as to the good which would accrue, even to the general mass of humanity, from the ascent of Mount Everest.

A porter on an underground railway might be considered as about as representative as any one of the general mass of humanity. 'The other day I heard one,' said Sir Francis, 'who laid it down as an absolute certainty the we could never reach the top. He had been with us in Tibet and had seen these Himalayan peaks, and "they might take it from him that the top of Mount Everest would never be reached."'

If the human race had always acted in the spirit of the general mass it would never have emerged from the primeval forest. We should be still timid uncultured people hiding in caves and forest depths. Fortunately, however, there were always daring leaders who struck out ahead of the general mass. They ventured out into the open plains, onto the rivers, onto the sea, even up into the air. And it was an uncommonly good thing for the general mass that they did. The leaders with spirit and imagination showed the way. The herd were glad enough to follow after and pick up all the benefits.

The advantage that would come from the ascending Mount Everest was this – that once the highest peak had been climbed we would pluck up courage to ascend all manner of other mountains. Even to the obtuse mass of humanity it would then be evident that men were capable of higher achievement than they had ever imagined.

Regarding the popular ignorance as to the location of Mount Everest, Sir Francis quoted the remark of a lady, who said she thought it was in Iceland, while another said to him, 'I do hope you will get to the top and then you may bring back a piece of the wood in the ark.' *(Laughter)*

A mountain war memorial

❄ JUNE 9 1924 ❄

On Great Gable, perhaps the most wholly beautiful of English mountains, there was dedicated yesterday one of the grandest and most appropriate of all war memorials. A tablet there will now record the names of those Lakeland mountaineers, members of the Fell & Rock Climbing Club of the English Lake District, who were killed in the war, and the summits of Great Gable itself and of several of its loftiest neighbours at the heart of the Lake hills have been bought and given to the nation as their monument. Those who have received this signal honour were all good soldiers. No other sport goes quite so far as mountaineering towards training men for the characteristic labours of modern infantry. The longest forced march in full kit has little to add to the physical experience of the guideless climber who has carried his full rucksack through many 18-hour days of scrambling and tramping up rough rock and over soft snow.

The mountaineer's broken sleep and rough feeding, the many little calls for steadiness of nerve, for alertness and improvisation, are all so much practice in the essentials of soldiering; what they leave to be added is little more than the handling of weapons and the rigid part of formal discipline needed in order to make man-power applicable in war at any desired spot. So it was that in the French, Italian, Austrian, and German armies alike the Alpine Corps were always found to be among the best of troops. And, though we had no such unit in our army, every British mountaineer who fell in the war is known to have had the record of a first-rate officer or man.

The instinct of comrades has put this tablet far out of the way of indolent crowds, in the midst of the crags where life used to run highest in those whom it commemorates, and where it will bring them back to our minds in some of our moments of happiest effort and most radiant health.

Leader

Rock climbing for women

❅ APRIL 2 1921 ❅

Sir, – The last decade has witnessed a notable increase in the number of women who are devoted to the pursuit of rock climbing. For some time it has been felt that women climbers required some organisation that would concern itself with their special interests, and serve the double purpose of promoting the independent development of the climbing art amongst women and of bringing into touch with one another those who are already united by the bond of common love for a noble sport.

To the end a club has been formed called the Pinnacle Club. The inaugural meeting was held at Pen-y-Gwryd in March 26, and the club already possesses 41 members.

Any women who are interested in the objects of the new club are requested to communicate with Mrs HM Kelly, at 29 Fountain Street, Manchester, from whom all particulars may be obtained. – Yours etc.

Eleanor Winthrop-Young, President
ME Kelly, Hon Secretary

Rock climbing for women

❄ APRIL 2 1921 ❄

A club that was certain to come has come at last. A letter, which we print elsewhere, tells us that the Pinnacle Club, for women rock climbers, was formed on March 26. Of course climbing on rock, snow, and ice has long been successfully practised by women. A Manchester woman was a member of one of the earliest parties to climb the Napes Needle; one of the most pleasant Alpine stories is that of the early traverse of the Sesiajoch, on Monte Rosa, by two resolute English spinsters, conducting a terrified 'guide', and rumour says that one of the most famous of Alpine pioneers used to divide peaks into three classes, in an ascending order of difficulty: (1) those which he climbed with other male amateurs, (2) those which he climbed by himself, and (3) those which he climbed with his aunt. A long time ago a club for women keen on climbing in the Alps was founded as, we understand, a sub-division or annexe of the Lyceum Club in London. The usual experience of men who have climbed much rock with women is that a woman of any experience, climbing second on a rope, is usually quicker and neater than the average man in that position, and that the efficiency as leaders is not yet fully tested – which is not to say that it is rather low, but simply that in mixed parties they have climbed in that position too seldom for their powers to be fully estimated. Of course it is the idea of the new club to help women to do more climbing than ever, no matter whom they do it with. But it will necessarily lead women, directly or indirectly, to do a good deal more of leading on rocks, or, in other words, to become

40

more complete climbers. It is also certain to lead to the appearing of a new club journal, and human experience up to now goes to show that of climbing journals there cannot be too many, though it is so easy for other periodicals to be superfluous. Only this week the eyes of Manchester climbers have been gladdened by the appearance of the excellent *Rucksack Club Journal* for 1921, laden with delectable reading matter about climbing and mountain walking – the only tolerable substitute for climbing. It can hardly be long before a *Pinnacle Club Journal* enables us to assess the proper place of women's climbing, as a distinct thing, in the sport as a whole. We can think of no British mountaineering or rock climbing club that, once started, has ever failed, perhaps because there is no other sport the active pursuit of which does so much to make club comradeship at other times pleasant and helpful. The Climbers' Club, the Scottish Mountaineering Club, the Yorkshire Ramblers, and the Fell & Rock Climbing Club of the Lake District have all had good careers, and the Rucksack Club has contributed enormously to make Manchester more interested, as we believe it is, in mountains and mountaineering than any other British city. From no other city will warmer good wishes go forth to the nascent Pinnacle Club.

Leader

Seven years' itch, then a legendary ascent

❄ April 2 1980 ❄

Hundreds of climbers who take to the Lakes and Peak over the Easter weekend will be following in the footsteps of one of the greatest climbers of all time, the legendary HM Kelly, who has died at the age of 96. His ascent of Moss Ghyll Grooves on Scafell in the 1920s was described as 'like the firing of a fuse to explode the latent energies of England's rock climbing youth'.

Moss Gyll Grooves was one of dozens of new routes he discovered and made famous in the Fell & Rock Climbing Club's guides, which he wrote for and later edited for nearly 30 years. Initially he was invited to write up the route he pioneered on Pillar Rock, which towers between Ennerdale and Wasdale in the western Lake District and remained his favourite crag. Later as editor, he did away with the editorial descriptions by climbers and replaced them with facts, splitting a climb into pitches, giving precise measurements and including photographs and drawings.

He used a graduated rope for climbing so the length of the pitches he measured was precise and starting points of climbs made clear. Just as important was the scaling down of the size of the book so that it could be slipped into the pocket and taken on a climb.

His climbing companion and friend Sid Cross, who for years kept the climbers' haunt the Old Dungeon Ghyll hotel in Langdale said that HM admired the guts of some of today's climbers but was not particularly enamoured of their methods, preferring the days when climbers set off in tweed jacket and boots, carrying only a rucksack, a length of rope, and a pair of plimsolls.

The plimsolls were HM's innovation. On difficult climbs when the rock was dry, changing from hobnailed boots to the more adhesive and flexible rubber-soled shoes meant climbers could go where no man had gone before. But climbers admired not just his style; neat, precise, and above all balanced. 'He was quite fearless and the most delicate mover; very beautiful to watch climbing and to climb with. You had such confidence in him whether he was in the lead or was second,' said Sid Cross.

Although Herford and Sansom just before the first world war heralded the start of British cragmanship when the empty mountains cried out to be conquered, it was HM's eyes for new routes and his determination to discover whether they could be climbed that make him a pioneer.

At Laddow Rocks above Longdendale in the Peak District he found the two gritstone classics Tower Face and North Wall. In the Lake District, Tophet Wall on Great Gable, and routes one and two on the Pillar, can be credited to his courage and skill. But above all, his name is associated with Moss Ghyll Grooves on Scafell, which he cracked after seven years' study and about which he wrote in the *Rucksack Club Journal* of 1927.

Describing the climb up to the Pedestal, he wrote:

'A pedestal some six feet away on the left looked hopeful but it seemed hardly attainable as the intervening space appeared destitute of even the minutest holds.

'A very close survey, however, did reveal something of the sort, for I got across somehow. An upright – but far from moral – flake of diminutive proportions was used for the left foot, though it was rather high up and far away; and a still more immoral rugosity was found for the left hand.

'To balance, in transit by the aid of these two points of attachment, was a ticklish business, and a breathless moment followed, as a rapid change of hands was made, so that the left could reach forward to the Pedestal and lodgment be gained thereon. The Pedestal was large enough to accommodate a life-sized saint but as I had no wish to remain there long enough to become an effigy and as, apparently, the difficulties of reversing the Stride precluded any possibility of retreat, my interest was concentrated on the route ahead.'

A glimmer of the rewards he found in climbing comes in his summing-up of the Moss Ghyll Grooves ascent, which he made with Mrs Eden-Smith of Grange and a young but inexperienced climber, JB Kilshaw.

'Thus seven years of intermittent hope and thought crystallised, almost unexpectedly, into achievement,' he wrote. 'Youth and Maturity found equal delight, from their several points of view, in victory. The climb opened up for Youth a new joy in life. Maturity gazed across those intervening years and recalled similar days. There had been times when the tide ran strongly and carried instant success in its wake, as on Kern Knotts and the Low Man of Pillar. There was also a memorable day when a close acquaintance with Pillar was the key with which the doors of routes one and two were unlocked.

'The gods which guard our crags were gracious to us that day, though they almost frowned on our effrontery. Then there were others like the present climb, and like Tophet Wall, when the reception was brusque and rebuffs a frequent experience.'

He had started climbing late in life, at the age of 30, when he was invited to try a rock climb on Tryfan in Snowdonia. His natural talent was obvious and with the Derbyshire Peak District only a 1s 6d train ride from his home in Manchester, he would set off at seven in the morning, climb all day, and take the train home at night. The luxury of owning a motor car in the 1920s allowed him to escape to the Lake District, although even before that he was not deterred by tram, train and foot journeys to the foot of the fells and the crag of his choice.

Sid Cross says he never knew of HM falling off a crag, but tragically Kelly's first wife, Emily, a clever climber and founder of the Pinnacle Club for women climbers, was killed in 1922 when she fell as they walked down Tryfan.

Perhaps that is why HM made it a rule always to climb rather than walk down the ascents he made. More likely he found it more exhilarating and a new dimension on his achievement. Often he would be lowered down a crag on a rope to assess if it could be climbed. To celebrate his 75th birthday with his friends Sid and Jammy Cross, he climbed Langdale's Scout Crag by route one.

'After we made the ascent, I was sitting at the top mapping out a gentle walk down,' said Sid Cross. 'He was aghast. "Walk?" he said. "We must go down the route."' And so they did, descending by route two.

On his 70th birthday they had climbed the Tophet Bastion on Great Gable, a route he discovered 35 years before. Sid Cross has an image of HM at his happiest climbing in plimsolls and shirt sleeves on a warm summer's day in the Lake District and singing *Sipping cider through a straw*, with the towering Pillar his goal and his beloved fells falling away at his feet.

While at the age of 80 and more he would turn up to talk mountains at Manchester's Rucksack Club, those close to him said he never seemed to pine for his mountains or the days of his youth. 'In his own phlegmatic sort of way he accepted that as you get older things have to change,' said his niece, Mrs Dorothy Caley. Perhaps that was easier because HM Kelly was more than mountain man; he loved music and was a champion of the Hallé, he was a member of Lancashire County Cricket Club and always had a seat at Old Trafford. And he painted – not mountains but figures.

Cynthia Bateman

Everest wins

❄ JUNE 28 1922 ❄

We fear there can be no doubt that the stout assault delivered against Mount Everest by General Bruce's party has been repelled at a point about 1,700ft below the summit. The final attack was to have been made on June 6, but on June 3 the monsoon broke, earlier than was expected, and when that happens on Mount Everest there is nothing to be done but to get off the mountain if you can. So ends – failing a miracle of luck and of skill in using it – the most serious attempt yet made to meet the most fascinating challenge still offered to the explorer by the surface of the globe. One need not be very old to remember a time when neither Africa nor Australia had been completely crossed, when neither pole had been reached, when even the Alps still abounded in untrodden peaks, and when the tip of Everest, though easily visible to Anglo-Indians at afternoon tea in the hills, was moated about with a belt of scores of miles unmapped and untrodden desert of stone, ice, and snow. At the beginning of this year the heart of one alone among these mysteries remained to be plucked out, and so it remains today. The Himalayan experience of many private parties of mountaineers has long made it clear that the enterprise is one either for millionaires of uncommon intelligence, vitality, creditable ambition, and physical fitness, or else for a more or less publicly organised and financed expedition.

Though success has not been achieved this year, the results gained are important. We now know that no 'technical' difficulty in the ordinary mountaineering sense stands between explorers and the top. The first man on Everest may quite well be a man who could not climb Scafell by Moss Ghyll or Mont Blanc by the Brenva route. On the other hand, we know more definitely than before that the intensity of the climatic or physiological difficulties of the last stage is very formidable indeed, and the ascent, when made, will be a feat of human endurance and determination more memorable than any masterpiece of rock or ice craft. When a skilled climber says, speaking more loosely than he should, that 'Everest is easy' to climb, he need not be understood to underrate the extreme severity of the final struggle with frostbite, exhaustion, and threatened suffocation. All that he means, if he be worth attending to, is that if the upper 15,000ft of Everest were a mountain of that height and shape, rising from sea level, it would not baffle any part of competent mountaineers. That, thanks to the information gained this and last year, is known to be true; but it leaves out nearly everything that is important in estimating the very gallant performance of this year's party.

Leader

Harry Kelly, the great rock climbing pioneer of the 1920s, climbing on Laddow Rocks

Limelight on Everest

❄ JUNE 20 1922 ❄

The reticent sport of mountaineering has been dragged almost blindingly into the limelight by the financial needs of the Everest expedition. We suppose there was no other way. And certainly the last successive stages of approach to the top of Everest are 'good copy'. Yet one may feel a sneaking regret for the passing of the times in which the thrilling international struggle for the first ascent of the Matterhorn went on unreported and unknown, and when no wider publicity was given to Mummery's two days on an ice slope than a record, some months later, in the *Alpine Journal*. But then those were days when fewer among us kept albums of press-cuttings about their sporting achievements of all kinds: 'publicitis' was a malady raging mainly among regular performers as platforms and stages – pushing politicians, actors and singers on the rise, etc., – and somewhat derided by the practitioners of most other professions and sports, though no doubt they sometimes found furtive satisfactions in unsought public references to themselves. No doubt the members of the Everest expedition are of the old mind still. They are all thorough mountaineers, and must have imbibed the tradition that there is a kind of vague prima facie case against a climber whose new ascents are first heard of through the lay press. But the new ways – new Europe at least – are too strong for them and for all of us; so strong, indeed, that submission to being fully reported and to have one's unconquerable daring daily lauded in a hundred leading articles may become one of the practical conditions on which alone a fine enterprise like that which General Bruce has so well organised can be carried out. So no mountaineer, however thoroughly endued with the old habit of keeping things to himself and his fellow-craftsmen, need grudge any of his sympathy and goodwill to the happy party now on Everest. If fully reported, they are also fully employed.

Leader

Cigarettes as an aid to high climbing
Everest experience
❄ November 21 1922 ❄

Captain GJ Finch, who took part in the Mount Everest expedition, speaking at a meeting of the Royal Geographical Society, London, last evening on the equipment for high climbing, testified to the comfort of cigarette smoking at very high altitude. He said that he and two other members of the expedition camped at 25,000ft for over 26 hours and all that time they used no oxygen.

About half an hour after arrival he noticed in a very marked fashion that unless he kept his mind on the question of breathing, making it a voluntary process instead of an involuntary one, he suffered from lack of air. He had 30 cigarettes with him, and as a measure of desperation he lit one. After deeply inhaling the smoke he and his companions found they could take their mind off the question of breathing altogether.

Probably the smoke acted as an irritant and took the place of the carbon dioxide in which the blood was deficient at these high altitudes. The effect of a cigarette lasted at least three hours, and when the supply of cigarettes was exhausted they had recourse to oxygen, which enabled them to have their first sleep at this great altitude.

Good ramblers
❄ January 22 1923 ❄

Anyone who is depressed by the thought of some 50,000 able-bodied men, in every great English city, looking on at a few others playing football every Saturday afternoon should be cheered by a sight of the just-published *Rambler's Handbook* for 1923. The mere list of societies included in the Ramblers' Federation, in the Manchester district alone, indicates the hold that the joys of mountain and moorland walking have on the more strongly individual and less sheep-like types of townsmen and townswomen. It may not be fantastic to think that the extremely small print of this annual handbook indicates also the average excellence of the hill walker's eyes, those eyes, as Mr Rudyard Kipling has described them, with the pupils blown into pin-points by the astringent cold of moorland winds.

Another surprising measure of the welcome ravages of the passion for upland rambling was furnished not long ago, when a walker was lost – and was afterwards found to have died of exposure – on Kinder, and many hundreds of men and women well qualified for the work turned out and scoured every square yard of a great tract of broken moorland till he was found. To live submissively in great towns, without ever going out to get an embrace of mother earth and renew one's acquaintance with solitude, is a deprivation, almost a creeping disease. In an appreciable degree one is remade, and made better, every time one spends a long day among the heather or the peat; a coating of the almost inevitably incipient parasitism that comes of living always in a crowd falls from you; you 'breathe deep and are yourself' – a phrase that underwent some mockery a few years ago and yet represents something not all unreal or ignoble. It is good to see that some thousands, at any rate, of northern townsmen have found out the secret.

Leader

Access to mountains

❄ MAY 15 1924 ❄

How little the need for an Access to Mountains Act may be understood in southern England is illustrated by an odd little article in yesterday's *Times*. It has to be referred to, because otherwise the deserved reputation of the *Times* for getting its facts right might lead innocent people to assume that in this case they were accurately stated. After some sneers at the bill as expressing (this is really a wonderful touch) the state of mind of urban football crowds who do not even want to see country places, the *Times* writer goes on to say that the whole of the present trouble is a 'bogey' and that 'as a general rule the man or woman or child who wishes to explore the waste places of this island can do so without let or hindrance from anyone.' Of Scotland, as every mountaineer or walker knows, this statement is quite untrue. Of the English Pennine moorlands it was almost true some 50 years ago, and it definitely ceased to be so since. The case of the higher parts of the Derbyshire Peak, over which anyone could ramble at will in 1890, and which now are strictly preserved, to the exclusion of walkers and climbers, is only typical of what has been taken away, at almost every part of the Pennine range, from the inhabitants of East Lancashire and the West Riding. There is no need now to repeat, for northern readers, the detailed evidence of this. To thousands of people, in all classes, it is a matter of painful weekly experience. But clearly there is great ignorance elsewhere, and lest such absurdities as have crept into the *Times* be taken by any members of parliament for the facts of the case, an effort ought at once to be made to remind all members for northern constituencies of the extent of the recent deprivations and of the deep feeling of injury among constituents easily distinguishable from football 'fans'.

The south of England has no mountains, and – thanks largely to a few pugnacious old Whig lawyers – it secured long ago its threatened access to such of its wilder common lands as had not already been misappropriated beyond recovery. The north has now to protect itself against a course of aggression as grave as any that was undertaken in the south under cover of the Enclosure Acts. We may not be rich in tough and public-spirited Whig lawyers, but we have among us scores, if not hundreds, of clubs devoted to mountain and moorland rambling, and it is for them, as well as for the unattached enthusiast, to see that members for all sub-Pennine constituencies are thoroughly instructed now and must expect this to be a 'test question' at elections until it is properly settled. There are any number of sophistries to be dealt with. There is, for example, the trick of asking 'Are not people free of all the Lakeland fells?' – when just the point is that the owners of many Pennine fells are failing to show the generous public spirit that the great Cumberland fell-owners, the Leconfields, Lonsdales, and Marshalls of the Lakes have, we think, invariably shown. Then there is the fanatical assertor of overstrained 'rights' of property, who cannot yet see that there is a difference between asking for freedom to cross a man's suburban garden of geraniums. So there is much educational work to be done, and if it is set about quickly and hard it may shorten by several years the time that will pass before the mid-Victorian freedom to roam throughout the Pennine moors is restored.

Leader

No mercy from Everest

❄ JUNE 21 1924 ❄

Only a few days ago we published a message in which Mr Mallory, after describing the second rebuff that the mountain had dealt out to the expedition, ended by saying, 'we expect no mercy from Everest,' and now comes the news that he and Mr Irvine, a young Oxford climber who has been frequently mentioned in the telegrams, have been killed in the last attack. Everest has shown no mercy. At the moment we do not know how the disaster came about, but the experiences of the climbers since the beginning of May have been such as to leave no scarcity of likely explanations. In the first two weeks of May the intense cold and prolonged snowfalls compelled Mr Mallory to abandon the advanced Camp No 3, which was at a height of 21,000ft. A week later Camp No 4 was pitched 3,000ft higher up, and there was only one more camp to be established (this with the aid of the oxygen apparatus) before the final attack was made. But No 4 also had to be abandoned. For nearly a week there were temperatures of 50 degrees of frost – on one day of 56 degrees – there were heavy falls of snow involving serious danger of avalanches, and on one occasion the intense frost was broken by signs of a danger even more threatening – a warm current of air which seemed to presage the early coming of the monsoon and with that the complete destruction of the expedition's hopes. The disaster which has befallen the expedition seems to have taken place about a fortnight later. We do not yet know its cause. We can only grieve that so much of combined youth and experience, of high spirit and determination, should not have sufficed to overcome the terrible weapons with which, as we have only this year learned, Everest is armed.

Leader

Was it victory?

❄ JULY 15 1924 ❄

The third act of the attack on Everest is over; the curtain falls on a tragedy, perhaps on a triumph. Mr Odell, in his report to Colonel Norton, throws considerable, though not a complete, light upon the last desperate push made by Mr Mallory and Mr Irvine. Through his glasses we can see the small black figures, belated but ascending, reaching as the afternoon wore on to the base of the final pyramid, known to be short and believed to be easy. And then, as Mr Odell looked for the supreme thrust upward, there came the film of cloud that has kept the mountain's secret. That victory was attained is considered probable by the man best qualified to judge, and we can only hope that his estimate of a sleeping, painless death for the night-trapped but victorious climbers is indeed the true solution. Terrible as that supposition is, it does not rob the victims of a swift savouring of their superb achievement as they rested for a moment on the pinnacle of the world and of their high ambition.

The curtain drops too soon, and it drops on mourning men. The mountain has taken yet another life, this time from the Nepalese who worked so well for the adventure. But the returning party comes with great records and with knowledge gained.

The amount of progress made is not to be measured in feet only. When this year's expedition started there was no definite agreement about the necessity of oxygen. Now there is the most accurate information, gained by sharp experience, as to the incidence of atmospheric pressure up to the height of 28,000ft. Should it be thought wise to attempt a consolidation of these gains and a confirmation of victory, the staff work about supplies and porterage will greatly eased.

All the climbers are suffering from heart-trouble by continued work at great heights. It is for them to decide whether the certification of triumph over Everest demands another battle.

Leader

A rock climbing phenomenon

❊ APRIL 27 1926 ❊

In the hope that some mountaineering reader of the *Manchester Guardian* may furnish a simple explanation, I relate the following experience on Sharp Edge when descending Saddleback with my two daughters on Saturday afternoon last. As we scrambled down the rocks I noticed that my ice axe (which I had taken to shed its rust rather than for use) was singing or 'sizzling', and on mentioning the fact to my companions they said that their hair was behaving in a similar fashion. On inspection I saw that all loose strands of hair (of which there were many) were standing out stiffly from the head. The air was still and snow was falling gently. I recollect a similar experience on the Furg Joch at Zermatt some 15 years ago. The phenomenon ceased as we reached the grassy slope below

Sharp Edge, and it would be interesting to know whether the disturbance was purely atmospheric, or whether the rocks – which in some places play such tricks with one's compass – were a factor in the situation.

Fell Walker
Grasmere

Re: A rock climbing phenomenon
❋ APRIL 29 1926 ❋

Sir, Your correspondent Fell Walker's experience of his ice axe 'sizzling' when on Saddleback has a simple explanation. If he had been in total darkness he would have seen that a luminous electric 'brush' was proceeding from the point of his axe, exactly like the 'brush' given off from the highly charged electric pole of a static electric machine. The electric condition of the atmosphere was such that his axe, similarly charged with one type of electricity, positive or negative, was discharging this into the atmosphere. Some years ago while crossing an arrete in the Zillerthal Tyrol in bad weather our axes and all sharp points of rocks around us were 'singing' loudly, and our guides insisted on covering our axes and made us descend as rapidly as possible for fear of lightning stroke.

As regards rocks playing tricks with compasses, the following may not be generally known. A few years ago I was on the Gornergrat, and found to my surprise that my compass was useless in taking my bearings. Wherever I walked on the small plateau the North Pole would point to one spot only on the plateau: and, investigating this, I found the spot was a large rock, presumably of magnetic ironstone, embedded in the ground. – Yours etc.,

Ernest S Reynolds
Manchester

Obituary: A camera on Everest — JBL Noel

❄ MARCH 17 1989 ❄

Captain JBL ('Jack') Noel, who has died aged 98, was an extraordinary anachronism and a last living link with the golden age of Himalayan exploration in the decades before and after the first world war.

He was born in Devon in 1890, son of a colonel in the Rifle Brigade whose military career was spent skirmishing along the eastern outposts of the Empire, and whose other main claim to fame was as military theoretician and author of texts such as *Gustave Adolphus – Father of Modern War*.

While Noel senior was serving the flag in Burma and China, young Jack was receiving his schooling in Lausanne, where the abiding twin interests of his life – mountaineering and photography – were kindled. With a school friend, and at a time when to do so verged on the unthinkable, he made guideless ascents of many of the major Alpine peaks.

In his late years, he recalled one incident during a descent from the Wetterhorn, in bad weather, that was inspirational:

'I met a 72-year-old Swiss guide, and he said to me, "Young man, if you are tired, lean on me and I'll take you down!" He has always been a model in my life. You should go on living until you die and that has always been my guiding principle.'

After school, Sandhurst, the Yorkshire Regiment, and India as a subaltern in 1909 were his allotted path. Every summer, when the garrisons retired from the heat of Calcutta and the plains, Noel explored the border valleys of India and Tibet, studied native lifestyles, and immersed himself in the obsession current in the army at that time of reconnoitring the approaches to Everest.

By 1913 he had formulated his own plan to 'seek out the passes which led to Everest and if possible to come to close quarters with the mountain'. With three hill tribesmen he planned to cross the mountains behind Kangchenjunga to the Arun Gorge, and thence to Everest's eastern glaciers. His men were armed; he himself, after the style of Murthwaite in *The Moonstone*, darkened his face, greased his hair with butter and wore native dress. The escapade ended with an exchange of fire between his party and Tibetan soldiers on the Tibetan–Nepalese border, and the long trek back to India as the sole remaining option. But he had approached closer than any white man had previously succeeded to the world's highest mountain. When he returned to his regiment two months overdue from leave, the explanation he offered his colonel was that his calendar had been swept away in the course of a river crossing. The colonel merely advised him to take two calendars next time.

The next time was almost a decade away, and in the interim Captain Noel, as he now was, married an actress and went to war. He survived two years on the western front without a scratch, fighting at Le Cateau, Ypres, and Hill 60. At Mons, 600 men of his battalion were wiped out in 20 minutes: 'It was very exciting,' he reminisced.

His war ended with him an instructor with the Machine Gun Corps, and shortly after it began his involvement in the three Everest expeditions of the immediate post-Great War period.

On the expedition of 1922 Noel was appointed official photographer. The idea was not received with unanimous enthusiasm. George Mallory, in particular, aired the view that he 'did not wish to be an actor on a film'. Nor did the film of the 1922 expedition made by Noel receive much critical acclaim. GBS [George Bernard Shaw] opined that it had all the appearance of 'a picnic in Connemara surprised by a snowstorm'. None the less, it made a profit, running for 10 weeks at the Philharmonic Hall, and ensured Noel's opportunity to film the next Everest attempt in 1924.

This expedition turned out to be one of the great heroic sagas of mountaineering history, and Noel was perfectly placed to capture it on film. His utter professionalism in spending long periods at altitude on both expeditions, and developing thousands of feet of film under conditions of great adversity, were exemplary. He captured the mood of the events by being there at the right time. Even Mallory's last note before he and Irvine disappeared in their summit bid was addressed to Noel – and recorded on celluloid.

The ensuing film, much of it hand-tinted by Noel, was a huge commercial success, which the entrepreneurial side of Noel's character exploited to the utmost by bringing to Britain a group of Tibetan monks to tour with it, 'to give it authenticity'.

This action incurred the wrath of the Dalai Lama and ensured that there were no further British expeditions through Tibet for nine years. It also effectively severed Noel's links with the prewar mountaineering establishment. He continued to make films on travel or Catholic hagiography for many years, but was invited on no other major expeditions. In the second world war, he served in Geographical Intelligence and retired to live on Romney Marsh.

Even as late as his 90th year, he was still going regularly to Kodak House in London, showing his work on half a century before, and being feted by younger mountaineering generations. He planned, too, to return to Everest, but it was just the flickering of an obsession. In his last years he was by turns charming, lucid, hospitable, rambling, autocratic and even occasionally litigious.

His memoir, *Through Tibet to Everest* (1927), has just been reprinted.

John Noel, born 1890, died March 12 1989

Jim Perrin

Meals out of doors

❄ AUGUST 27 1925 ❄

Lunch in the Alps

The best lunch out of doors is the lunch carried in a rucksack and eaten at the top of a mountain pass before one descends into the new world on the other side: where the austerity of the snow-patch is tempered by the timid soldanella, where the rock waste is relieved by clusters of forget-me-nots and anemone, and where the silence is broken only by the strangely human whistle of the sentinel marmot as he keeps watch for his little tribe.

Tea in the Highlands

The perfect tea out of doors is the tea freshly made over a fire of sticks in some sheltered nook beside a running stream or on the wooded shore of a mountain loch. The wood is redolent to me of the moorland lochs of the Central Highlands: Loch an Eilean, Loch Garten, Lochs Laggan, Insh and Alvie; with the heather in full bloom, the leaves of the birches twinkling, and a gentle soughing in the pine. In the uncertain glories of a Highland summer one takes the foul weather with the fair, and I remember with a thrill my last tramp in the Highlands when, having ascended the Garbh Allt in drenching showers to the Saddle in the fastnesses of the Cairngorms, I snatched a hasty thermos flask of tea in the shelter of a friendly rock, and uplifted by the sight of a herd of deer running along the skyline, descended to Loch Avon and returned to Nethy Bridge by the Little Lairig and the Revoam Pass.

Dinner in the Dolomites

The al fresco dinner is a rarer proposition and is only possible in Alpine lands when one is on the tramp and freed from the restrictions of the *table d'hote*, but when it is attained under perfect conditons it is one of the greatest of earthly joys. Memories of wiener schnitzel with various appetising accessories and perhaps a kirsch-torte to follow, eaten in the shady Gartenwirtschaften of Western Germany after a long day's tramp in the Black Forest or in the side valleys of the Rhine, seem now to belong to another world than this. Fontainebleau and certain little townships on the Seine understand the art of open air dining, but in all my memories of travel Botzen (or must we now say Bolzano?) stands supreme. To get the full flavour of Botzen one should spend a week tramping over the passes of the Dolomites, sleeping in the Alpine Club huts and enduring Spartan rigours. Then one can relish to the full its Capuan amenities.

AJA

Eerie experience on mountain
Professor's story of invisible companion
The 'Big grey man of Cairngorm'

❆ DECEMBER I 1925 ❆

An eerie story of Ben Macdhui, the highest mountain in the Cairngorm range, has been told by Professor J Norman Collie, Lecturer in Organic Chemistry, London University, the hon president of the Cairngorm Club, which held its annual meeting on Saturday in Aberdeen.

Professor Collie, who has done much original exploration and climbing in the Himalaya, Caucasus, Alps, Canadian Rockies, and Black Coolin of Skye, confessed to the club members that he had experienced the most intense fear of his lifetime while climbing Ben Macdhui some 35 years ago.

He was returning from the cairn upon the summit in a mist when he began to imagine he heard some other things than merely the noise of his own footsteps in the snow. Every few steps he took there was the sound of a big crunch, and then another crunch as if someone was walking after him but taking steps three or four times the length of his own. He reassured himself that this was all nonsense, then listened and heard it again. Nothing could be seen in the mist.

As he walked on, and the eerie crunch, crunch sounded behind him, he was seized, he declared, with an overwhelming terror – why, he did not know, for he did not mind being alone on the hills – and began to run, staggering blindly among the boulders for four or five miles nearly down to Rothiemurchas Forest.

The spectre appears!

This was an experience, he said, that made him feel that on no account would he ever venture back to the top of the Ben Macdhui alone. About 12 years later he told this story to the late Dr Kellas, and found that the doctor had had a weird experience at the top of the same mountain about midnight one month of June. Dr Kellas saw a man appear and wander round the cairn near which Dr Kellas's brother was sitting. The man was almost the same height as the cairn, which was at least 10 feet. The man descended into the ground when Dr Kellas asked his brother what on earth was that man doing walking round the cairn. The brother replied: 'I never saw any man at all.'

A good many years after that, Mr Colin Phillip met an old man living at the edge of Rothiemurchas Forest who knew the Cairngorms very well. When Mr Phillip told this man Dr Kellas's story he was the least surprised, but simply remarked: 'Oh, aye. That would have been the *ferla mhor* [the big grey man] he would have been seeing.'

'That is the end of the story,' said Professor Collie. 'Whatever you may make out of it I do not know, but there is something very queer about the top of Ben Macdhui, and I will not go back there by myself.'

From our correspondent

CHAPTER THREE

AN ALMOST RELIGIOUS FERVOUR

In the fevered, highly politicised atmosphere of prewar Europe, attempts to climb the north face of the Eiger mirrored the intense nationalist rivalries taking place across the continent. The mountain, a monstrous wall of rock and ice rising behind the Swiss village of Grindelwald, was one of the last great challenges in Alpine mountaineering and the Reich was to sponsor several German attempts on the route during the 1930s. Raked by avalanches and loose rocks, many climbers lost their lives on this notorious Mordwand ('murder wall').

After the deaths of four climbers in 1936, a *Guardian* leader was highly critical of the attempt; both for what was seen as the distasteful continental practice of using pitons (hammering metal pegs into the rock for aid) that led the climbers into danger, and the fact that they were driven on by an 'inflamed nationalism that regards mountaineering as a field for the moral aggrandisement of one's own country'. No doubt this was influenced by recent events (Germany had just concluded a gentleman's agreement with Austria and had recently sent troops to the Rhineland).

In the first half of the decade, it was the ethics of reporting all things mountain that was to concern the *Guardian* writer and editor, Patrick Monkhouse. Paddy Monkhouse, as he was known, joined the paper as a reporter in 1927 on the recommendation of CE Montague. He became a leader writer in 1930 and news editor in 1932 but while a serious journalist, he was also a keen outdoorsman and member of the Rucksack Club. According to one historian, Monkhouse spent much of the 1920s wandering over every inch of the Peak District, climbing on most of its crags. The fruit of this labour was the publication in 1932 of the much-acclaimed *On Foot in the Peak* and two years later he produced *On Foot in North Wales*. (Another *Guardian* man, Donald Boyd, wrote *On Foot in Yorkshire*.)

Monkhouse always felt a new climb was worth at least 20 lines in any paper but he deplored inaccurate and sensational reports of mountaineering accidents in the printed media. In 'Mountaineering and the Press', a thoughtful article he wrote for the *Rucksack Club Journal* in 1933, he set out a code of practice for the reporting – both for reporters and practitioners of the sport – of climbing that seems as relevant today as it did 70 years ago. He began by saying that newspapers, on the whole (and this included the *Guardian*), are more inaccurate on the subject of climbing than any other. One reason for this was that the sport had an air of mystery, which meant to the uninitiated 'the impossible seems no stranger than true'. Also, remote locations often meant that there was less chance of checking the probability of story, especially when up against a deadline.

Monkhouse's remedy was that, after an accident, a responsible climber should draw up a sober and succinct account of the events to give to a news agency or a reporter. Reporters should also be sent out climbing to familiarise themselves with the subject. Finally, in a statement that would gladden the heart of the modern-day readers' editor, readers should write in to report errors, as 'no paper can remain indifferent to a rash of complaints against mis-statements of fact.'

One fact reported in 1932 was that Bob Graham, a Keswick guest-house proprietor, had climbed 42 Lakeland peaks in 24 hours, a record that was to stand until 1960. A Harry Griffin, an esteemed Country Diarist from 1951 to 2004, later wrote about this and so popularised the 'Bob Graham round'. Elsewhere in the area, a new generation of working class climbers such as Sid Cross, his wife Alice 'Jammy' Nelson and Jim Birkett were putting up hard routes.

After the Everest disaster of 1924, there wasn't another attempt on the mountain for nine years. This was partly because, irritated by the repeated incursions, the Tibetans had banned all expeditions. By the 1930s, relations had thawed just enough for climbers to be allowed back into the country and during the decade three expeditions plus a reconnaissance trip made the long trip up the Central Rongbuk Glacier. They all failed but each added another piece of knowledge to Everest jigsaw.

The fifth abortive attempt to climb the mountain in 1938 took a radically different approach to all its predecessors. Instead of the large, siege-like expeditions of the past, a lightweight attempt was to be made under the leadership of Bill Tilman. The Everest Committee, after funding three successive trips to Tibet, was almost broke, but Tilman also wanted to climb it without the scientific experts and 'an intolerable burden of tinned food'. In the end, the expedition had to retreat in the face of an exceptionally early monsoon. However, he proved that a lightweight expedition could get as high as the previous larger ones; a point that was mostly ignored until the 1970s.

An expedition that was most definitely in the grand style was the 1930 attempt on Kangchenjunga, the third highest mountain in the world. This was an international venture led by the Swiss GO Dyhrenfurth and included the British climber Frank Smythe. Smythe also led a successful expedition to the Himalayan peak of

Kamet in 1931, which saw four climbers making it to the summit. The *Times* had exclusive rights to reports and photographs from the expedition, but offered the northern rights to the *Guardian* for £80 plus the cost of the runners to carry the dispatches from 'base camp to civilisation'. The *Guardian*'s news editor, WP Crozier, (who became editor in 1932) got Monkhouse to knock them down and the paper did a deal for £50. Correspondence from the time reveals much moaning about the lack of a decent map of the area and that fact that the promised pictures from the *Times* didn't always turn up.

More and more people may have been exploring the uplands of the Peak, but they were restricted as to where they could ramble and climb. Monkhouse, in *On Foot in the Peak*, warned his readers that on the approach to Edale Cross from South Head, 'There is a faint path, but no right of way, and on populous Sundays a gamekeeper may be seen sitting with a dog and a gun … His presence is usually an adequate deterrent, and the gun has not yet been used.'

While the *Guardian* was supportive of an access to mountains bill, its attitude to the Kinder Scout mass trespass of 1932 was slightly more ambivalent. The paper provided a detailed eyewitness account of the events where 400 ramblers trespassed onto private moorland to demand that walkers be allowed when the land was not in use. However, it made a point of distancing the established Ramblers' Federation from the trespass, emphasising that it was organised by the British Workers Sports Federation – made up of members and supporters of the Communist Party and largely working class. Jim Perrin (probably the UK's most acclaimed climbing writer and from the 1980s a contributor to the paper) suggests that it was felt that, with more time for negotiation, the landowners were gradually being brought round to understand the need for legislation and that the mass trespass would jeopardise the chances of the bill in parliament.

Paddy Monkhouse left the paper for the *Evening Standard* in

1936, but returned after the war, becoming deputy editor in 1948 and in 1957 the first journalist to sit on the Scott Trust. Through a succession of leaders and articles, well before it became fashionable, he carefully examined the best use for Britain's limited countryside.

New Lakeland climb
Keswick party in first ascent
A Dungeon Ghyll crag

❋ August 14 1930 ❋

A new climb in Lakeland is as rare as the golden eagle, so thoroughly has the whole district been explored and mapped out. Only on what have been declared to be unsafe crags are new routes likely to be found, and attempted only by the greatly daring.

Such a new climb has recently been proved by Mr Stanley Watson, the new Lakeland mountain guide at Ambleside. It is on Raven Crag, Dungeon Ghyll. Several attempts have formerly been made to scale the crag, but a fatal accident caused it to be pronounced unsafe, and it was left alone. Mr Watson believed that there was a way up towards the left and that the rock was sound there. His first attempt was foiled by wet rock and a thunderstorm, but the next day was fine and sunny, and a party of climbers from Keswick joined him for a second attempt.

A second attempt

From the first, Mr Watson found the going extremely difficult, and about 80ft up, the holds became smaller and smaller until he was brought to a standstill. He returned to the bottom safely, and after a short rest made another attempt, on rubber-soled shoes.

When he reached the point where he had previously been checked, he found a small hold for the left hand, and pulled himself up to easy going and quickly reached a ledge at the top of the first pitch. The others climbed up to him.

The second pitch proved easier than the first, but now the route lay up perpendicular and exposed slabs, which had intimidating overhangs. Mr Watson found the 'holds' to be fairly large, and the rock sound and clean. The rope ran steadily out until a jutting 'overhang' of exceptional severity was encountered. Persistent searching revealed a foothold on the very tip of the overhang, and was used to gain a comfortable six-inch ledge for a rest.

Record length of rope

Farther on, many of the mossy holds gave trouble through their wet state from the rain of the previous night, and Mr Watson found that his rubber-heeled shoes would not grip the wet 'holds'. By moving to the right, Mr Watson found some smaller but dry holds, and was able to rejoin the obvious route above the wet moss. Some idea of the extreme difficulty of this movement can be gathered from the fact that although only a few feet it took a quarter of an hour to accomplish. The whole of the 100ft of rope had now run out and there was no sign of a safe ledge to which to bring the second man. A second rope was tied on the end of the first to allow Mr Watson to continue on. It was not until 115ft of rope had been run out that a small platform with a 'belay' was reached. This is believed to be a record length of rope in the history of British rock climbing, but it is hoped to find a way to divide that extremely long pitch into two, so as to avoid the great downward drag on the leader of such a length of rope and the risk it entails.

The rest of the party was up easier slabs, and all the party reached the top. One of the party was Miss N Middleton, a member of the Pinnacle Club, who is only 19. The others were Messrs Wiliam Cowen, Dunbar Usher, Robert Holmes, and Stanley Schofield, Keswick.

From our correspondent

*Pioneer rock climber Peter Harding, making the first ascent
of Goliath's Groove, Stanage Edge in 1947*

A Lakeland climb
The Raven Crag

❋ AUGUST 27 1930 ❋

Was it a new climb on Raven Crag, Dungeon Ghyll, Langdale, that Mr Stanley Watson, Ambleside, discovered recently, and on which he made such a thrilling ascent? Local people say that Raven Crag has never been climbed before, but Mr JEB Wright, Keswick, chief of the Lakeland Mountain Guides, in an interview states that Mr Watson's discovery was no discovery at all. 'Guide AJ Hope, of Preston, and I,' he said, 'made an almost identical ascent of Raven Crag on June 29 1928, and we were certainly not the pioneers, for bootnail marks were in evidence in several places on parts of the route followed by the 1930 explorers.'

From our correspondent

The lonely man of the mountains

❋ JULY 26 1985 ❋

Mallory said of Everest before trying to climb it for the third time in 1924, that he was doing so 'because it's there'. Much the same might have been said by others as far back as Moses before he climbed Mount Sinai (8,561ft), some 4,000 years earlier.

The motives of mountaineers are many, and perhaps not always clear to the climbers themselves. John Menlove Edwards, one of the outstanding rock climbers of the early 30s, wanted to go as far as he could towards attempting the impossible. He was a medical psychiatrist and wrote with clarity. As a result of his writing, his climbing achievements and the recollections of his friends provide exceptional insight into one man's impulse.

His biography has been written by a much younger mountaineer, Jim Perrin, and it makes extraordinary reading. That Menlove

70

Edwards eventually became mentally unstable, ought not to detract from its fascination, even for ordinary mortals, although his frustrations as a homosexual are one key to his climbing as he himself well knew. But his early achievements, at least on a simple reading of the evidence, derived from sheer physical enjoyment of the challenge of hard rock and from love of the scenic architecture of mountains in all weathers.

He achieved his first new route at the age of 20, on Lliwedd in North Wales, after an Alpine summer holiday. From the start he understood that climbing required extreme physical fitness and intellectual drive. He was a medical student at Liverpool University, and trained each day in the gym below the Adelphi Hotel, improving his balance and strengthening his muscles.

North Wales and the Lake District were his favourite areas, being near Liverpool. But he was also the first to make a solo traverse of the whole Cuillin ridge in Skye, including outlying peaks of Blaven and Clach Glas, in 12 and a half hours.

Menlove attempted other near-impossibilities and some of these are attributed by Perrin to periods of sexual or mental strain. The chronology bears him out. In December 1932, after the collapse of his first homosexual love affair, he went with another climbing companion to Mallaig, hired a rowing boat and rowed across to Skye in ferocious weather. The pair were lucky to survive. The following spring he insisted on swimming in icy water down the Linn of Dee, near Braemar, on a day when the weather was too bad for climbing.

Two years later, again in March, he crossed alone by canoe from the Isle of Man to the Lake District. That summer he tried to sail solo from north-east Scotland to Norway but was forcibly stopped by two fishing drifters. In December 1935 he rowed alone from the Scottish mainland to the Outer Hebrides – 40 miles of open water that took him 28 hours – and then rowed back again.

Afterwards he wrote about that expedition in cool terms. 'Somehow all that year, I don't know, one thing had come on top of another and now there was nothing for it, one must clear out, get right away somewhere, under the stars, and have another look at oneself from the angle.'

He attributed his loneliness and periodic unhappiness above all to the bitter experience of being a boarder at Fettes, which forced him to 'bury' his emotions. He wrote about it in terms of the 'murder' of his feelings and those of others. He sought a platonic marriage, but the girl turned him down – 'wisely', Perrin says, though Menlove seems to have thought that human comradeship could have made him happy.

These were his darker moments; mercifully they were only part of his life. More often he could be a friendly and patient companion of others who were less skilled in climbing than he was, and a stimulus to them. He was well respected as a clinical psychologist.

As a student he had intended to be a medical missionary, but he moved away from Anglican orthodoxy. Perrin says of his religious poetry that it is 'closer to Blake than conventional Church teachings'.

It is as a great climber that he should be remembered, the originator of many routes. He saved the life of Wilfrid Noyce on Scafell in 1937, by extreme physical exertion, will power, and medical care. Noyce went on to be another great climber, until killed in the Alps in 1962. Many years after the Scafell accident, someone climbing with Menlove in Snowdonia noticed that the rope they were using was primitively patched. It was, Menlove said, the rope that had held Noyce.

Alastair Hetherington

Obituary: Pioneer of rock and ice – Sid Cross

❄ APRIL 30 1998 ❄

Sid Cross, who has died aged 85, was one of the most outstanding of the new breed of tough and innovative working class climbers to emerge in the interwar years.

Cross was born in Kendal, the son of a cobbler. By the 1920s, with his school friend Charlie Tatham, he had begun climbing the Lakeland's mountains. For their first climb they borrowed a 'coffin line' – used to lower caskets into the grave – from Tatham's father, an undertaker.

Cross soon revealed himself to be a natural rock climber and came to the notice of HM Kelly, one of the key players leading a post-Great War renaissance in Lakeland rock climbing. He invited him to join the Fell & Rock Climbing Club. In the mid-1930s, Cross went to work for K Shoes in Kendal, and met Alice Nelson, also a natural mountaineer, and destined to become his wife. They formed a formidable climbing team, mastering rock, snow and ice climbing, and skiing.

Their climbing entered a new dimension in the winter of 1937–8 when they attempted an ice-sheathed Bowfell Buttress. This climb, probably the most difficult winter route climbed in Britain before the war and now graded 5 – still one of the highest categories of difficulty – is characterised by strenuous crack climbing and delicate moves on sloping, thinly iced rock. Cross and Nelson were breaking new ground technically, but rose to the occasion by improvising a repertoire of techniques familiar to any modern winter climber.

Cross tackled the crux pitch using Nelson's ice axe as a foothold while torqueing his own axe – an ancient implement given to him by the famous Lakes pioneer climber George Bower – in a crack and using it as a hold. Later on in the climb, he used a Scout knife, which he carried on climbs for splicing hemp rope, as an ice dagger with which to haul himself over the difficulties.

The fun and beauty of climbing was the impetus behind these ascents – 'the most perfect winter evening with a pure duck egg blue sky' – rather than the competitive drive that was then afflicting Alpine climbing. Cross and Nelson went on to climb another Grade V route, Scafell's Pisgah Buttress, in the winter of 1937, with Albert Hargreaves and then, to round the decade off, made an ascent of the extremely serious Steep Gill, on Scafell, again Grade 5, and again with Hargreaves, together with his wife, Ruth. Steep Gill is today regarded as the most difficult and serious of the traditional Lakeland gully climbs, with sparse protection on the crux section and unthinkable consequences in the event of a fall. Despite this, Cross recalled the ascent as 'fun'.

They bicycled to and from most of their epic adventures. Walking 12 miles, ascending 3,000ft, doing a Grade V climb and cycling 20 miles would be tough test for any modern professional triathlete. Doing it for fun and still being at work the next day indicates astonishing levels of fitness and enthusiasm. They were arguably the finest all-round British mountaineers of their day.

Sid and Alice married in 1939 and, after the war, with the responsibilities of a growing family, they put their energies into building a hotel management career. First, with their friends the Hargreaves, they turned a moribund inn at Boot, Eskdale, into a highly popular pub that was included in the first *Good Food Guide*. In 1949, the Crosses took over the Old Dungeon Ghyll Hotel in Langdale, where they created a climbers' bar out of an old cowshed. The 'ODG' became one of the key base camps from which the explosion of post-war talent was unleashed on the crags.

Cross became an unofficial guardian to the gangs of unkempt and impecunious climbers, among them such luminaries as the young Don Whillans and Joe Brown, who dossed in Wall End Barn next to the hotel. His good-humoured authority sorted out the scraps that inevitably followed the activities of such high-powered company. He helped set up what became the Langdale Mountain Rescue team and pioneered the use of dogs to locate casualties in the Lakeland mountains. He was later appointed MBE in recognition for his services to mountain rescue.

After retirement in 1970, Sid and Alice spent many winters in adventurous travel across the wilder reaches of Europe but their home near Ambleside remained warmly welcoming to visitors. To spend a few hours in Sid's company was deeply pleasurable. His memory made for fascinating discussions about the climbing and characters that had peopled his long and busy life.

Sidney H Cross, climber, hotelier and mountain rescuer, born March 18 1913, died March 31 1998

Colin Wells

Mass trespass on Kinder Scout
Battle with keepers
Police detain six men

❄ APRIL 25 1932 ❄

Four or five hundred ramblers, mostly from Manchester, trespassed in mass on Kinder Scout today. They fought a brief but vigorous hand-to-hand struggle with a number of keepers specially enrolled for the occasion. This they won with ease, and then marched on to Ashop Head, where they held a meeting before returning in triumph to Hayfield. Their triumph was short-lived, for there the police met them, halted them, and detained five men. Another man had been detained earlier in the day.

For a week past, Hayfield had been looking forward with anxiety to today's events. Last Sunday, members of the British Workers Sports Federation, which has no connection at all with the Ramblers' Federation, distributed handbills among Hayfield's usual Sunday population of ramblers urging them to 'take action to open up the fine country at present denied us'.

County police called in

This morning chalked notices on the roads, and leaflets distributed at the station, urged ramblers to meet on the Recreation Ground at two o'clock for a meeting before the much-advertised mass trespass.

Forewarned is forearmed, and Hayfield parish council at its meeting on Tuesday had taken steps to stop this meeting. Numbers of Derbyshire country police had been called in, and special new copies of the bylaws, one of which prohibits meetings there, had lavishly been posted in the recreation ground. The deputy chief constable of Derbyshire and Superintendents McDonald and Else came to see that the regulation was observed, and Mr Herbert Bradshaw, the clerk to the parish council, was there to read the bylaw publicly if the ramblers attempted to make speeches.

They thought better of it, and punctually at two o'clock the 400 or more ramblers who had gathered there set off for Kinder reservoir and Kinder Scout. As they marched they sang. They sang *The Red Flag* and *The International*.

By the time we got to Nab Brow we saw our first gamekeepers dotted about on the slopes below Sandy Heys on the other side of William Clough. In a few moments the advance guard – men only, the women were kept behind – dropped down to the stream and started to climb the other side. I followed. As soon as we came to the top of the first steep bit we met the keepers. There followed a very brief parley, after which a fight started – nobody quite knew how. It was not even a struggle. There were only eight keepers, while from first to last 40 or more ramblers took part in the scuffle. The keepers had sticks, while the ramblers fought mostly with their hands, though two keepers were disarmed and their sticks turned against them.

Keeper injured

Other ramblers took belts off and used them, while one spectator at least was hit by a stone. There will be plenty of bruises carefully nursed in Gorton and other parts of Manchester tonight, but no one was at all seriously hurt except one keeper, Mr E Beaver, who was knocked unconscious and damaged his ankle. He was helped back to the road and taken by car to Hayfield and to Stockport infirmary. He was able to return home tonight after receiving treatment. After the fight the police chiefs, who had accompanied the mass trespassers, left them alone to their great though premature relief. The fight over, we continued uphill, passing on the way a police inspector bringing down one rambler, who was subsequently detained at Hayfield police station.

Soon we turned to the left and continued along the hillside towards Ashop Head, the summit of the public footpath from Hayfield to the Snake Inn on the Glossop–Sheffield road. Before we regained the footpath a halt was made for tea and the Manchester contingent was joined by a party of about 30 from Sheffield, who had marched from Hope over Jacob's Ladder, from the top of which they had watched the battle with the keepers. The trespassers were urged not leave any litter about, and to their credit it must be said that they were particularly neat in this matter. On Ashop Head itself, a victory meeting was held, and the leader who at an earlier stage had asked us to trespass in spite of all danger now congratulated us on having trespassed so successfully. We were warned that some ramblers might be unfortunate enough to be fined, and for their future benefit the hat was passed around.

The march back

This done, we made our way back to Hayfield, keeping religiously to the footpath this time. Near the Stockport Corporation Water Works we met the police once more. One policeman made a movement as if to detain one of the leaders, but he immediately took to his heels and was closely followed by a large number of ramblers, who so crowded the way that the policeman could not have got near him if that indeed had been his intention.

At the first beginnings of the village, the ramblers were met by a police inspector in a 'baby' car. At his suggestion the ramblers formed up into a column and marched into Hayfield, still over 200 strong, singing triumphantly, the police car leading the procession.

It was their last happy moment. When they got properly into the village they halted by the police. Still they suspected no ill, and it was not until police officers, accompanied by a keeper, began to walk through their ranks that they realised they had been caught. Five men were taken to the police station and detained. The rest of the now doleful procession was carefully shepherded through Hayfield while, as the church bells rang for evensong, the jubilant villagers crowded every door and window to watch the police triumph.

From our correspondent

A climbing feat

❄ JUNE 14 1932 ❄

Ascending 41 [it was actually 42] district 'tops' within 24 hours, Mr Robert Graham, a young Keswick fruiterer, yesterday broke the Lake District fell walking record set up some years ago by Mr Eustace Thomas, of Manchester.

Mr Graham started his walk, like most of his predecessors, from Keswick, but he reversed the usual sequence of peaks; he began with Skiddaw, and finished with the Newlands Fells. He left Keswick town hall at 1am on Sunday and climbed successively Skiddaw, Great Calva, and Saddleback. The Hellvelyn ridge was followed at full length, and Dunmail Raise was reached by way of Fairfield and Seat Sandal.

After a short halt, Mr Graham then climbed Steel Fell, on the west side of Dunmail Raise, and polished off half a dozen or so minor 'tops' on the way to Bowfell. Thence he went by Esk Hause to Scafell Pike, on to Scafell by Broad Stand, and so down to Wasdale, where he stayed some 20 minutes. The last round he began by climbing Yewbarrow: thence over Red Pike, Steeple, Pillar, Kirk Fell, and Great Gable to Honister Hause, and over the Newlands Fells to Keswick. The last four and a half miles into Keswick were done in 47 minutes along the flat. Mr Graham reached Keswick town hall at 12.39am, just 23hr 39min after setting out. He finished very fit.

The effect of reversing the normal route is that the easier walking is taken first, and the rougher walking later on. Mr Graham is estimated to have walked nearly 140 miles and to have climbed 30,000 feet in the day.

A Country Diary: The Lake District

❄ OCTOBER 28 1996 ❄

The most exclusive club in England recently admitted its 1,000th member. No subscriptions are required. All you have to do to get in is to walk – or run – up and down 42 Lake District mountains within 24 hours. The Bob Graham Club commemorates the achievement of a 43-year-old Keswick guest house proprietor who, in 1932, broke the Lake District 24-hours fell record by ticking off his 42 peaks, starting and finishing in Keswick marketplace. This made a total height ascended and descended of at least 27,000 feet – almost the height of Everest. Despite several bold attempts, nobody was able to equal or improve on this until 1960, when Alan Heaton, a young Accrington man, got round in rather less time than Graham and so, when the club was formed years later, he became member No 1. Another Lancashire mountain runner, Stan Bradshaw, now aged 83 and still active, became member No 2, but five years later the number of successes was still only a handful. Later, the pace gradually hotted up and now, every summer, around the longest day in June, dozens of people attempt the round – Skiddaw and Blencathra first, then the Dodds and Helvellyn, the Langdales, Bowfell and the Scafells, the Pillar round, Kirk Fell and the Gables, the Buttermere fells, Dale Head and Robinson and back to Keswick. Three supermen have even been round twice; actually, a few have done this, going round on two occasions, but these three heroes did their second round immediately after their first, clockwise and then anti-clockwise. The record now stands at an incredible 76 summits, while the women's record has reached no fewer than 62 summits. Remember all this when next you set off to climb Scafell Pike from Borrowdale or tick off the Langdale Pikes.

In fact it was an article by A Harry Griffin in the Lancashire Evening Post *that inspired Heaton to break Bob Graham's 28-year-old record. Griffin was also one of those to suggest the formation of the Bob Graham 24 Hour Club in 1971.*

A Harry Griffin

Death on the Eiger

❄ JULY 24 1936 ❄

For the second successive year, an attempt to climb the formidable north face of the Eiger, a peak in the Bernese Oberland, has ended in the death of the climbers concerned. In August 1935, two Germans were caught by bad weather on the face, and died of exposure; their bodies are still hanging there, suspended from the pitons that they drove into the rock to assist or safeguard their progress. This week four climbers (two Germans and two Austrians) died on the same precipice, two of them by falling, two by exposure. The sinister repetition will distress but will hardly surprise those who have kept in touch with the more recent developments of European mountaineering.

There are two marks of the extreme modern school – one technical, one moral. Technically, these climbers are distinguished by the regular use of iron pitons, pulleys, hooks, and rope engineering not only to safeguard their ascents but actually to make progress where the steepness of the rock, or the lack of natural rock holds, makes an ascent impossible by ordinary methods. Morally, they are moved by a kind of fanaticism, an almost religious fervour, probably counting death as nothing in comparison with the glory of possible achievement – a sentiment often aggravated by an inflamed nationalism that regards mountaineering as a field for the moral aggrandisement of one's own country. Both characteristics are equally distasteful to the average British mountaineer, to say nothing of the layman. But neither has passed its zenith in Europe, especially in the Fascist countries, where the heroic virtues are officially admired.

The technical development of this school of climbing is not yet comprehended in this country. Over three years ago an Austrian cragsman, Dr Leo Maduschka (since killed while climbing), wrote in the *Mountaineering Journal* two articles on the piton technique on rope and on ice, but he has made few converts here. The principle is simple. The climber hammers into small crevices in the rock an iron piton with a ring attached to its head. He secures himself to it by a hook fastened to his waistline by two feet or so of rope. Planting his legs against the rock, he is now free to drive in another piton in a few feet higher and repeat the process. A pulley piton may be used instead of a simple ring piton. But it is not the piton technique itself that leads to disaster. It may not please the scrupulous sportsman, but as a method of overcoming a short stretch of very difficult rock it is not peculiarly dangerous. Its real danger is that it lures men into attempting expeditions of great length on rock of a kind that makes it impossible to secure adequate protection against the elements at night or to retreat if bad weather comes on.

Leader

Everest 1938

❄ JANUARY 25 1937 ❄

Everest has in the past been attacked by something like a siege train. The expedition of 1936, with a nucleus of 12 British mountaineers, recruited 65 porters at Darjeeling and nearly 100 more at

Sola Khombu. These, naturally, were not all with the expedition throughout; but even if they accompanied it for only part of the way they added greatly to its cost. Besides these porters there were 250 pack animals, which had also to be paid for and fed. The whole business cost nearly £10,000. But there have been, from several sides, suggestions that a less elaborately equipped party would not only be much cheaper but would also stand at least as good a chance of success.

The reconnaissance party that visited Everest in 1935 and the British-American party that climbed Nanda Devi in 1936 both found it possible to dispense with much of the paraphernalia that make the big Everest expeditions so costly. The Nanda Devi ascent was particularly interesting, because it exploded the idea that Europeans are incapable of carrying loads at great heights. It does not follow, of course, that tactics successful against a peak of 25,660ft would be appropriate against Everest's 29,002ft. Previous Everest expeditions have reached 28,000ft. But there is a clear case for trying, on Everest too, the small party at fairly frequent intervals instead of the big party at longer intervals.

Leader

The 1938 attempt on Everest
Mr HW Tilman and a pointer to success

❄ OCTOBER 12 1938 ❄

People who attended the two lectures in Manchester yesterday by Mr HW Tilman, leader of the latest attempt to climb Mount Everest, had the 1938 expedition presented to them as something more than one more in a the series of gallant failures, and as a pointer to the confidently expected success of the future. Mr Tilman made it a significant break with previous Everest traditions. The earlier attempts were all expeditions on a large scale, with many scientific experts, a non-climbing leader and 'an intolerable burden of tinned food'. The 1938 expedition consisted of far fewer people and cost only a quarter of the sum spent on the previous expedition. Its members avoided tinned food, which Mr Tilman said he had found tasted all exactly alike after one had lived on it for a good many days. They took instead large supplies of bacon, ham, cheese, and butter, and were able to buy eggs for a great part of their journey, and had eggs laid up in waterglass for a later stage. Thus they were able, almost to the end of the climb, to have bacon and eggs for breakfast.

Food did not become a problem until after about 23,000ft. At that point the difficulty was that they had no appetite, and yet must eat to keep going. If they had been able to eat a good meal they would not have been able to keep it down.

Mr Tilman told how they had planned to be at the base camp 10 days earlier than the 1936 expedition because of the experience that year of the unexpectedly early break in the monsoon. After that effort, the monsoon broke still earlier and the lull between icy winds and snow – the only period in which an attempt on the summit is possible – did not come at all.

The party was delayed by snow even before reaching the Tibetan border, and Mr Tilman described how at a later stage they lay at night listening to avalanches, which told of the hopeless conditions above. He described, stage by stage, the journey to the different camps and the returns for supplies, until finally one section had reached 27,300ft and had to return saying that the snow was still so bad that an attempt on the summit was impossible. Mr Tilman and another member of the expedition set out to try to climb the summit ridge, but that also had to be abandoned, and as one of the porters had pneumonia, it was decided to descend.

Mr Tilman claimed that the 1938 effort had shown that a small party was as likely to get to the top as a large one. Commenting on the idea of dropping supplies from aeroplanes, Mr Tilman said the logic of it would be to drop men also, and 'if we could not refrain from dropping bombs on to towns, we might at least refrain from dropping tins, tents, and men on to the mountains.' Life was so cluttered with 'gadgets' that no lover of mountains wanted to introduce them into so simple a matter as mountaineering. Some people had been horrified because they did not take a wireless, but a transmitter would have cost £1,000 and added greatly to their burden, and a receiving set, though it would have told them something about the weather in advance, would not have altered their plans. Mr Tilman also has little use for oxygen apparatus. He said a climb with oxygen would only inspire somebody to do it without, and was in any case of less value to the physiologist.

The lectures were arranged by the Manchester Geographical Society, and Houldsworth Hall, Manchester, was filled both in the afternoon and in the evening. In the afternoon the audience was largely of children. The most impressive of the lecturer's many striking lantern slides were those that in effect were vertical picture maps of the expanses of snow and ice with the climbers making their way across them. The most charming were the informal studies of Tibetan life, some of them in colour.

Himalayan outfit

❄ AUGUST 7 1937 ❄

The city's pride in its own achievements, which is good enough even now, would be almost intolerable if the public knew of all the unusual things that Manchester makes. One of these is equipment for first-class mountaineers. There is lying in a city workshop at this moment a suit of wind proof and rain proof material, which will shortly be dispatched to India for a man who is to do some mountaineering in the Himalaya.

The head of the firm that is making this suit is Mr Robert Burns, who knows the needs of the mountaineer from his own experience.

He is a member of the committee of the Rucksack Club and assistant editor of the club's journal. Mr Burns supplied the tents and sleeping bags for the Everest expedition of 1935 and the Nanda Devi expedition last year. Anyone who has read of the conditions that these mountaineers had to face will appreciate the importance of their choice of equipment.

Climbers' feat
First ascent of Cumberland crag

❄ APRIL 5 1939 ❄

The central face of Castle Rock of Triermain, a Cumberland crag that has never been climbed before, was scaled today by three members of Cumberland and Westmorland Guides Organisation. The crag is 340ft high and overlooks the Vale of St John, and the difficulty of climbing it is due to the large overhangs and the sloping holds, which make rubber-soled shoes the only practicable wear.

The climbing was led by RJ Birkett, of Langdale, whose companions were CR Wilson, of Carlisle, and L Muscroft, of Thursby. Previous attempts to climb it have always been abandoned before halfway.

Birkett and his companions took three hours in the ascent. The route increased in severity as they went on, and when the leader was 220ft up the overhang was so great that a stone dropped from the hand did not touch the rock face in its fall to the bottom.

At the critical point of the climb, about 50ft from the summit, Birkett left Wilson and Muscroft belayed at a pinnacle and with great coolness and skill climbed a narrow chimney and forced his way up the overhang into which the chimney merged. This brought him to a small recess, which served as a safe stance, and Wilson and Muscroft were drawn up after him, all three then reaching the top without mishap.

This is the most difficult of three new routes opened by Birkett recently. The others are on Great Gable and on Scafell East Buttress.

From our correspondent

Climbing the Castle Rock
Some early ascents

❊ APRIL 10 1939 ❊

Sir,

A report has recently been published that the Castle Rock in Lakeland had been climbed for the first time. In justice to people who have been climbing this rock since 1928, I wish to correct the inaccuracy. The first ascent was made by Miss MM Barker and GG Macphee, both members of the Fell & Rock Climbing Club, on March 31 1928. During the same year, four other new climbs were made up the rock. I myself led a party on the second ascent of the direct route. Evidence of these earlier ascents appears in the *Journal of the Fell & Rock Climbing Club* for 1929, and details of the climbs are given.

Yours, etc.

Stanley Watson
Chief of British Mountain Guides
Borrowdale

Obituary: Champion of the crags –
Jim Birkett

❊ JANUARY 29 1994 ❊

The motorcyclists lose heart as the cart track begins at Bowness Knott, gateway to climbers' Ennerdale. Only one continues to burn on up it, pointing the girder forks of his steed over the ruts to leave his companions far behind. The firs of the Forestry Commission plantations are scarcely handlebar-high, and the lone rider – known as 'Mad Jack' to more than one farmer, cloth cap pulled back-to-front – is not yet the celebrity he is to become in the climbing world. But his style is in character; a role he will play as one of Lakeland's great climbers. Jim Birkett presses on ahead: Pillar Rock, first stop that day; another crag the next.

In the years around the war Birkett, who has died aged 79, made 45 new rock climbs in the Lake District, most of them in the harder grades of 'difficult'. He had a tremendous eye for a line and most of his routes are now classics and still immensely popular.

'There were no local climbers then,' he said. 'You were looked on as rather silly if you climbed for fun.' Not that Jim, who lived in Little Langdale and worked in the local quarries, was ever stuck to the exclusion of other mountain regions. From the age of 14 he cycled as far as Glencoe, 'pedalling like mad and hardly ever stopping', before becoming also in his own words 'motorcycling mad'. His eyes gleamed as he talked of blinding over Wrynose Pass, then a grit track behind his house, on a succession of Velocettes, Nortons, Aerials, BSAs and a solitary Cotton that came his way – some with sidecars. If climbing had not appealed it would have been TT racing instead.

Jim did not begin to make new climbs until he had climbed all the hardest challenges going. These included the painfully thin Diagonal on Dinas Mot, Raven's Gully in Glencoe and Central Buttress on Scafell. This he did in nailed boots, only the second time it had been climbed that way: the first such ascent having been done by Menlove Edwards in 1931. As Jim said: 'It was a point of honour to try the hardest routes in nails.'

Birkett, who started his vintage climbs when he was 22, ushered in the harder level with climbs like Harlot's Face on Castle Rock, the first 'extreme' in the Lake District. And by other test pieces like Do Knot on White Ghyll, Leopard's Crawl on Dow and Overhanging Bastion, also on Castle Rock and a route he rated 'one of the six best climbs in the Lakes'.

He made his mark elsewhere during the war with a first ascent of the ferocious-looking Morgue Slab on Helsby Crag (still graded a respectable 5c today), the sandstone bluff that juts above the Cheshire plain. Until then it had repelled all comers.

Jim, who became manager at Moss Rigg quarry, perched on the skyline above his home, once told me: 'Money isn't everything. I would have liked to have gone on Everest in 1953, of course, but it's no use saying lack of cash or the "proper" schooling had anything to do with it. Nor that I would have climbed well above 22,000ft if I had gone. I wouldn't have a million pounds for all the fun and enjoyment I've had from climbing and work exactly as it happened.'

Robert James Birkett, born April 22 1914, died December 30 1993
Tony Greenbank

CHAPTER FOUR

A CHANGE OF WEATHER·

With many climbers away fighting and leave from the forces sparse, the war years were a quiet time on the British mountaineering front. Post-1945, a rock climbing revolution was to take place, with improvements in equipment and rising standards. More people than ever were to participate in the sport, with many of the recruits drawn from working class backgrounds.

The social composition of the climbing world had already begun to change in the 1930s. Rambling clubs such as the Sheffield Clarion Ramblers were introducing more of the general population to the fells, some of who 'graduated' to climbing, while the new Youth Hostels Association provided cheap accommodation. In the book *High Peak*, Eric Byne records, Sheffield climbers 'often wore workmen's overalls or cast-off plus fours bought for a song in the city's rag-market. A good rope was a treasure, worn-out ropes were passed down and used until the very threads curled up in disdain.'

After the war, the gradual rise in prosperity resulted in more people being able to afford to get out into the countryside – there were more cars to hitch rides from and some could even afford motorcycles. Coupled with this was an improvement in equipment. Army surplus material such as karabiners, nylon ropes (which were first used in parachutes), rucksacks and rubber-cleated boots could all be bought cheaply.

This all led to a growth in a kind of climber who was as likely to work in a factory as in a school or law firm. New, primarily working class, clubs such as the Rock and Ice in Manchester or the Creagh Dhu in Glasgow were formed, where competition among members within the clubs led to extremely hard routes being put up.

The most famous of this new breed were two Mancunians: Don Whillans, a plumber, and Joe Brown, a jobbing builder. Classic routes such as Brown's Cenotaph Corner in 1951 or Cemetery Gates (with Whillans), set a new level for achievement in rock climbing and they are still respected to this day.

The rise in the numbers climbing led to an inevitable rise in the number of accidents. Cast an eye over the entry for mountaineering in the *Guardian* index for the years following the second world war and there are scores of references to climbing accidents, often as a result of poor technique. This reporting may well have been down to the fact that 'the mountaineer's death seems more tragic', as a 1947 leader put it, than, say, a car accident, thus warranting more column inches. Other articles suggested that the hordes of new climbers from the city needed to learn the basics of ropework and rudiments of safety from established climbing clubs.

Mountaineering: A British Council

❄ AUGUST 7 1945 ❄

A British Mountaineering Council has been formed by the various mountaineering clubs of Britain. Its chief objects are to encourage the sport of mountaineering and to make it more widely known that it is by no means expensive; to give advice and help on clothes, equipment, bivouacking, food, and the best climbing centres; to put climbers in touch with local clubs and leading mountaineers; and to provide instructors for training leaders for recreational organisations, for whom there is already a considerable demand.

The council is working closely with the First Aid Committee of British mountaineering clubs, which maintains first aid equipment and rescue organisations at various centres in the country, and is cooperating with other bodies in the defence and protection of mountain scenery and in advancing the cause of national parks. It points out that expeditions into the mountains by inexperienced and ill-equipped persons may be a menace not only to their own lives but also to the lives of those called upon to go to their rescue and is preparing for publication, at a nominal price, a book to be entitled *Climbing in Britain*, which will contain all essential information and advice.

Death on the hills

❄ APRIL 8 1947 ❄

Why is death on a mountainside more interesting, more poignant, than death in the street or bed? Why does every newspaper record, with such detail as it can gather, that a man has died on Snowdon or the Pillar Rock, and dismiss briefly or omit altogether the death of another, knocked down by a car on a main road? The distinction may be illogical, but it is instinctively made. Perhaps it is because accidents on British hills are fortunately rare, as traffic accidents regrettably are not; perhaps because though mountaineering, now far more popular than it was, is still to many people something novel and bizarre. The mountain background, too, may lend to death something of its own solemnity and august beauty. But there is also a deeper factor. The mountaineer's death seems more tragic because, though still an accident, it is in a way less accidental than a death on the road. A car that knocks a man down is something irrelevant to his whole previous life. It strikes him as he does what he had done a thousand times without thought of mischance. The mountaineer certainly does not seek his own death, he is often in no way at fault; but he dies in a situation to which he has brought himself of his own free will and for his own happiness. The causal element, leading up to the moment of death and linking it with past life, this 'peripateia' as the Greeks called it, is what bestows the dignity of tragedy on what was else a mere accident, a slip of the foot, a loose fragment of rock, or a change of weather. It is a turn of the screw if the accident falls on a great climber, perfect in technique and bodily condition, such as Frankland and Linnell, or to go farther afield than British hills – Mallory on Everest or OG Jones on the Dent Blanche.

It must be recognised that mountaineering, even in the mild form of walking on British hills, brings men into closer relation with death than any other sport (except possibly motor and motorcycle racing). Death from a fall or from exposure and exhaustion is risked in some degree by all who attempt more than they can do; it is the constant limiting factor. No one that ever had the mountain fever in his blood would be deterred by that from the noblest of sports. The risk is willingly accepted. But it must be deliberately accepted and then minimised by skill and judgment. The mountaineer owes this to others besides himself; both to his kin and friends, and to those who must spend their strength and perhaps risk their lives, too, in bringing him aid. A farmer whose only contact with climbing is the toil of bringing down the dead or injured may look on the sport with a jaundiced eye; but his point of view is to be respected. One cannot admit the suggestion, which has been seriously made, that walkers should be debarred from the hills to save them from getting into difficulties; it could hardly be done, even if it was right to attempt it. The responsibility lies on the mountaineer himself. He must approach the hills with a certain humility and an underlying seriousness, knowing that a walk or an easy scramble may by a turn of the weather be trans-formed into an exacting expedition. He must be willing to learn. There is among walkers and climbers, both in the older climbing clubs and the newer and bigger bodies like the YHA and the Ramblers' Federations, a fine tradition of readiness to help the newcomer and to guide his early steps. But the need for prudence and judgment dies not end with apprenticeship. It is lifelong. For this reason, if for no other, it is in the public interest that the facts of mountaineering accidents should be fully and accurately described. A danger recognised is already half-discounted; and it must never be far from the consciousness of the mountaineer that he carries his life on his feet.

Leader

Miscellany

❄ JULY 28 1943 ❄

A little bit off the top

That popular and sonorous phrase 'the everlasting hills' has just suffered a nasty knock with the announcement that a heavy landslide has changed the shape of the Matterhorn. It is stated that, owing to a big avalanche, one of the rocks of the Furgggrat, a lower peak of the Matterhorn, has been torn off, giving it a more vertical and smooth appearance. But if the news comes as something of a shock to simple people it will be welcome to the experienced rock climber, who with every change in the shape of a mountain perceives a new and attractive obstacle to be overcome. Usually he has to be satisfied with the wearing out of a foothold or the displacement of a chock-stone, which advances a rock climb from 'difficult' to 'severe', but a wholesale alteration like the Furgggrat accident is pure jam. It is fortunate that the Furgggrat is not near Rome, or the Italian radio would be sure to blame allied bombers for the avalanche.

The Rucksack Club
Fifty years of British climbing
❄ MAY 10 1952 ❄

The Rucksack Club is 50 years old this year; and its annual journal, which has just appeared, recalls many milestones in the history of British mountaineering. Indeed, the club has set up some of the milestones itself. It was not the first mountaineering club to be formed outside London, where the Alpine Club was already well established. The Yorkshire Ramblers came a few years before it, and so did the Scottish Mountaineering Club and the Cairngorm Club. Even in the north-west, the Kyndwr Club (named from a romantically Gaelic version of Kinder Scout) had cut, as it were, the first sod. But it took root quickly and – though its roots have remained in Manchester – was not long in acquiring what may be called national status.

It began with a modest letter to the *Manchester City News* signed by JE Entwistle and AE Burns (Mr Entwistle is still an active member and this year's vice president; Mr Burns died some years ago). Describing themselves as 'novices with a good walking record and a secret ambition to handle a rope and axe,' they described the activities of the Yorkshire Ramblers Club, then 10 years old, and asked why Manchester should not have something on the same lines. There was response enough to justify a start.

Gritstone climbing certainly began before the Rucksack Club did. There is a well-known photograph by George Abraham of OG Jones climbing on Cratcliffe, near Youlgreave, and Jones died in 1898. But it would be fair to say that the Rucksack Club members have done more than anyone to make gritstone a serious and distinguishable, though minor, part of British rock climbing – naturally, as many of the best gritstone crags lay at their threshold. There have been several successive waves of exploration. The first, which found its chronicle in Laycock's *Some Gritstone Climbs*, published in 1911, put this variant of the sport recognisably on the map. There was a concentration on gritstone just after the four years of war.

The experience of the gritstone crags had an interesting by product – the girdle traverse. Most gritstone crags are relatively wide and not high. You get a longer climb by working from one end to the other, without touching the bottom, than by climbing up and down. JH Doughty has suggested that Laycock and Herford drew from their climbs on gritstone the idea of the girdle traverse, which they later applied to Scafell, setting a precedent which has been followed on most of the great crags. (The girdle traverse of the Pillar Rock, one of the most notable, was made in 1931, with a Rucksack Club man on each end of the rope.)

Mountain rescue

The mountain rescue movement, which is so active in mitigating the consequences of mountain accidents, also derives in large part from the club. The need was brought home to the members in 1928, when their president fell while climbing on Laddow Rocks and broke his leg. Bringing him down to the road without proper equipment proved so exacting that it was later necessary to amputate his leg. Moved by this and a similar incident on Snowdon, the club appointed a stretcher better suited for mountain work than the ordinary type. The Thomas stretcher, designed by a Manchester engineer and Rucksack member, was the outcome. Nor was that all. It was found that the Fell & Rock Club was thinking on similar lines. A joint body was formed, other clubs came in; and out of it grew the present Mountain Rescue Committee and its chain of rescue posts, each with its stretchers, first aid equipment, and nucleus of voluntary rescuers.

One mentions these points particularly, because of their impact on British climbing at large. But of course the essence of a climbing club is to climb. It is impossible here to list the important rock climbs first led by members of the club; an article by AS Pigott gives some account of the members' activities between the wars. It is enough to say here that they made the first serious breach in the most formidable of Welsh crags, Clogwyn Du'r Arddu, and played a leading part (particularly in the person of the late Maurice Linnell) in domesticating the hardly less ferocious East Buttress of Scafell; and that a Rucksack man, HM Kelly, was (as Mr Pigott says) 'for many years the dominant force in the exploration of the Lakeland crags'.

Patrick Monkhouse

Growing toll of mountain accidents
Dangers of ignorance and over-confidence

❄ AUGUST 19 1948 ❄

The growing frequency of accidents to climbers and ramblers in mountain country is causing serious anxiety to the organisations most closely concerned.

Untrained climbers

Sheer ignorance caused few accidents in the days when the normal approach to climbing was through a mountaineering club. Today, however, our hills are swarming with town-bred youngsters who have no idea how quickly and inevitably their untrained muscles and ill-clad bodies would succumb to exhaustion and exposure if they were trapped for the night without shelter in a blizzard or a freezing mist. For the most part they do not venture on rock climbs, but they blithely run the greater risks of scrambling on steep dry grass in plain leather shoes or glissading down a slope of soft snow into a sunless gully, where they find themselves out of control on a sheet of ice.

From our correspondent

96

Clothes line used on climb
Youth's 400ft fall

❄ JUNE 19 1951 ❄

At the inquest at Bethesda yesterday on Thomas Edward Bibby (20), apprentice engineer, of Penmaenmawr, who was killed while rock climbing above Lake Idwal, Caernarvonshire, on Saturday, it was stated that the rope he was using was normally used as a clothes line. The rope snapped when he fell about 400ft.

Miss June Sheila Gladdish (19), of Agnes Road, Higher Tranmere, Birkenhead, who was roped to Bibby, said they were attempting for the first time the 'Lazarus' climb. She saw him 40ft above her, hanging onto a rock with his hands, He slipped, regained his balance, then fell. 'I tried to hold onto the rope as tightly as I could to arrest his fall, but it broke.'

Miss Joan McKenna, warden of the Idwal youth hostel, identified the rope as the one used in the drying-room. She did not know the rope had been taken and did normally issue ropes to climbers.

Recording a verdict of accidental death, the coroner (Mr E Lloyd Jones) said Bibby should not have attempted to lead on the climb without having previous experience of it. Too much emphasis should not be laid on the rope, but, had it been in good order, the prospects of lessening the severity of the fall might have been better. There was no negligence on the part of those in charge of the hostel.

Miscellany: Trips round Everest

❄ AUGUST 27 1952 ❄

The forthcoming Swiss and British attempts on Mount Everest have reminded a correspondent that somewhere in the world are several amateur explorers who have taken a good look at close range at the summit of the mountain. Apparently, during the war there were several airfields conveniently situated in north-eastern Assam as bases for reconnaissance in the Himalaya, and it was from one of these that inquisitive airmen flew round Everest as a feat to recount to their grandchildren in old age. Flying over neutral Tibet was strictly forbidden but irresistible, for the view from the air of this mysterious land is one of the wonders of the world. In briefing, the embargo on crossing the frontiers into the Forbidden Land was always stressed, but, once having left the ground heading in a permitted direction, no power on earth except his conscience, could prevent a pilot from changing course to indulge in amateur exploration.

All in half a day

One or two airmen admitted off the record on the Air Force equivalent of the military maxim 'no names, no packdrill' that they had heard the call of the great peak and had succumbed, and it seems that the maps of the area were drawn from store in quantities that could not be matched with the pilots who had 'not' flown round that particular parish. How many airmen took an opportunity of inspecting one of the mysteries of this world is not known, but it seems that enough visited Everest to persuade her that her secret had been revealed to what might be described as half-day aerial excursionists round the tip and back.

'Easy rock'

❄ JULY 29 1947 ❄

The West Cumberland deputy coroner spoke yesterday of the dangers of scrambling on rock – in the instance on the Pillar Rock – not classified as a difficult climb. The warning is timely and sensible. Walkers in mountainous country (like the Lake District and Snowdon Forest) should never forget that between rock climbing and plain walking there lies an intermediate zone, often called scrambling, which has something in common with both and may be riskier than either. (Carr in his *Mountains of Snowdonia* calls it 'Alpine going', as resembling those easier Alpine ridges where the whole of a roped party can move at once.) This has to be taken seriously. The dangers of steep, difficult rock are obvious and systematic precautions of roping and belaying are taken against them. On scrambling ground the technical difficulties are much slighter; a slip is therefore far less likely and the same elaborate precautions are not taken against it. But if a man does slip, his fall is just as dangerous as a fall from difficult rock; often more so, for there is no rope to save him. A novice is safer climbing a fairly difficult climb behind an experienced leader than he is scrambling by himself on what a climbers' guide would call 'easy rock'. There is no reason why good walkers, used to finding their own way across rough and trackless country, physically fit and equipped with properly nailed boots, should not attempt the 'easy rock' routes (as hundreds of them do) so long as they realise that they are crossing the frontiers of walking and maintain an alertness and concentration that the plain walker rarely needs. For their early ventures, at least, in this field they should be content to wait for fair weather.

Leader

A Country Diary: Cumberland

❄ DECEMBER 23 1946 ❄

The house in the dale will be full to overflowing tonight, when the last of the travellers, with an enormous rucksack over his back, having been deposited at the nearest railway station, ends his long tramp over one of the mountain passes. Whatever adventures on ski and climbing boots await visitors, the not inconsiderable number of men and women gathered here will begin their day's wayfaring having breakfasted well and will return in the evening to hot baths and plenty of good cheer. Some austerity may be practised, but the plum pudding for 24 persons contains a pound each of suet, bread-crumbs, sultanas, raisins, one quarter-pound of flour, eight eggs, seasoned with mixed spices, and flavoured with a spirit that is said to have been shipped from the West Indies. This is the dish of dishes. There are, however, other sweetmeats that are not lightly to be neglected. The Christmas cake is as good as it looks and it loses nothing for having been pricked with skewers, so that there may percolate through it tiny streams of a liquid not wholly unknown to seafaring men. And there are, of course, mince pies, and ice cream from the nearby separator. Our eyes looked wonderingly at the home-cured hams and sides of bacon hung out of our reach, and at the turkeys, geese, and guineafowls being plucked and dressed, and at the huge round of beef, which Cook pronounced to be tender and far better than the white flesh she had ready for the oven. Said the mistress: 'This is nothing; we had a wedding feast for 200 yesterday. It's all in a day's work. There's nowt so queer as fowks, but if our Christmas fowk aren't thankful for this fare, Heaven help them.'

GWM

Helsby Hill

❄ AUGUST 22 1951 ❄

An appeal has been made to rock climbers not to use nailed boots on Helsby rocks, near Chester. Helsby is one of the few sandstone crags to yield any climbing. The rock is softer than most climbing rock, and it is feared that boot nails may wear out the footholds. Three local officials of the Youth Hostels Association, writing in the monthly newssheet of the Merseyside group of the YHA, say: 'It would only take a year or two of climbing in nails on the soft sand-stone to remove many of the best climbs irretrievably.'

From the road between Frodsham and Chester the rock face of Helsby Hill looks remarkably like the frowning profile of some primitive giant. This outcrop of red sandstone provides one of the very few climbing grounds between the Pennines and the mountains of North Wales. There are more than 30 recognised climbs around the fault in the face known as the Clash Hook, some of them extremely difficult, a few accessible to the unequipped novice.

A guide to the Helsby rocks says: 'Boots should be taboo for they wear away the holds. Rubbers are usual, and under wet conditions socks and Kletterschuhe' (felt- or rope-soled boots).

French success in Himalaya
Annapurna Conquered
❆ JUNE 30 1950 ❆

A group of French mountaineers, led by M Maurice Herzog, has, it is claimed, successfully climbed one of the great peaks of the Himalaya, the Annapurna, which is 26,496ft high. This is the highest mountain yet scaled, as the previous best performance was the conquest of Nanda Devi, which is about 835ft lower. Somerwell and Norton, however, in 1924 climbed considerably higher than this on Mount Everest, though they died before reaching their objective.

The expedition had set out to climb either the Annapurna or the Dhaulagiri peak (26,826ft) near by, both of which lie in unexplored territory in Nepal. They began by investigating the latter, but finding it too difficult turned to the Annapurna, the top of which they finally reached 10 days before the beginning of the monsoon.

Only one of the party, the photographer, had ever taken part in a Himalayan expedition before. Though the assault was successful at the first attempt, the going was not easy, according to M Lucien Davies, president of the French Alpine Club, interviewed in *Le Figaro*. The biggest obstacles – apart from the atmospheric difficulties, the height, the cold and the thin air – were an ice wall 4,200ft high between camps 2 and 4 and a very steep final gulley leading to the summit. M Herzog means to return to the Himalaya in 1952.

The reference to Somerwell and Norton should have been Mallory and Irvine.

From our correspondent

Horoscopes and mountaineering

❊ JANUARY 16 1947 ❊

It is reported that a proposed expedition to Mount Everest will have to be postponed because the authorities in Tibet regard the omens for that country as generally unsatisfactory. 'Difficult times in Tibet' are predicted 'for the next three years', and the 10-year-old Dalai Lama has ruled that mountaineering cannot be allowed 'until the horoscope improves'. It seems a reasonable assumption that the next three years will not offer very easy going for any country in the world, so that misgivings on the part of Tibet fit quite naturally into the general picture of international affairs.

The message that reports that misgiving gives no information about why the horoscope for the Himalaya is regarded as particularly unpropitious; indeed, casting a horoscope for a mountain range sounds rather a novelty in the way of white magic. But as attempts on Everest offer a tough enough proposition at the best of times, there may be something to be said for waiting until the Tibetan omens offer a more favourable complexion. In any event, the Dalai Lama's word is law, and, odd as the report about the Himalayan horoscope sounds, the mountaineers will have to await his permission to advance.

John Menlove Edwards, greatest of the pre-war rock climbing pioneers, 1932

Obituary: Heinrich Harrer

❄ JANUARY 10 2006 ❄

Heinrich Harrer, the mountaineer and champion of Tibet, who has died aged 93, first arrived in Lhasa in January 1946 as a penniless refugee, wearing a tattered sheepskin cloak. Accompanied by a fellow mountaineer, he had made a terrifying trek from the Indian border across the high Tibetan plateau.

One of only a handful of foreigners in Lhasa, Harrer soon caught the eye of the young 14th Dalai Lama, then aged 11. Before long he was coaching him in English and mathematics, fixing a broken projector to show the film of *Henry V*, and transcribing BBC news bulletins for the Tibetan government. Harrer left Tibet when the Chinese invaded in 1951, and embarked on a new stage of his mountaineering career, tackling new heights – from Mount Hunter in Alaska to the Carstensz Pyramid in New Guinea – though Tibet remained his passion.

Harrer and his colleague Peter Aufschnaiter had escaped from a British camp in India, where they were interned (because of their Austrian nationality), after an abortive assault on Nanga Parbat. Their epic tale, when Harrer told it in his book *Seven Years in Tibet* (1953), became an instant classic.

Harrer omitted to mention, in this or subsequent works, that as a young man in Austria he had joined the Nazi party, and with his fellow climbers had been congratulated in person by Hitler after making the first successful ascent of the north face of the Eiger. The story of his Nazi past came out in 1997, ironically just before the release of the Hollywood film of *Seven Years in Tibet*, starring Brad Pitt. Harrer said he regarded his involvement with the SS as the biggest aberration of his life: it belonged to the past, and his personal philosophy grew entirely 'out of my life in Tibet'. This episode marred his final years, and there were allegations that he was understating the strength of his past Nazi connection. The affair was also seized upon in hostile Chinese propaganda against Harrer and other western advocates of Tibetan independence.

Harrer was born in Huttenberg, in the Austrian province of Carinthia, and studied geography and sports at the Karl Franzen University in Graz. He competed as a skier in the 1936 Winter Olympics, and ascended the north face of the Eiger two years later. His book *The White Spider*, about his own Eiger climb and ascents before and after it, was published in 1958.

Whether he believed in Nazism or was just naive, it seems likely that the connection helped secure him a place on a German-Austrian expedition to the Himalaya. After escaping from the British, he and Aufschnaiter spent more than a year roaming the fringes of Tibet, where local officials refused them permission to head inland. Finally, they pretended to obey, but instead fled eastwards, in the depths of winter, across the high plateau to Lhasa. Granted leave to stay, they soon made themselves useful. Aufschnaiter was commissioned to design a sewer system for Lhasa, and Harrer surveyed the entire city.

Although he was a fervent admirer of Tibetan culture, Harrer's recollections were unsentimental. A fluent Tibetan speaker, he had many friends in Lhasa and observed from within. His photographs, in *Lost Lhasa* (1992), show ordinary Tibetans at prayer, work or play: they include prisoners in chains, begging for food.

Harrer criticised the monastic feudalism of Tibet, which, he felt, stood in the way of reform: he also acknowledged the sheer dirt and filth of everyday life. 'The Tibetans didn't wash,' he would tell me, 'and they had no toilets. Imagine Lhasa at New Year, when there were 25,000 Lhasans and 20,000 nomads as well as 25,000 monks.'

Harrer also admitted that many younger Tibetans believed that internal change was impossible and welcomed the Chinese – at first. But he insisted that if the Dalai Lama had remained in an independent Tibet, 'he would have made the changes anyway in spite of the monks.' Besides, what did Chinese 'progress' really amount to?

'Much is as it was before,' he concluded in *Return to Tibet* (1984), after finally managing to revisit Lhasa in a tourist group.

Harrer mourned the commercialisation of Lhasa and the destruction of traditional areas such as Shol village, beneath the Potala. A replica of the mostly vanished pilgrims' circuit of Lhasa stands in the Harrer museum, which he set up in Huttenberg to celebrate Tibetan culture: the museum was opened by the Dalai Lama in 1992. The two men had resumed their friendship after the Dalai Lama fled to India in 1959.

On the last page of *Seven Years in Tibet*, Harrer wrote soon after leaving Lhasa of his homesickness. He could 'still hear the wild cries of geese and cranes ... as they fly over Lhasa in the clear cold moonlight'. Forty years later he would observe that 'the landscape has not changed, but there are no more birds.' He is survived by his third wife, Katharina.

Heinrich Harrer, mountaineer, born July 6 1912, died January 7 2006

John Gittings

CHAPTER FIVE

A NEW, TIMELY
AND BRILLIANT JEWEL

After hailing the 1953 ascent of Everest by a British expedition as a 'new, timely and brilliant jewel in the Queen's diadem', the *Guardian* concluded that the mountain 'is in its nature a terminal point ... It is doubtful whether anyone will ever try to climb Everest again.'

This echoed a sentiment felt by some in the mountaineering world that now Edmund Hillary and Tenzing Norgay had 'knocked the bastard off', as Hillary so delicately put it, an era had come to an end. Climbers could now get back to ascending mountains without the pressure of having to stick a flag on the top merely for national prestige. In fact, this high point of nationalism in Himalayan climbing merely heralded the beginning of a period of competition that was to last for several decades. In particular, the 1950s were a golden age of Himalayan climbing, with 12 of the world's 14 peaks over 8,000 metres (26,247ft) being scaled.

Although it couldn't match the exclusive dispatches of the *Times'*

James Morris, who was actually with the 1953 Everest expedition, the *Guardian* gave plenty of coverage to the ascent. Most interesting were the leaders, which dwelt on the treatment of Tenzing once the team were down from the mountain. Unlike Hillary and John Hunt, the expedition leader, who both received knighthoods, it was decided to give him the lesser George medal.

Everest wasn't the only Himalayan peak to be making the news in 1953. In July, Hermann Buhl, as part of a German-Austrian expedition, had got to the top of Nanga Parbat, the 10th-highest mountain in the world. He made an incredible solo bid for the summit, which was in many ways a much greater climbing achievement than that of Hillary and Tenzing. On the descent, Buhl had only one crampon and no ice axe, which, in his exhausted state, he'd left on the top flying the flag of Pakistan.

Britain had more mountaineering success in 1955 with the ascent of Kangchenjunga, the world's third-highest mountain, by, amongst others, Joe Brown. Despite having put up numerous classic rock climbs, and making an audacious ascent of the Petit Dru in the Alps with Don Whillans, it wasn't until Brown succeeded on a traditional expedition that his exploits began to be reported. The same applied to Whillans, who came to within 150ft of the top of the Himalayan peak of Masherbrum in 1957. This expedition had been organised by the Rucksack Club and was partly sponsored by the *Guardian*. Initially, the club wanted £500 in exchange for a number of features and pictures, but the paper's offer of £300 was accepted even though the climbers knew they could probably get more from one of the 'more sensation-loving papers'. It was agreed that Bob Downes, a talented young climber, would write the reports but unfortunately he died of pulmonary oedema on the mountain.

In the autumn of 1956, Alastair Hetherington was appointed editor of the paper. He was brought up in Scotland and, after Oxford and six years in the army, he returned there as a journalist on the Glasgow *Herald*. A passionate hill walker, he was also an active member of the Scottish Mountaineering Club and later on in life compiled a hiking guide to Arran. On joining the *Guardian* as a leader writer in 1950, his thirst for the hills was met by Paddy Monkhouse, who introduced him to the Pennines. When, along with most of the *Guardian* editorial departments, he moved to London in 1964, Hetherington brought a sharp outdoor asceticism to the world of 1960s Fleet Street. His abstentions were famous and he was known to refuse cream with fruit salad at lunch because he wanted to keep a clear head while duty editing that night. Staff must have dreaded being asked to join him in brisk walks at lunchtime, irrespective of the weather, rather than meet in the pub, their natural habitat.

Women too were now climbing, and dying on, the highest peaks. When in 1959 the distinguished French climber Claude Kogan was killed on Cho Oyu, the paper, while disapproving of all-female teams, stated that 'men should be readier to accept women of her gifts and experience as equal companions in a common venture.' On the home front, Gwen Moffat was breaking down barriers by becoming one of the first female climbing guides. Stories about female climbers also gave the leader writers an opportunity to wheel out an old saying, 'an easy day for a lady'. Coined by the Victorian mountaineer and literary critic Leslie Stephen (father of Virginia Woolf and Vanessa Bell), and popularised by AF Mummery, it suggested that climbs go through three stages, ending up easy enough for ladies. In fact, Stephen had meant it as an ironic tribute to his brilliant climbing partner Lily Bristow.

In 1958 a long article appeared about the climbing scene based at the famous Pen-y-Gwryd hotel near Snowdon, by James Morris (going some way to redressing the balance for so many Lakeland articles).

After leaving the *Times*, Morris had joined the paper in mid-1956 as a special features writer, although he was also used in foreign emergencies such as Suez. The arrangement also allowed him a few months off each year to write books. Commenting about the

Guardian in 1974, Morris wrote, 'it let me go more or less where I liked, and seldom cut a word or changed an adjective.' In the end, however, Morris found the paper 'too wet for my taste' and departed in 1961.

The 1950s also saw the appearance on the pages of A Harry Griffin, who was to file his fortnightly Lake District-based Country Diary for the next half-century or so. Another Lakeland character, Alfred Wainwright, made his first appearance in the paper in 1955 with a short review of the first of his pictorial guides. It was illustrated with a reproduction of one of the famous 'vertical sketch maps'.

Everest

❄ June 3 1953 ❄

The ascent of Everest by a British expedition is a new, timely and brilliant jewel in the Queen's diadem. The warmest congratulations are due the whole team, British and Sherpa, who have shared in this superb achievement. It has called for a combination of mountaineering skill, resolution, scientific study, and logistic planning, such as no comparable enterprise has received. The credit of the two climbers who actually reached the summit – E Hillary and Tensing Norgay – is only in the final stage a personal one. It is much more the flowering of a collective effort in which all have shared – not forgetting the members of the 11 previous expeditions for, as Mr Murray put in his recent book, each team that goes to Everest stands on the shoulders of the one before it. Colonel Hunt, the leader of the successful expedition, would be the first to pay his tribute to the pioneers; but it must be said that he had shown a wonderful grasp of the essentials of the Everest problem, the more remarkable in a man who has not set foot on the mountain before. Hillary, the New Zealander, was with Shipton's party in 1951, when it was first shown that the icefall of the Khumbu glacier could be made to yield a practicable approach to the south ridge; his success shows the value of the New Zealand Alps as a training ground for mountaineers. Everyone will rejoice that Tensing was with him. A year ago, he and Raymond Lambers, the Swiss climber, came nearer to the summit than any before them; and he stands as the personification of his people, the cheerful and hardy Sherpas, whose qualities have contributed so much to the final conquest of the mountain. The evolution of the Sherpa from a mere load carrier to a mountaineer has been one of the main factors in the advance of Himalayan climbing. It is proper, too, that Everest should have yielded to a citizen of Nepal, for it would be unclimbed still if the Nepalese government had not laid aside its ancient policy of seclusion to permit the climbers to approach the mountain through its territory.

Another factor in the ascent has certainly been the better and fuller use of oxygen equipment by this party. Whether Everest could be climbed without oxygen was long debated by mountaineers. Some high authorities (among them Norton, who reached 28,000ft in 1924) thought it unnecessary. But the debate was conducted on too narrow a question, the value of oxygen to the assault party on the last stage of the climb. Colonel Hunt applied two new and fruitful ideas. First, if oxygen kept the climber in better trim while climbing would it not also improve his general condition if he breathed it as he slept? So equipment was devised that allows a man to inhale oxygen while sleeping, for use in the higher camps. The other idea was not less important. If oxygen aids the climber at 28,000ft, would it not also aid the porter to say, 25,000ft? Would it not so improve the stamina, speed, and load-carrying capacity of the Sherpas to guarantee a really strong assault camp on the South Col, the real prerequisite of success? The Sherpas are to some extent naturally acclimatised to great heights, through living normally about 12,000ft above sea level. But even they found their energies redoubled by the use of oxygen over 20,000ft or so: to quote a letter from a member of the expedition during the period of preliminary training, they were to be seen 'dashing about the mountains like steam engines'. These expedients have called for oxygen equipment on a bigger scale than ever before, and a British firm designed and supplied an improved pattern to the expedition without charge. But these scientific advantages do not detract from the great credit due to the climbers themselves for a unique achievement.

The ascent of Everest may be, in a sense, less fruitful than some other first ascents, of the Matterhorn, for instance, or even of Napes Needle, which has inspired innumerable others. Everest is in its nature a terminal point; it is like one of those great peaks that stand a little aside from the main chain of the range. It is doubtful whether anyone will ever try to climb Everest again now that it has been done. So the triumph of the British expedition of 1953 may remain unique and complete as the greatest event in the history of mountaineering.

Leader

Everest honours

❄ JUNE 17 1953 ❄

Colonel Hunt's arrangements for the climbing of Everest were a masterpiece of organisation and forethought. One cannot say the same about the arrangements for honouring the victors. The knighthoods conferred on Colonel Hunt himself and Hillary were announced, with commendable promptitude, on June 7; the position of Tensing remains embarrassingly obscure. It is true that, as he is not a British subject, it is necessary to consult his own government before a British honour can be bestowed on him. But it was obvious from the start to anyone with the least knowledge of mountaineering that he was quite likely to be a member of the assault party, in view of his fine performance with Lambert in the Swiss expedition of 1952: and soundings could surely have been taken in decent time. Since June 7, nothing more has been said at this end. From Kathmandu come reports that it is proposed to award him the George medal. Colonel Hunt's comment is apposite: 'He deserved it, and more.' A good deal more, many people think. The George medal is given in recognition for such acts of gallantry as, for instance, the arrest by police officers of armed criminals. (The arrest of Craig and Bentley was rewarded by one George Cross and two George medals.) It seems hardly appropriate to Tensing's feat. Would it not be wiser, since Hillary and he stood on the summit side by side, to honour them in the same way? Honourary knighthoods conferred on foreigners are rare but not unknown; Douglas Fairbanks is an instance. And it is objected that Tensing was with the expedition as a 'professional'; how did Gordon Richards and Jack Hobbs earn their laurels?

Gordon Richards was a very successful jockey; Jack Hobbs played cricket for England

Leader

Down from Everest

❄ JUNE 23 1953 ❄

The controversy over Tensing and his part in the ascent of Everest is an absurdity that might nevertheless develop into an ugly quarrel if it is not checked. The questions cut across each other. Is Tensing a citizen of Nepal, where he was born, or of India, where he now lives? And what was his share in the final stage of the ascent? The first bedevils the answer to the second. The people of Nepal, not unnaturally, are making the most of Tensing. They don't often get a chance to shine in the world and this is a golden opportunity to put Nepal on the map. (We ourselves, after all, are not unwilling to proclaim the success of the expedition as a triumph for Britain.) So the poor man is pestered to declare himself a lifelong Nepalese, and to claim an exaggerated share of the credit for the climb. India is no less anxious to welcome Tensing as her own, and some Indian newspapers have joined the Nepalese in exaggerating his share of the credit. Nepalese zealots, in reply, are threatening with violence anyone who calls him an Indian. While Tensing receives a specially struck gold medal from India and the Order of the Nepal Star from Nepal, there is still nothing known for sure about the way the British government proposes to recognise his feat – perhaps because it wishes to secure the consent of his government before honouring him, and cannot decide which his government is. This delay, of course, makes the Indian and Nepalese zealots think the Tensing is being slighted by the haughty British, and play him up all the more. It is a silly business. In a feat like Hillary's and Tensing's one cannot distinguish degrees of credit. If Hillary led the way on the upper slopes, Tensing's high-altitude climbing was done on top of his work as sirdar [leader] of the porters, which itself made a great contribution to the expedition's success. If Hillary was the first on top, by a few yards, as we believe he was, that is nothing to Tensing's discredit. They should be honoured alike by all countries that wish to honour them: without jealousy between the nations, as there is none between the men.

Leader

The man who peaked at 40

❄ JUNE 2 1977 ❄

Tenzing Norgay Sherpa spent a quiet Sunday in Haslemere in Surrey lunching off soup and cold meats and toasting his memories in Coca-Cola. His memories of course, were of May 29 1953, during which he spent what should have been lunchtime, burying a toy cat, a pencil and some sweets at the summit of Mt Everest. Today is the 24th anniversary of Coronation Day, when the news reached Britain that the highest mountain had been scaled, and Tenzing is in London signing copies of his timely autobiography, *After Everest* (Allen and Unwin, £4.95).

Although as a young village lad he used to take his yaks to pasture at 18,000ft, he learned nothing of mountaineering until he obtained work as a porter on the fifth British expedition to Everest in 1935, when he carried loads to the North Col at 22,000ft. He worked for number of expeditions in the Himalaya region for the next two decades, getting at one stage, with the Swiss, to within 800ft of the summit. On his seventh try, as one of the assault team led by the then Colonel John Hunt, he made it.

Hunt warned Tenzing, not long after he and his climbing partner clambered down the mountain and Sir Edmund Hillary announced 'We've knocked the bastard off,' that his troubles had only begun. Just as the London papers jubilantly announced that 'Britons' had conquered Everest, and just as the people in New Zealand were seized of the fact that Hillary had climbed it (assisted by a fellow New Zealander, George Lowe) so the Nepalese and the Indians made Tenzing the hero of the climb.

And even today, Tenzing is cautious about saying exactly who got to the top first. His English is limited, but he has answered the same question so many times in the past two decades that the phrases slide out smoothly: Everest is not a pinnacle up which one man must go first and then climb down to make room for the other.

The summit is flat, like a table, and the two men who have been working as a team and who are roped tightly together arrive together. (Hillary, who has reported that he became annoyed during their triumphal procession of India to see crude banners depicting Tenzing hauling up a recumbent Hillary, says in his own autobiography that he got to the top 'on a tight rope from Tenzing'.)

He looks back on those days with just that fresh, cheerful face that captured the world's imagination in 1953, but there is a slightly sour note to his story. He fell under the spell of Pandit Nehru on their first meeting. Nehru appointed him field director of the newly formed Himalayan Mountaineering Institute and told him: 'Now you make a thousand Tenzings.' Since then he has supervised the training of more than 4,000 students.

Eight Indian HMI graduates have climbed to the top of Everest, and a ninth student, a Nepalese and nephew of Tenzing, has been there twice. And yet, he reports a little wistfully, he personally has never been invited to take part in an Indian expedition to the mountain. Jealousy, he thinks. And in the 20 or more years he has served HMI he has never had a wage rise: his salary is still the same 1,400 rupees a month it always was.

Furthermore, he has been forcibly retired, although he is still retained as an adviser by HMI. In Nepal, he finds himself regarded with mixed feelings, probably because he worked with, and identified himself with Indian mountaineering, although he has done a lot for the reputation of the Sherpa people. But he says that Edmund Hillary, in raising funds for schools, hospitals and bridges, has probably done more for the Sherpa people than he has.

He achieved another kind of fame as a dog breeder – of Lhasa absos – but he gives them away, because Sherpas are superstitious about selling dogs. A good Lhasa abso can fetch $5,000.

Tenzing feels he could still climb Everest again (he was almost 40 when he climbed it) and he enjoys meeting people, although he diplomatically expresses no preferences. Everest has made him a lot of friends, he says, and when he is told that the famous photograph that Hillary took 24 years ago in now printed on dozens of Jubilee souvenirs, he looks pleased, and says he must get one.

Tim Radford

Tenzing – with 'z' – in Snowdonia

❋ MAY 24 1973 ❋

Tenzing Norgay, Sherpa and George medallist, flew to London yesterday, six days before the 20th anniversary of his ascent of

Everest. Small, dapper, and now 59, he was en route for Snowdonia, where the British Everest team of 1953 will celebrate the occasion with mountain rambles and a dinner party on Saturday night. All subsequent but less successful British Everest expedition members have been invited.

Mr Tenzing pointed out good-naturedly that the British press has spelt his name wrongly over all these years: it has a 'z' not an 's' in the middle, and he produced his business card to prove it. Colonel Charles Wylie, who was secretary of the 1953 expedition, said that neither was it correct to call him Sherpa Tenzing – Sherpa was the name of his tribe. It was like addressing the prime minister as Broadstairs Ted.

Rosemary Collins

Gamesmanship on mountain?
Nanga Parbat climbers fall out

❄ AUGUST 7 1953 ❄

The leader of the Austro-German expedition that conquered Nanga Parbat, Dr Karl Herrligkoffer, has obtained an injunction against Hermann Buhl, the man who climbed the mountain, and the Munich *Abend Zeitung* to restrain them from publishing a series of articles entitled 'The truth about Nanga Parbat at last'.

The injunction will put a stop, for a few days at least, to a quarrel that seems to have been going on ever since the climbers left the mountain. The lord mayor of Munich tried in vain to stop it at a press reception there on Monday. There has, too, been much adverse comment in the press on the cantankerous way in which the climbers have behaved since returning from their bold adventure.

The ground for the injunction is a contract between Herrligkoffer and all members of the expedition, who are said to have promised not to publish independent accounts of their experiences on Nanga Parbat. The *Abend Zeitung* has given notice of appeal, having heard from its lawyers that the contract is invalid. The paper says today that the public has a right to know what really happened.

Climbers' oath

It seems to have been a curious expedition, though successful. Before leaving their base camp, the climbers swore a sort of oath. After that, according to one of their number, they felt themselves to be subject to some kind of martial law. This may or may not have been the case. It seems to be true, however, that neither the oath nor their 'iron determination' to get to the top prevented them falling out among themselves.

The oath, as quoted by the expedition's cameraman, Hans Ertl, declares:

'We promise to be honourable fighters in the struggle for one of the highest 8,000-metre mountains in the world, for the glory of climbers the world over and for the honour of our homeland.'

This oath was sworn on the morning that the climbers left their base camp. Soon after they had established higher camps. Herrligkoffer is reported to have ordered them to withdraw to refresh themselves for the assault on the summit. Two climbers, Buhl and Frunberger, together with Ertl, are said to have disobeyed this order because they felt in good form, they thought the weather was improving, and they did not wish to postpone the final assault.

Conflicting reports

Herrligkoffer has since explained that his order was not meant to be final and that he withdrew it when the weather got better. Be that as it may, Buhl and one companion, Kempter, set out for the summit together, but only Buhl arrived. Buhl says that he was unable to awaken Kempter on the morning of the assault and decided to go on alone: Kempter says that Buhl left him in the highest camp. Buhl also complains that Kempter had most of the rations in his rucksack and failed to leave any behind when he started his descent.

Tenzing Norgay and Edmund Hillary drink tea in the Western Cwm, Everest, in 1953

These and other, conflicting and unfriendly, reports have led people to believe that the spirit of the climbers left something to be desired. So far, however, the reports have been contradictory. All that is known for certain about the final assault is that Buhl was by himself and that he embellished the summit of Nanga Parbat with the flag of Pakistan.

From our correspondent

Disputing the hills

❄ AUGUST 10 1953 ❄

The dispute over Hermann Buhl's proposal to give his own version of the Austro-German ascent of Nanga Parbat is one of many in the history of mountaineering. What was perhaps the earliest kind involved Marc Théodore Bourrit, an ambitious and none too courageous Alpine pioneer, and Michel-Gabriel Paccard, the first man to climb Mont Blanc. In 1783 Paccard and Bourrit joined in an abortive expedition up this, Europe's highest mountain, but Bourrit's performance was so uninspiring that Paccard vowed that he would never again climb in his company. There were other attempts, but in 1786 Paccard and Jacques Balmat, a chamois-hunter, reached the summit.

Almost immediately the jealous and affronted Bourrit published a 'Letter on the first journey to the summit of Mont Blanc', claiming (untruthfully) that Balmat had led the climb and in places had had to drag Paccard with him. Paccard published articles contradicting Bourrit's story, but the damage was done, and only in the last few years have historians been able to give Paccard full credit for his part in the climb.

From our correspondent

Top women

❄ NOVEMBER 2 1957 ❄

Those who believe that anything more hazardous than the Chilterns is a male province must have been rather startled by the news that Mrs Joyce Dunsheath has climbed Mount Elbrus in the Caucasus. Great women climbers are admittedly few and far between. Nevertheless they span the entire range of modern mountaineering short of Himalayan adventures. Henriette d'Angeville, an intrepid aristocrat, led the way in 1838, when, on her first serious climb, she conquered Mont Blanc. It was really an outrageous piece of bravado. The only advice she could get were appeals begging her drop her foolish notions or she would certainly freeze to death. So, for a summer climb, she designed a costume better fitted for Arctic conditions. As the going became more difficult, the stops became more frequent. She kept dropping off to sleep and in the end the kindly but perplexed guides more or less dragged her to the top. Once there, however, she revived and was with difficulty persuaded to come down, she was so busy writing triumphant notes to her friends with one of the six pencils sharpened at both ends which she carried, along with a parasol, a fan, a large straw hat, and field-glasses, so that she could spy on those who were watching her from below.

Henriette later became an accomplished climber. In her 70th year she climbed the 10,500ft Oldenhorn peak in 10 hours, a record that withstood younger blood for many years.

Maid of the mountain

To be a pioneer mountaineer presupposed a degree of eccentricity. For the most part they were not Amazons, but generally rather frail, cautious, and quite oblivious to ridicule or scandal. Their great problem, of course, was what to wear. The majority compromised between comfort and convention. Elizabeth Le Blond, who was the first to make a 'manless' ascent in the Alps and who founded the Ladies Alpine Club 50 years ago, wore a skirt until she could safely reveal the riding breeches underneath. One of her difficulties was that she had never taken off or put on her own boots. There was only one thing a society woman could do; she always took her maid with her as far as possible. Lucy Walker, of the famous Liverpool family who spent their summers hopping from Alp to Alp, refused to wear anything but skirts. They did not, however, prevent her from ascending the Matterhorn in 1871 or making 98 other major ascents in the Alps. Nor did mountain sickness, which afflicted her above 12,000ft, manage to put her down.

'Easy day for a lady'

❄ SEPTEMBER 3 1956 ❄

There is an old saying among mountaineers that Alpine climbs go through three stages; 'the hardest climb in the Alps' becomes in time 'a sound climb for a strong party', and ends up as an 'easy day for a lady'. Is the same natural process at work in the Himalaya? The question is prompted by the almost simultaneous publication of two books largely concerned with Himalayan climbing by women. *White Fury* records an expedition, led and chronicled by Raymond Lambert and Mme Claude Kogan, a distinguished French mountaineer, which began as a reconnaissance of Gaurisankar and ended as an attempt on Cho Oyu; *Tents in the Clouds,* by Monica Jackson and Elizabeth Stark, describes a much more modest but no less significant expedition by three members of the Ladies' Scottish Climbing Club, who with four Sherpas but no male Europeans cleared up a very respectable peak of 22,000ft. Two morals are pointed. Mme Kogan (who had already shown her mettle on the first ascent of Nun Kun in 1953) has proved that a first-class woman mountaineer can hold her own on a major peak; Cho Oyu is the sixth or seventh summit in the world in height, and she would almost certainly have reached the top but for an appalling gale on the crucial day. The Scottish party has shown that quite ordinary women climbers can enjoy themselves in the Himalaya (if they can raise the fare) as readily as they could in the Alps, or in the Highlands. One may expect to see both examples followed – though Cho Oyu is unlikely ever to become an 'easy day'.

Leader

Women mountaineers

❊ NOVEMBER 18 1959 ❊

But for a bad break in the weather, Mme Kogan and Mlle van der Stratten might well have reached the summit of Cho Oyu instead of dying on the mountain – this was the opinion expressed yesterday at Kathmandu by Countess Gravina, who took over the leadership of the party after Mme Kogan's death. It may be so, but the weather is apt to be very bad on Cho Oyu after the monsoon, as Mme Kogan herself found in 1954. It would be a great pity if this rebuff scared off women from the Himalaya. But it might be still more lamentable if it was to spur them beyond their strength of skill in an attempt to prove their mettle. Countess Gravina is reported as saying that Cho Oyu is a 'challenge to international womanhood, and must be climbed by a team of women'. Surely this is a perilous spirit in which to approach great mountains, and half akin to the nationalist rivalries that at one time led young men to immolate themselves on the Alps. Women have had less than their fair share of Himalayan climbing, perhaps rather from social convention than from lack of ability; Mme Kogan's status was unique, though there have been some brilliant women climbers, like Mme Morin and Mrs Underhill, at the Alpine level. But her great achievement was to show that a woman could hold her own in a strong party of men. The moral of her career is not that women as such should enter into rivalry with men, but that men should be readier to accept women of her gifts and experience as equal companions in a common venture.

Leader

Mecca of climbers: Everest view in Wales

❄ JUNE 23 1958 ❄

Two men on the hillside outside my tent this morning, away above the road junction at Pen-y-Gwryd. The younger of the two was a tatterdemalion Welsh shepherd, a cheerful, cloth-clapped scarecrow of a man, driving his sheep down to the road with a clatter and a scurry, calling to his dog, shouting guttural Welsh encouragements, and waving his thick stick like an apparition. The elder was a scholarly looking man in plus fours.

He was setting off through the rain for a day's scrambling, carrying his packed lunch in a haversack and wearing on his face, as the raindrops streamed off his bushy eyebrows, an expression of unyielding enthusiasm. He was evidently a believer in rhythmic breathing, for as he walked he whistled to himself, under his breath a monotonous Bach-like melody: two beats to a footstep, round and round, over and over again, in an endless, classical cadence.

The two men passed each other as I gaped at them. The shepherd brandished his stick and grunted casually; the scholar interrupted his fugue to utter a greeting in a reedy academic voice; and so they disappeared into the rain. Neither seemed in the least surprised at this improbable confrontation, nor paused for a moment in his progression; for the truth is that, though my sodden tent looks homely enough, this is no ordinary hillside.

Climbers' inn

Pen-y-Gwryd, the little hamlet at the road fork below me, looks like many another old Welsh posting station – an inn, a clump of trees, a petrol station, a pond, a signpost, a cluster of gently smoking chimneys: but in fact is the unofficial Vatican, the homegrown Mecca of British mountaineering, a sport that has never been without the individualists and eccentrics. From this small place the climbers had gone out to the four corners of the earth, to Everest and the Andes, to the Ruwenzori and the High Rockies; and on a weekend in June, even when the Glyders are shrouded in cloud and the tents on the hillside are dampened and depressed, Pen-y-Gwryd is thick with passions and prejudices and rhythmic breathings of the mountaineers.

Last night, for instance, as we crowded into the small smoking-room of the inn, or loitered with our mugs around its trestle tables, the talk ranged over the whole gamut of alpinism, from pitons to Kangchenjunga, by way of the Radcliffe camera. Here were the brave beginners, festooned in equipment, shrouded in anoraks, reliving their moments on Tryfan in the afternoon, when the face of that long-suffering protrusion echoed with the shrill altercations of the tyros. Every kind of accent fills the room, Lancashire and Etonian and clerical, and even Welsh; and there are lots of sprightly but muscular girls, and a few young men with beards, and one or two more elderly practitioners rather scout-masterly in style, mingling breezily with the chaps.

This is a classless, gregarious assembly, perhaps a little self-satisfied in its fraternity. It smells heartily of the outdoor, with suggestions of campfires and canvas and Kendal mint cake. It provided the prefects at school. It drinks beer. It says the newspapers usually get things wrong. It votes Liberal, I shouldn't wonder.

Sometimes there is a hush and a murmur, as one of the great mountaineers edges his way modestly through the crowd. (Braggadocio is not encouraged at Pen-y-Gwryd.) Joe Brown, that legendary virtuoso, cannot be here tonight, for he is up the road at Pen-y-Pass, nursing a damaged ankle in a tent; but here is George Band, a smiling bespectacled giant, in breeches and suede shoes and no socks. He is off on Wednesday to the Caucasus, he hopes, and he and some of his colleagues of the Caucasus climbing party are up here for a last preparatory weekend, still keeping their fingers crossed for their Russian visas.

One of their nice, white shooting brakes, kindly lent by the makers and suitably emblazoned, is parked outside the inn, and upstairs another member of their team is lying in bed, suddenly frustrated by an attack of tonsillitis. The rest of them are planning an unusually hideous enterprise tomorrow, entailing the climbing of 14 3,000ft tops in 12 hours; but they are a little reticent about their plans, in case the *Daily Express* sues them for breach of copyright.

Inside the cosy smoking room, where a fire burns merrily, the sedater habitués are gathered. There is a rubicund old admiral, the spark in his eye miraculously undimmed in spite of half a century of mountaineering. There is a genial accountant from Liverpool momentarily laying aside, as he buries his nose in an enormous beer mug, a new translation of St Paul's Epistles. There is a shy man with spectacles who says he is 'a civil servant, not altogether unconnected, in a remote kind of way, with a distant branch of the ah, Foreign Office'. There is a senior army officer in tweeds, who comes for the fishing and has a funny clown-like dog. And there are a few simple travellers, men with pleasant Midland anecdotes and women in flowered rayon, who sit beside the fire in attitudes of suppressed bewilderment, for they thought they were just getting a bed for the night, and they found themselves in Shangri-La.

Endless and delightful are the anomalies of Pen-y-Gwryd. Not long ago, two Sherpas with pigtails were attached to the staff of the inn, and once began rounding up all the sheep from the surrounding hills to save them from the wolves.

As we sat there last night, we knew that all around us in the mountains, from Bethesda to Capel Curig, were the tents of the weekend climbers; huddled against the rocks or defiant beside a river, yellow and white and brown, with the lights of their lanterns shining beguilingly through the night.

Pen-y-Gwryd lies at the heart of the climbers' country, the marketplace of their craft. When a climber wants a drink in the Snowdon country, more often than not he tramps down the road, or traverses a hill, or begs a lift to Pen-y-Gwryd, where he knows they speak his own language, and will not look askance at his muddy breeches. When an Everest team wants to celebrate an anniversary, it brings its wives, its titles, and its high memories to this little hamlet in Caernarvonshire. And only yesterday Mr Briggs, the proprietor of the inn, stormed off with his mountain rescue team to help an injured mountaineer, like a big mechanised St Bernard delivering the brandy.

So the old posting station is instinct with the traditions of mountaineering, and its tentacles of memory or experience reach out to the far places of the world. On the walls of its inn are immortalised the alpinists of the past, in their Norfolk jackets or long, demure skirts, with their splendid English moustaches and their donnish poses: and there is hardly a British mountaineer alive, not an ambassador in Helsinki or a head of the Third Programme, or a ridge walker in Nottingham or a stout girl rock climber from Reading University, who does not look with affection towards the road junction at Pen-y-Gwryd.

Thus it was pleasant to contemplate those two passing figures on the hillside this morning, and collate them with all the bustling contrasts in the inn below, where the poor Caucasus man was cursing his tonsillitis, the admiral was lacing up his boots, the accountant was packing St Paul with his ham sandwiches, and all the ghosts of the alpinists were finishing a long, leisurely Elysian breakfast.

James Morris

Strong rope

❊ AUGUST 15 1957 ❊

The BBC has assembled a strong team for its *Eye to Eye* television programme on rock climbing on Friday week. The undisputed star, of course, is Joe Brown, though one keeps hearing of new geniuses who may challenge him in a year or so. In case modesty prevents him from doing himself justice there is his chief chronicler, Geoff Sutton, who contributed the account of his feats to the book *Snowdon Biography* earlier this year, and there is also that gallant octogenarian G Winthrop Young, who wrote on the early history of Welsh climbing.

The growth of feminine interest in the sport is justly marked by the inclusion of Monica Jackson, who led the first all-woman party to the Himalaya, and of Gwen Moffat, probably the only woman in the world to earn her living as a rock climbing guide. Both are small and fragile-looking, but no one who has watched Gwen Moffat generaling a party up the Idwal Slabs could doubt her high professional competence. And there is her husband, Johnny Lees, to represent another form of professional mountaineering. He is a sergeant in the RAF rescue unit based on Valley in Anglesey, and though its primary purpose is to rescue crashed air crews, many a rope come to grief has found Sergeant Lees and his stretcher-bearing team, appearing out of the mist or twilight, a sight for sore eyes.

Climbing revolution

❆ SEPTEMBER 25 1957 ❆

At both ends of the mountaineering scale there has been something of a revolution in the last decade. The great Himalayan peaks have been climbed one after another; and in the relatively miniscule art of rock climbing on British hills there has been an advance hardly less remarkable on its own small scale. Two current books bring the point home. In *Snowdon Biography* (Dent, 25s), Geoffrey Sutton gives an account (sandwiched between historical and literary sections by Winthrop Young and Wilfrid Noyce respectively) of recent climbing in Wales. After speaking of the 'balance technique' of climbing, which flowered between the wars, he goes on, 'In 1950, the technique of out-of-balance climbing came into its own, and the overhang epoch began.' The new climbs made in the last few years – by a handful of exceptionally gifted climbers, and often with the artificial aids already familiar in the Alps – have been much more difficult than any made before. Yet slowly these remarkable first ascents are beginning to be repeated by others. The gritstone edges of the Peak are even smaller in scale than the crags of Wales. Yet the same story is told of them. In his introduction to *Further Developments in the Peak District* (Willmer Brothers, 10s 6d), Eric Byne says: 'Perhaps gritstone climbing has now reached its peak in the standard of difficulty that has been attained – a standard that 15 years ago would have seemed fantastic.'

Climbing with pitons has appeared even on gritstone! Not on all the crags, fortunately; but Millstone Edge near Grindleford is now accepted as a 'piton climbing ground', where the technique can be practised near at home. There have been some spectacular results. Such climbing should not be derided as a sort of carving of cherrystones. Joe Brown, who has stood out among the new climbers on Snowdon and in the Peak, was the first man up Kangchenjunga.

Leader

Kangchenjunga

❄ JUNE 3 1955 ❄

The ascent of Kangchenjunga is a tremendous achievement. Sir John Hunt described it in prospect as 'the greatest feat in mountaineering', for it is almost as high as Everest and its technical difficulties have always been reckoned greater. What makes the success of Charles Evans's party the more remarkable is that it was attacking a face of the mountain that was, in its upper part, almost unknown. All serious attempts on the mountain have been made from the north side, not because of political difficulties, like those which for so long barred access to the south side of Everest (and now bar the north approach), but because the leading mountaineers considered the south side impossibly difficult and dangerous. In 1905, an ill-equipped party visited the Yalung Glacier and studied the side of the mountain by which Evans's party had gone; but this was hardly a serious attempt. Nearly 50 years passed before Kempe, in 1954, took a close look at this face and saw a possible route up the steep glacier that leads to the Great Shelf, stretching across the southern face at 24,000ft. His judgment proved correct. The icefalls were found practicable, though not quite by the route he had tentatively suggested. In all, the party seems to have covered 10,000ft of virgin ground, a feat probably without parallel in Himalayan climbing. Evans, who had the distinction of reaching the South Summit on Everest, has shown himself a brilliant leader as well as a fine mountaineer.

Leader

We knocked the bastard off

❄ MARCH 13 2003 ❄

Settled into an armchair with his back to Auckland's Hobson Bay, Edmund Hillary is still recognisable as the lanky beekeeper who climbed Everest with Tenzing Norgay in May 1953. His eyebrows have unfurled into patrician crests, and the black of his hair is losing out to the white. The voice is slow, considered and slightly wheezy – if he ever sounds tired, it is probably because he has spent the past 50 years reprising the same old anecdotes about Everest.

Were he 33 now instead of 83, he is not sure that he would even bother with tackling the famous peak. 'There wouldn't be any of the feeling of achievement. It's been dealt with. So much is known about it.' He pauses. 'I suppose I would want to climb it,' he smiles.

He talks about his experiences with the bluff modesty of a Boys' Own adventure hero. When he set off for the Himalaya, he was a 'reasonably good climber'. Of his achievement, he concedes that he and Tenzing 'did a pretty good job'.

On reaching the summit of Everest, he initially went to shake hands manfully with Tenzing before the Sherpa threw his arms around him and slapped him on the back. 'I wasn't extremely excited,' he says. 'I didn't jump around, but I had a pretty strong feeling of satisfaction. It was a very good moment in that sense.'

It seems almost underwhelming to be greeted with this matter-of-fact attitude from arguably the most famous mountaineer of all time. The most serious climbers are popularly believed to have an almost mystical dedication to the peaks they attempt. Reinhold Messner, the Italian who became the first to scale Everest without oxygen, in 1978, described a 'state of spiritual abstraction' at the summit. 'I no longer belong to myself and to my eyesight,' he wrote. 'I am nothing more than a single narrow gasping lung, floating over the mists and the summits.'

Even John Hunt, the stiff British army colonel who led the 1953 expedition, refused to talk about the 'conquest' of Everest, only the 'ascent' – a concession to Tibetan reverence for Chomolungma, the goddess mother of the earth, that carries a whiff of superstition about it. Hillary's down-to-earth attitude is the exception to this rule. 'When you go to the mountains you see them and you admire them. In a sense they give you a challenge, and you try to express that challenge by climbing them,' he says.

It is a long way from Mallory's own sonorous metaphor. 'If you cannot understand that there is something in man which responds to the challenge of this mountain and goes out to meet it,' he wrote, 'that the struggle is the struggle of life itself upward and forever upward, then you won't see why we go. What we get from this adventure is just sheer joy. And joy is, after all, the end of life.'

Hillary's response to reaching the summit was more succinct. 'Well, we knocked the bastard off,' he told his companions on returning to base camp.

I ask him if standing on the peak of the highest mountain in the world felt qualitatively different to conquering another, equally difficult peak, but he bats it away. 'Oh, I definitely knew I was on top of Everest,' he says.

He seems impatient of too much self-analysis, disliking all the symbol and metaphor that has accreted to the mountain. But for all this self-effacement, in 1953 Hillary found himself caught up in a stage-managed moment of high patriotism. No matter that the pioneers had been a New Zealander and a Nepalese, the expedition was British: in the photograph taken at the summit, the British, Nepalese, Indian and United Nations flags flutter, but Hillary's native country goes unrepresented.

Amid the dying remnants of the empire, the news of this final grand exploit acted like a tonic. The first reports of the ascent arrived in London to coincide with the Queen's coronation. A week later,

Hillary and Hunt were knighted (Tenzing missed out on this honour, because he was not a British citizen).

It was no accident that the triumph coincided so neatly with the coronation. The Himalayan Committee, which sponsored the ascent, was an avowedly nationalistic body. Eric Shipton, the great mountaineer who had been Hillary's inspiration and mentor, was thrown off the expedition in favour of Hunt because of fears that he would not push the Nepalese authorities hard enough to start the climb in time. The French were booked for 1954, the Swiss for 1955, and, as a favourite mountaineer's dictum has it, 'No one remembers who climbed Mount Everest the second time.'

Their success sparked a brief golden age of mountaineering. Of the 14 mountains above 8,000m, only Annapurna had been scaled when Hillary and Tenzing stood on top of Everest. Just five weeks later, the world's ninth highest peak, Nanga Parbat, was topped, and by the end of the decade only Shishapangma, which lay off-limits to western alpinists in Chinese Tibet, remained unconquered.

Since the early 1970s, the trickle of adventurers making it to Everest's summit has become a flood: 1,500 pairs of boots have trekked their way to the top, ropes and tents lie abandoned in the snow, and glacial crevasses are bridged by aluminium ladders. Two years ago, the Nepalese government began a clean-up operation on the mountain after nearly 100 tons of rubbish was discovered on its slopes.

Hillary's son, Peter, has climbed the peak twice, and three generations of Tenzings have stood at 29,028ft. There have been husband-and-wife ascents, climbs by siblings, even a climb by a blind mountaineer. In 2001, two people snowboarded down from the summit.

It is a highly profitable business. A guided tour to the top of Everest costs between £12,500 and £40,000, not including the equipment you will need. There are even plans afoot to open an internet cafe at the Everest base camp.

'I find it all rather sad,' says Hillary. 'I like to think of Everest as a great mountaineering challenge, and when you've got people just streaming up the mountain – well, many of them are just climbing it to get their name in the paper really.'

In one 1993 expedition, 40 people reached the peak in the course of a day, more than did so during the first 20 years after the 1953 ascent. 'They might as well have provided a bus,' Hillary commented at the time.

'I do believe that many of the climbs on the mountain now lack that sense of success and exhilaration that we gained from going up,' he says. 'There was a much bigger challenge for us than there has been for later expeditions.'

Maybe he is just in a good mood, but as the 50th anniversary of the ascent approaches, he is talking with the circumspection of an ambassador. On May 29, he will be surrounded by 800 other Everest climbers for the celebrations in Kathmandu, many of whom may be uncomfortable with the gruff views of the pioneer who declared a few years ago: 'It's all bullshit on Everest these days.'

He never returned to the summit after 1953, setting off instead on fresh adventures to the south pole and the source of the Ganges, before dedicating the rest of his life to charitable work among the Nepalese mountain villages.

He says it is this charity work, and not the Everest ascent, which gives him most pride, although he thinks pride an 'awful thing'. It would be easy to dismiss the comment as a platitude, were it not for the fresh animation with which he talks about Nepal's mountain people.

Perhaps it is the wisdom of age, but there is no trace of self-aggrandisement or razzmatazz in Hillary. He speaks about his achievements with a phlegmatic honesty. It seems almost unnatural: when so many great climbs have been attempted out of jingoism or personal egotism, he appears to have become a climber purely for the physical and mental challenge.

The house in which he lives in Auckland is beautiful, but far from plush. His wife, June, flits around making tea and conversation, answering phone calls and proffering oatmeal biscuits.

Next to Hillary's bear-like presence, she seems positively sprightly. She suggests he can take off his jacket now the photographer has gone, and he does so.

He gets up again, his 6ft 2in frame still towering. June telephones for a taxi, and we walk to the bottom of a short staircase leading up to the front door. He is leaning heavily on the banister as he offers his hand.

David Fickling

CHAPTER SIX

CLASSLESS CROWD ON THE CRAGS

The 60s were to see climbing become both more anarchic and develop a professional side. There were more climbers than ever, with people exploring new areas both at home and abroad. The social structure of climbing was changing again, with the *Guardian* reporting in 1969 on the 'Classless crowd on the rocks'.

Working class 'hard men' climbers had arrived in the 50s, but in the 1960s the sport drew many of its recruits from higher education. Thanks to the 1963 Robbins Report into the future of higher education, there were now thousands more students attending the new universities and vastly expanded old ones. University mountaineering clubs grew and, armed with a grant and long holidays, student climbers began to play an important part in development. Evidence of this can be seen in the naming of new routes. Whereas in the past climbs had been named after rock features or someone's name, the latter part of the 1960s saw all manner of bizarre sexual and narcotic references being used.

Also, as part of this building expansion, it became de rigueur for each university to have a state-of-the-art climbing wall built in the sports facilities. At walls such as the one at Leeds University, the concept of the 'rock athlete' was to develop. Here climbers trained hard and practised moves before going on to real rock to put up incredibly hard climbs. The full effect of these walls was to be felt in the 1970s.

The decade also saw the sport become more professional, with local education authorities around the country opening outdoor education centres. These required instructors and so qualifications were introduced. The growth of these centres introduced thousands of children and young people to the sport.

As car ownership increased, the geographical location of rocks was no longer a problem. New climbing areas such as disused quarries and sea cliffs, away from the traditional mountain crags and outcrops, began to be opened up. Often in these areas there was an absence of 'natural' protection, such as rock spikes or stones jammed in cracks, so climbers used artificial means such as pitons to protect dangerous sections of the route.

One area where pitons were a necessity was the north face of the Eiger. During the decade, various firsts were achieved on the German mountain; in 1962 Chris Bonington and Ian Clough were the first Britons to climb the classic 1938 route, in 1964 the German climber Daisy Voog was the first woman to climb the north face and two years later the Scottish climber Dougal Haston helped put up the direct 'Harlin' route. As part of a new band of elite climbing stars, Bonington and Haston were invited, along with Joe Brown and others, to climb the Old Man of Hoy, a sea stack in Orkney, as part of a BBC televised climbing extravaganza in 1967.

A similar event had been held in Switzerland to commemorate the centenary of the first ascent of the Matterhorn, by Edward Whymper, in 1865. The *Guardian* gave this great occasion plenty of coverage, although the gently mocking feature by the paper's versatile features writer, Geoffrey Moorhouse, probably best caught the mood of the jamboree. Mocking too, was a certain Gyula Nagy, a Parisian house-painter who, in 1964, at the climax of the Eiffel Tower's 75th birthday celebrations, upstaged 10 of France's finest alpinists, who were planning to climb the metal mountain, by scrambling up it before them.

Another celebration was that of 10 years since the ascent of Everest. James Morris, despite having left the *Guardian* in 1961, contributed a delightful piece about a reunion of the 1953 team at the Pen-y-Gwryd hotel in North Wales. In the Himalaya itself, most of the 8,000m peaks had been climbed by 1960, and interest was turning to more difficult routes to top of peaks. In 1966, cold war reverberations were felt in the climbing world when the Nepalese government stopped all large expeditions to their country. Climbers, however, were exploring new horizons. In 1961, a piece appeared about an expedition to the Towers of Paine in the Andes, an area that had hardly been climbed before. According to Jim Perrin in *The Villain: The life of Don Whillans*, this article aroused considerable interest amongst climbers of the day, most notably Whillans. In 1962 a team including himself and Chris Bonington returned to the area, although it was later claimed that the expedition had been marred by various members taking their wives and babies along.

Andean Towers

❄ October 6 1961 ❄

In the remote southern tip of South America lie some of the greatest prizes left for the modern mountaineer. Two hundred miles north of the Magellan Straits is the Cordillera del Paine, a mountain range no bigger than Snowdonia and separated from the Pacific by only 20 miles of desolate icecap. Recently I was a member of the first British expedition to visit this area.

The expedition was first inspired by a photograph seen in the British Museum of the Towers of Paine, and we were tempted by the huge faces and ridges – rock climbers' dream mountains, just waiting to be climbed. Only one party before us, an Italian millionaire's expedition in 1957 with unlimited resources, had achieved any measure of success in these southerly Andes, but the two biggest Towers were still unclimbed. The richest of these Andean plums were thus waiting to be picked when we arrived.

The Paine range is like a fairyland, a Walt Disney fantasia where towering rock peaks with incredibly sharp ridges leap straight up from green meadows and blue lakes. In the valleys it is calm: the temperatures are those of an English summer and thousands of sheep graze on the vast pampas. In the mountains the weather, our greatest enemy, reigns supreme. Hardly a day passes when the wind, blowing unheeded from the Pacific, fails to lash the Towers with devastating force. We had hoped for a good summer, but a Chilean farmer told us it was the worst he had known for 15 years.

We planned to attack the South Tower and after initial reconnaissance we established Camp 2 behind it. We had three 'Everest' mountain tents and spent two days digging an ice cave for cooking and stores. From this camp a two-hour plod over moraine and up snow brought us to the initial 'bad step' of the Tower – an 800ft wall that would give access to the northern ridge. It was on this blank wall that our first attempt on the Tower failed. Climbing under appalling weather conditions, we advanced 300ft up the snow-covered slabs until blizzards forced us to retreat. We were attempting in 'duvets' (eiderdown jackets), heavy clothes, and over trousers, in bitterly cold weather and snowstorms, rock climbing that would be classified as excessively severe in North Wales.

After a fortnight of waiting and more attempts, it was obvious that we were wasting our time on this side of the mountain. A fortnight later we were in another ice cave on the opposite side of the mountain – waiting for the weather under the only possible ridge.

Our camp was high on the mountain at 6,000ft, and there was no question here of pitching tents outside. The tents had been ripped in the other valley and only given temporary patch repair, and it was out of the question to expect them – and us – to survive the full fury of the Patagonian winds and blizzards in the open.

We arrived at Camp 4 in the teeth of a snowstorm at 6pm ... now we had to burrow into the huge wall of snow with ice axes and light shovels to make a hole large enough to house two tents. By midnight we were established – two tents, five people, and a wee space in the middle for cooking.

We spent two four-day periods in the cave. We were on the doorstep of the Tower. There was a half-hour scramble up the scree, then the slabs, the steep wall, and the final summit ridge – we were sure it would go. We could see our way. Two fine days, that was all we asked for. We did not get one.

Yet we did attempt the Tower on this side twice, and we were both times driven back at the top of the slabs 500ft from the summit by ferocious blizzards at midday. To continue was impossible, and to climb down was a desperate struggle for survival, as the snow blinded us and the wind tore our fingers from their minute and tiny holds.

And so these rich plums of the Andes remain unplucked, the Towers remain inviolate. But in spite of our retreat this year, we are convinced by our experiences and reconnaissance that the South Tower can be climbed – by another party, another year.

Derek Walker

A Country Diary: Napes Needle

❄ MARCH 14 1966 ❄

The most famous bit of rock in England is Napes Needle, perched high up among the ridges on the side of Great Gable and looking down on the patchwork fields of Wasdale Head nearly 2,000ft below.

It was first climbed just 80 years ago by WP Haskett Smith, a young Oxford graduate who was later to be revered as the 'father' of climbers, and its ascent was the first significant landmark in the development of the new sport of rock climbing. Haskett Smith climbed it alone, leaving his fell pole at the foot, and left his handkerchief jammed in a crevice on the top block to prove it. Fifty years later, at the age of 74, but roped this time between two distinguished climbers, he went up again and, seated at the top block, made an extempore remark that has since passed into history. 'Tell us a story,' shouted somebody from the admiring crowds below, and the old man, never at a loss for words, replied on the instant: 'There is no other story. This is the top storey.'

Since the first ascent all sorts of indignities have been heaped upon the old Needle. It has been climbed thousands of times by at least eight different routes, small boys and girls have been hauled up, stunt climbs and speed record attempts have been perpetrated on its smooth walls, and it has been photographed, sketched, filmed and televised. People have lit fires on top, stood on their heads, eaten meals, shaved and danced jigs, and, if there are three of you on the edge of the top block, you can gently rock it. I know, I've done it. But the other day the Needle looked none the worse for its harsh treatment, except a little polished here and there.

A Harry Griffin

Classless crowd on the rocks

❉ SEPTEMBER 28 1969 ❉

'Geoff, you look a treat hanging up there by your eyelashes.' The burly young man had apparently reached a critical point of no return on a sheer rock face, and was hanging motionless in the wind, undecided about his next move. The remark is typical of the good humour that crackles among the climbers who come to Stanage

Edge. The Edge is a sudden outcrop of steepish rocks at the lip of a long plateau above the cosy little Hope Valley near Sheffield in the Derbyshire Peak Park. The climbers chaff one another mercilessly with repartee that is both witty and crude.

A whole host of people, mainly young and husky with with beards and jeans, students and apprentices, but some older seasoned souls, come to Stanage Edge every weekend. The black granite rocks are like a magnet. They swarm with enthusiasts. The road below can have as many as a hundred cars and there may be anything from 300 to 400 people climbing. Viewed from a distance, it's a multicoloured antheap. Voices echo back loudly from the rock face. Ropes crisscross the rocks like the tendrils of creepers. There are children playing below while fathers and mothers hang above them. Non-climbing girlfriends try to huddle out of the wind and rain, and are ready to hand out hot coffee or tea from a Thermos whenever required.

It's a classless crowd. Voices have Lancashire, Yorkshire, Cockney and Scots accents. People come from Salford, Derby, Manchester, Sheffield, Leicester – by bus, motorbike, car. Students, office types, steel workers, doctors, school teachers, they're part of a crowd that moves around a lot. This weekend here, the previous one at Langdale in the Lakes, the next in North Wales. People get to know each other. It's really a new kind of set, the climbing crowd. But one that isn't dependent on money or position. There's only one standard when you're being judged on a rock face: whether you can get up or down.

Stanage Edge is indeed a kind of nursery. It's an ideal place for climbers to begin their first hesitant handholds because the rocks, though sheer, aren't very high – perhaps 60 to 70 feet – and there is wide variety of grades of climb. 'You can't come to much harm here,' said one schoolboy. 'It's not very far to fall.' He and his friend were supposed to be at home studying for approaching examinations. But having started only about a year ago, they couldn't resist the temptation to drive over from Wilmslow. The other two they usually climb with had chosen to remain behind and swot.

Neither of them seemed to have inhibitions about climbing, even at this stage. A fear of heights was something that just didn't seem to arise. The reason why so many are there is a mixture, obviously, of excitement, a contact with sympathetic people, a sort of camaraderie which is instant, with a common language of enthusiasm, the gaining of a sense of achievement at the end of a good day, when you've managed to get the better of a particular buttress or chimney.

Everywhere you look on Stanage Edge there are people spreadeagled on a rock face, lodged in a crevice, inching along a ledge, or just hanging at rope end in a curious taut limbo. It's a kind of climbers' Blackpool. The talk flies back and forward, the words carried by a wind that sighs and whistles from the west over the Pennines. 'Jack, did you know that you've got a hole in the seat of your trousers?' 'Oh, I wondered why my crotch was so cold.' The reply comes from a point halfway up Ellis's Chock, where all that can be seen is a jean-clad bottom and a rope hanging out over space. Figures above stand braced like statues against the skyline and the whirling clouds, carefully watching their climbing partners inching up from below. Someone gets stuck on the Flying Buttress and there are ironical handclaps and cheers.

Lunchtime is a moment for swapping stories, experiences, and comments over sandwiches and chocolate. 'John did that climb with a touch of elegance, I thought.' 'Next time I'm going to do that buttress *direttissimo* – be damned if I'm not.' The talk is full of words – of abseiling, handholds and crampons, and traverses. The clothes that are worn are colourful – red, blue, orange, and green anoraks, and a variety of headwear including both knitted and hard helmets. Rope lies about everywhere. You can't get away from the stuff. It's an all-nylon world today. There's a lively discussion about whether the new type of braided rope is better than the traditional three-stranded type. 'The braided handles better and you don't get kinks.' 'Ah, but what about the centre of this new braided stuff – what about the grit getting in between the outer sheaf and working through the inner sheath where you can't see it? What about that, eh?' 'But the British Mountaineering Council have given the braided kind an excellent report, haven't they?'

A man passed with an anxious look on his face. 'Has anyone seen my wife?' he asked. 'I saw something stuck in a crack back there,' was the reply, as stringent as the wind, and without a smile he went on his way. Then, peering over the edge, he saw her. 'But she's down there and I'm up here,' he said plaintively.

The pale lemon sunlight faded and the vivid colours in the surrounding landscape dulled. The clouds were building up as the afternoon passed on. It started to rain.

But that didn't seem to disturb the climbers. 'Ready to climb?' 'Ready.' 'OK.' The shouted formalities continued, and would do so into the early Sunday evening, until darkness came. The climbers then would go away, happy, muscles all aching and tired, but with a lungful of fresh Pennine air.

David Morgan Rees

The man on the Eiffel Tower

❊ MAY 4 1964 ❊

The climax of the 75th birthday celebrations of the Eiffel Tower, an ascent by 10 alpinists in full mountain gear for the delectation of Eurovision's 50 million tele-watchers, was privately sabotaged by a house painter who suddenly appeared from the second platform (346ft) and shinned up, in his best Sunday suit, another 243ft of beams, bypassing the heroes, before he was nabbed by the police.

Europe's tele-fans missed the historic moment. The director of the carefully prepared television programme remarked: 'Drunks don't interest me,' with a fragile air of insouciance. But the painter, a Hungarian, Gyula Nagy, aged 36, was received with shouts of glee by the 6,000 spectators at the foot of the tower and since then his life has been the subject of tender investigation by the Paris popular press. His life story is gratifyingly romantic.

Nagy's childhood ambition was to be a violinist and composer, and he spent 10 years of his youth with the appropriate ear slanted over the resined box listening intently for the arrival of sounds which would, by his own coaxing, gave voice to his mournful hopes. He was indeed found in this position by reporters who tracked him down to his hotel room by the Bastille.

Nagy's violin studies were interrupted by the war. He was conscripted; ran away when his company was ordered to Russia; crossed Austria on foot; and ended up in a German refugee camp where there was no violin. He took to expressing his flights of spirit concretely: in other words, he became the daring young man on the camp's homemade flying trapeze, and would trot across a bar in his hands as an encore – still dreaming of better things. His ambition now was to go to Paris and thrill that effete and perfumed populace with death-defying tumbles through space in the shade of the tower.

His dream materialised a little crookedly. He was given a 24lb pot of paint and told to hurry up the tower – on the outside. This was 1954. For 15s an hour he helped to preserve that gangling Parisian lady, scorning the regulation safety belt. After the usual seven years' interval he was back again, and he admits to having developed a fondness for the tower. 'She is very beautiful,' he said simply. 'I became exasperated when I saw the big production they made out of climbing her – boots, ropes, and tackle, the prefect of police threatening to call it off just because the beams were a little slippery! Cameras! Ten solemn alpinists! I could stand it no longer – so off I went.'

The blow to the prestige of the alpinists has been painful. In vain they protested that they had never meant to pretend to the world that it was a hazardous feat, although the descent, using a new rope technique was tricky. France's No 1 alpinist, M Frison-Roche, who had not been invited to take part in the exhibition, sneered that alpinism was an occupation that gentlemen practised alone not for the '*tout* Paris'.

Enraged, one of the climbers, Guido Magnone, pointed out that Frison-Roche was in no position to complain about exhibitionism, since he made his money going around showing films of himself climbing. And Magnone proposed a duel: a summer dawn, over any chasm in the Alps. Frison-Roche accepted. But Nagy has refused to be drawn, over any chasm in the Alps. With one ankle athletically stretched over a bar stool in his local bistro he gave his answer: 'A chimney,' he said. 'A bridge. A high-tension cable. Or if Magnone likes I'll race him up the Tower. But not Mont Blanc – every man to his trade.'

Peter Lennon

Ten years after Everest

❄ MAY 27 1963 ❄

'You're late,' they said to me at Pen-y-Gwryd, handing me a pair of boots; and sure enough, when I started along the Pig Track there was the Everest party high above me, halfway up Snowdon.

I could not see much of them, only the blue and red of their anoraks, Hunt's mop of sandy hair, and the gleam of Tenzing's camera, and from that distance they looked much as they used to look on Everest – moving with the same slow, deliberate rhythm of mountaineers, in the meditative single file necessary to their calling: but golly, said I to myself, panting a little already, here we are in 1963, 10 years gone already, and a new world all around us.

A new world? Well, of the men who were on Everest in 1953, seven had assembled in North Wales on Saturday to celebrate the 10th anniversary of the mountain's first ascent, and for all of them life had shifted with a vengeance in the decade since the adventure.

The mountain air smelt sweet as ever, the squelch beneath my boots was just as squelchy, and the young climbers I sometimes met greeted me with reassuring brogues of Birkenhead or Black Country; but as I laboured up the track, I counted the roster in my mind, and marveled what 10 years can do.

Two of us, Tom Bourdillon and Wilfrid Noyce, have died beloved and honoured on other mountains. Three more are household names in every corner of the world, so that there is almost nobody who does not want to shake the hand of a Hunt, a Hillary or a Tenzing. The rest of us are not only older but distinctly grander, too, elevated partly by the progress of our professions, but partly, too, by the very fact of our connection with Everest. There is the head of a college on our roll now, and a military attache, and two oilmen of substance, and a surgeon as dashing and distinguished as ever peeled off his rubber gloves in Dr Kildare's hospital.

We are scattered always across the face of the earth, climbing in Russia, or photographing in Peru, or schoolmastering in Chile, or filming in Persia, or extracting oil in Venezuela, or wandering foppishly through Spain. We are mostly authors by now, all married, nearly all proud fee-paying fathers – some of us greying, some of us balding, Tenzing a grandfather, all of us moving steadily, crampons firm and pitons acock, up the long plateau of middle age.

I stopped for a moment, at this point of a rather breathless reverie, and while pretending to do up my boots looked sidelong up the hill – to find to my satisfaction that those champions of the high peaks above me seemed to be taking just such a breather, too.

'You all right?' asked a passing adolescent, practically offering me his arm and an aspirin, so I stepped indignantly off again, I reminding myself that if we have changed, so has our England, too. How merrily the news from Everest ran through London, on that Coronation morning long ago! How touching, somehow, were the cheers and the congratulatory telegrams, as we bravely entered our New Elizabethan Era! How nearly untarnished was the British view of the monarchy, in the days when John Osborne had hardly been heard of, and kingship still possessed some last suggestions of divinity! Ours was an adventure of a lost kind, out of a vanished English age – straightforward, above board, rather boyish, and still faintly Imperial.

For we were just old enough, in 1953, still to be Sahibs of the Raj. Several of us spoke Hindustani, a last echo of old responsibilities, and however hard and sympathetically we tried, our relationships with the Sherpas were necessarily tinged by the fading fact of Empire. We were essentially a respectable party in the old sense, pre-eminently Marlborough, Oxbridge, or army, pre-destined to marry doctors' daughters and go into Shell. We were quintessentially British, tempered by the aberrations peculiar to alpinists but with our fair share of the stiff upper lip, the straight back and the under-statement. We sheltered no wild rebels or eccentrics, and the most flamboyant among us were always the New Zealanders; but we did, in our corporate self, represent a civilisation – that old, cultivated, comfortable civilisation of certainties evolved by the prosperity of Victorian Britain.

Wilf Noyce was a civilised man, if ever I met one – a very gentle man, rather mystical, the kind of figure you expect to see sitting rapt in an English cornfield in the corner of a Samuel Palmer picture. John Hunt, up there above me on the hillside, represents no less clearly a whole culture, manner of thought, scale of values, set of principles. Charles Evans was born in a home where Welsh was the natural medium of conversation, with no nonsense about nationalism or alien oppression. We were not, by and large, racked by doubts or anxieties, upon that higher mountain. Even I myself was so dedicated to the ends of competitive journalism that if any Fleet Street rival had brought a radio transmitter to base camp, I was seriously prepared to demolish it with the sharp end of my ice axe.

Here my thoughts were interrupted again, for at that moment five young men strode past me, very fast, and I heard the first one declaiming, in a fine organic tone of voice, that what they needed at the bottom was 'food, girls, booze and fags'. I winced a little, for I was sure they had got the order wrong, but it made me laugh, too, to think how changeless are the human yearnings. On Everest, also, our intentions were simple. There was nothing satirical about our adventure, nothing iconoclastic. It shattered no totems, burst no bubbles, advanced no scientific cause, breathed no fierce spirit of protest.

Indeed, there was, it seems to me now, something actually innocent about the thing, and it was with a certain relieved simplicity that the world, from Moscow to Los Angeles, accepted and shared our pleasure. Almost nobody scoffed, when the news reached London on Coronation Day. Nobody seemed to question our values.

Outside the Waldorf Astoria, New York, one autumn evening in 1953, I timorously asked if I could possibly gate crash a taxi queue, because Ed Hillary was late for some posh luncheon or other. Instantly an elderly American gestured me into his own place at the head of the line. 'For Sir Edmund, sir,' he said, 'it will be a privilege!'

And that same autumn my neighbour at a state dinner in London, a retired diplomat of eminence, drew my attention to Tenzing, still the most modest and sweet-natured of celebrities, who had never tasted a French wine before in his whole life, and was particularly enjoying the experience. 'Ah, Mr Morris,' said my neighbour approvingly, 'how good it is to see that Mr Tenzing knows a decent claret when he has one!'

But as I laboured up Snowdon on Saturday, and remembered that old glow of glory, so I began to wonder how much we had altered after all, how much those figures up there had really aged or hardened, how harsh our contemporary satire really was, how deep our cynicism: for it is an odd thing that even now, 10 years later, when people are climbing Everest right and left, and circling the great globe itself in capsules – even now our old adventure seems somehow to take the fancy of the world. Even now it rings true. Even now the small boys still queue for John Hunt's autograph, and the very cynics will still occasionally relax, to hear a tale of Everest.

For there was something good to that experience, something simple, human and understandable; and when at last I struggled to the top of Snowdon on Saturday, and found those friends assembled by the summit cairn, by God, suddenly I discovered that nothing had changed at all: Bourdillon himself waved to me through the wind burly in his anorak, and Wilf Noyce smiled at me above his Penguin Dostoyevsky, and there the snow gleamed still on the great face of Lhotse, and all was the freshness of youth, sunshine and excitement. Grizzled Hunt was grizzled still, and over the ridge below the great kind world expected us home. Better sharpen your ice axe, said I to myself, and helped myself to tea.

James Morris

Schools for Sherpas

❄ MARCH 2 1963 ❄

Sir Edmund Hillary is on the way to lead another Himalyan expedition. Its purpose is not to climb – though he may take time to tackle a relatively minor peak – but to build two schools, to carry out a medical survey, and to lay on a fresh water supply for Khumjung, the village near Everest from which so many of the Sherpa climbers have come. He is honourably repaying a little of the debt which the mountaineers of the west owe to these indispensable partners. This is not the first instalment to be paid. On his last visit in 1961, he started at Khumjung the first school ever seen in the Sherpa country. This has proved popular. Now Thami, birthplace of Tenzing Norgay, his companion on Everest, and Pangboche, near the great monastery of Thyangboche, on the way to the Western Cwm of Everest, will have schools too.

This expedition is a sign of an important change in human attitudes. A generation ago it could hardly have been thought of, let alone performed. The Sherpas have played an increasingly important and responsible part in Himalayan climbing since the earlier attempts on Everest. But before the war, their home in Nepal was forbidden to Europeans. They appeared at an exhibition's starting point as if mysterious beings from another world; personally admirable, but devoid of social background and imposing no social obligation but to pay them for their work (and sometimes, alas, to compensate the families of those who lost their lives in the course of it). Postwar expeditions have been able to enter their country and to see them not merely as heaven-sent high-altitude porters but also citizens, members of a primitive but strongly organised community, almost untouched by the outside world and isolated from its life and thinking.

It could be argued that the Sherpa's life is idyllic and unspoiled and should be left so as long as possible. But the 20th century catches up with everyone sooner or later, and it swamps those who cannot come to terms with its influence. Not all Sherpas, of course, are illiterate. Those who mean to become lamas learn in the monasteries to read the Buddhist scriptures in classical Tibetan, an accomplishment of limited use except for the purpose of serving as a lama. (No Sherpas are known at present to be learning to read the Communist scriptures in classical Chinese; but many things have entered their country from Tibet before now.) Secular learning began there only 18 months ago in the Khumjung school, where 40 or 50 young Sherpas are learning to read and write their own language under a Sherpa teacher born in Darjeeling and acquainted with both worlds. This modest provision will be trebled after Hillary's visit this year.

Leader

Cold war in the Himalaya

❋ APRIL 27 1966 ❋

The cold war has odd reverberations. One of them is the freezing – in a metaphorical sense – of the Himalayan range by order of the

Derek Walker looking towards the Towers of Paine, 1961

Nepal government. The best that can be hoped for, it was indicated in a message from Kathmandu this week, is that climbers may be let in again in the spring of 1968. With India and China as neighbours, King Mahendra of Nepal sits – again metaphorically – in a hot seat. He has to be cautious. He may allow China, India, Russia, Britain and the United States to vie with each other in bringing up to date his capital of Kathmandu, where he can keep an eye on them. But who knows what mischief a party of foreign mountaineers might be up to, slinking round peaks and passes, inaccessible to the police, and accompanied only by Sherpas who, since Hillary started teaching them to read, are little better than New Zealanders? So the Japanese (little better than the Americans) may have to give up their plans for an attack on Everest this year. And the Sherpas must refrain from making their often substantial contribution to the Nepalese economy.

The only consolation, for the mountaineers, is that this obstacle has arisen so late in the day. If there were still 8,000m peaks awaiting first ascent, it would be exasperating to be denied the chance of being the first to climb them. (Gosainthan was always out of bounds, but the Chinese climbed that themselves.) Now that there are only second ascents and variations to be made on the great peaks, it is less intolerable to have to wait for them. They will still be there when the cold war ends.

Leader

Exercise in mountaining

❄ JANUARY 22 1962 ❄

It was not an everyday problem, but it faced us: our Morris 1000 van was stranded at the top of Honister Pass with a ribbon of verglas winding down into Buttermere on one side, Borrowdale the other. If you drive up, you should be able to drive down. But not even the

Land Rover had reached the slate quarry on the summit that day; nor the works lorry; nor us.

We had topped the pass four days previously on dry tarmac, then joined our Outward Bound boys on the skyline above. We had four days of climbing on increasingly snow-plastered hills from a drift-enclosed hut, and now the quarry men were adamant that we would never drive the van down in one piece. But we could not leave it. There were kitbags, rucksacks, and ropes to go back to Eskdale. In any case, we had to reach the Mountain School before the boys and so check their return. John began to drive down, tyres almost flat, and brakes only just gripping.

The tyres bit through snow crust into the gravel of the quarry track; the gradient was gentle. In 10 minutes we had bypassed the icy steep summit rise of the main road, and were crawling along the easy, curving section above Seatoller. John braked gingerly to a stop by the first warning sign, which loomed through the frosted windscreen. Directly below were one-in-four gradients, S-bends, and a deep ghyll to one side.

There was not a chance of driving safely down this strip of ice – at least not without artificial aids, possibly ropes. While I uncoiled the four 100ft nylon lines and knotted them together, John lashed an oily length of towing rope across the rear springs. Tying one end of our now lengthy rope to this, we then passed it round the far sign support, and I stood in the road with it round the small of my back, ready to pay it out round the 'pulley' with both hands.

John looked dubious, but eased himself into the driving seat and let off the brakes. Slowly he rolled down as the rope slid round the metal post. By the time he was out of sight round the corner three knots had jumped round the road sign, and we were on the last 100ft. I blew a whistle and heard his horn somewhere below.

The next road sign we used said, YOU HAVE BEEN WARNED. It was a strong affair, however, and once more the van sledged away from it, now on the steepest section, and with the back wheels turning as though in reverse. A farmer with a flock of sheep passed. 'Nay, you're wasting your time, lad,' was his comment. 'There's none of them lower down.' He waved his stick at the sign.

He was right about that. But in place of metal tubes we used the trees and boulders on the verge. Once John thought he was away and the door flew open, his face peering back to where I had just untangled a snarl in the rope and caused his swift drop of six feet. Otherwise there was ample friction to hold the van. After three hours of inch-by-inch progress we were filling the tyres and assuring an astonished man at Seatoller that, yes, we had just come down the pass.

Tony Greenbank

Eiger north face

❄ SEPTEMBER 1 1962 ❄

Chris Bonington and Ian Clough yesterday climbed the north face of the Eiger. The news of their success will give the greatest pleasure to all their fellow climbers here. They are the first men from this country to succeed in a climb which – though its reputation is not quite as fearsome as it was 20 years ago – still holds its place as a supreme test of mountaineering skill, endurance, and courage. British climbing has held its own well in the world; in the Himalaya its record is still unsurpassed. But there was still something lacking so long as the Eigerwand, which had yielded to Germans, Austrians, French, Swiss, and Italians, still held out against the British. That gap in the record has now been filled.

One is particularly glad of Bonington's success. Only a few weeks ago he was robbed of a good chance of climbing the face. He and Don Whillans had gone a good way up the climb when they found that disaster had overcome another British pair, Nally and Brewster; a falling stone had struck Brewster, who fell and eventually died on the mountain from his injuries, leaving Nally in a position of great danger.

Naturally Bonington and Whillans abandoned their own attempt to do what they could for the others, and they helped Nally safely down. It might well have been his last opportunity to do the climb. Happily it proved otherwise; success was merely postponed, not lost by the act of succour. Don Whillans has not been so fortunate.

Leader

Making room at the top

❄ OCTOBER 27 1967 ❄

Joe Brown, one of the great climbers of our time (or any time), has written an autobiography that no mountaineer should miss. From the gritstone edges of the Peak to the summit of Kangchenjunga, which he and George Band climbed in 1955, he has had a go at innumerable exacting crags and peaks, made innumerable first ascents, and has been a pioneer in the technique of artificial climbing, which has opened up so many new possibilities. He has lived hard, climbed hard, and talked hard, and the book is full of his personality, frank, irreverent, and uncompromising. He must have puzzled the Russians sorely in the misbegotten Anglo-Russian Pamirs expedition of 1962; but he got to the top all right. He would get to the top of anything.

Mountaineering used to be reckoned mainly an upper-middle class kind of sport. He's smashed that mould. He was born and brought up in desperate poverty, and his work as a property repairer never took him much above the subsistence line. When he went out to the hills, he slept out. He wasn't apprenticed to climbing by a senior mountaineer; with his companions in the Valkyrie Club, just after the war, and in the Rock and Ice Club a few years later, he developed his own techniques, his extraordinary muscular strength and endurance.

He climbed instinctively, until he became an instructor for a while at Whitehall (Derbyshire's centre for outdoor pursuits) and had to think about how he climbed in order to be able to explain climbing to others. That was good. He couldn't have written this book without it, any more than he could have climbed all the overhangs without knocking in pegs.

And now he lives in Llanberis (nearest inhabited spot to Clogwyn Du'r Arddu), sells climbing gear, and is breaking in the sea-girt cliffs of Anglesey. The hard years are not quite over yet. 'I don't think I'll ever settle down completely,' he says. You bet he won't.

The Hard Years by Joe Brown (Gollancz, 42s)

Patrick Monkhouse

Limestone climbing

❄ APRIL 11 1963 ❄

Old-fashioned climbers in this country distrusted limestone crags as treacherous, slippery, and a great deal too perpendicular. This does not deter the modern school. A short guide to *Climbs in Yorkshire Limestone*, edited by Mr MA Mitchell (Dalesman Publishing Company, 3s 6d), is mainly concerned with climbs first made in the last six or seven years. Overhangs are characteristic of limestone, and are surmounted with the help of pitons, etriers (short rope ladders hung from pitons), rawlplugs (are these what householders commonly call 'rawlplugs'?) and 'golos', which are steel bolts driven in drilled holes. A distinction is made between climbs dependent on these aids and 'free climbing', which may use pitons for belays but not for upward movement.

Such climbing may be exhilarating, especially for the pioneers; it must call for great skill, daring and ingenuity; and artificial aids are now widely accepted in mountaineering, great and small. But is it fair to ask how far climbs depending almost wholly on such aids should be admissible? Some of the routes described are on the great crag of Malham Cove. Most of these are in its low flanking wings.

But the Central Wall is in a class by itself. Its height is 270ft; the time taken, 'possibly several days'; it has been ascended only three times, and on the first ascent the bottom pitch took 24 hours. The guide comments that: 'It is unnecessary to give any route description as the route is clearly marked by previous ascents. The route depends entirely on rawplugs and golos.'

This seems a denatured sort of climbing. Was there not at one time a convention, which might be revived, that climbers were entitled to use artificial aids but must put them in for themselves, and knock them out as the party moved beyond them? But it would be impossible to knock out a golo.

Leader

Not yet an 'easy day for a lady'

❄ SEPTEMBER 5 1964 ❄

The ascent of the Eiger north face by a woman is one more milestone passed in the subjugation of the mountains by mankind. Frl Voog has earned the warmest congratulations for her unique and superb achievement. She was, of course, climbing second on the rope throughout, and her companion, Herr Bittner, had the greater share in the work and the responsibility. But this is not a climb on which a strong leader can carry a passenger. The scale and exposure of the climb (which took this party more than three days), the long traverses in which the second climber is in as much risk as the leader and the great technical difficulties, which each must independently overcome, must make great demands on both members of a party of two. Voog must be remarkably fine climber in her own right to be able to enter into such a partnership.

There is an old saying – attributed to Leslie Stephen – that all Alpine ascents pass through three stages of repute: 'The hardest climb in the Alps – for experienced climbers only – easy day for a lady.' The Eiger north face may have stepped down a fraction from the highest position while remaining well above the second; it will never drop into the third. But indeed the third group is losing its derogatory sense as the number and skill of women climbers grow.

A great many men would have been hard put to it to follow climbs led by the late Mme Claude Kogan, unhappily lost on Cho Oyu after reaching nearly 25,000ft on it; while women climbers like Nea and Denise Morin, or Miriam O'Brien and Alice Damesme, blithely disposed of men altogether in tackling successfully ascents, which, in their day, could have been classed as 'hardest climb in the Alps'.

The success of the women mountaineers is one aspect of the general growth of mountaineering. A less happy aspect is the increasing number of fatal accidents. More than 100 people have been killed this year on the Mont Blanc range alone, more than double last year's figure. The range is, of course, much more than Mont Blanc itself; the term would include the innumerable Chamonix Aiguilles and the formidable buttresses of the Grandes Jorasses. Some of those killed may have been not so much mountaineers as sightseers venturing beyond their limit of safety; and it is believed that the dry winter of 1963–64 has created unusually difficult conditions on the mountains. For all that, it is a shocking record, to be set off against the high peaks of achievement.

Leader

First step to the summit

❄ MARCH 20 1965 ❄

An artificial crag of brick will, it is hoped, be built at Liverpool University's new recreation centre, for instruction and practice in rock climbing. This is an engaging idea. Well-designed and furnished with excrescences and recesses, it could be a useful aid to the acquisition of various climbing devices – movement on small holes, lay backs, jamming, mantlepieces and so on. The novice thus instructed could take his place on the rope more confidently; he would soon find that there was plenty more to learn on real crags.

Why stick at brick? It is, of course, solid and durable, and relatively cheap; and the architect of the centre hopes to find a climbing bricklayer to plan and build it. But if the idea catches on, other materials may be found more attractive. Sheets of some hard, rough plastic material would have advantages. They could simulate natural rock more closely. And they might be moved to present fresh problems and combinations. The novice who had successfully climbed a slab tilted at 65 degrees could then try it again at 75 degrees; two strips standing side by side could be rotated to form a corner or a chimney; a face that became too familiar would present new problems if turned upside down.

One risk must not be overlooked. Artificial climbing (in this new sense) might become so popular as to draw climbers away from the real crags, with their handicaps of distance, wet and cold, and occasional loose rock. It may seem improbable. But has not skating on artificial ice quite overshadowed the skating on natural ice that was so much enjoyed by, for instance, Wordsworth and Mr Pickwick?

Leader

Camera on the rock face

❄ JULY 10 1967 ❄

It was magnificent, but was it climbing? The Old Man of Hoy has seen many strange sights in his time – from Norse longships of a thousand years ago, with striped sails and slender sails and slender oars, to the BBC television men this weekend, with portable cameras and a professional cast of climbers. But mostly the Old Man stands alone. He looks over an empty, if turbulent, Atlantic, and he is backed by the huge desolate cliffs of Hoy.

The climbing of this slender pinnacle, 450ft high, is itself a feat. To accomplish it encumbered with microphones and transmitters – and to keep up a drily humorous commentary while doing it – is a greater feat. Chris Bonington, Joe Brown, Tom Patey, Dougal Haston, and others of the team put on a memorable performance. They must have given millions of people a secondhand sense of what great climbing is like. Not only the technical difficulties of overhangs, loose rock, rope control – and of bombardment by angry fulmars – but the architectural grandeur of the pinnacle were brought out. Vertical shots looking down past climbers to the crashing Atlantic swell 300ft below, vertical shots looking up at the overhangs ahead, and panoramas past the pinnacle to the cliffs and the ocean horizon, these told the story.

But we also saw how the technique of climbing has changed. Clattering ironmongery, web and canvas slings, hammers and expansion bolts – these were the weapons. It is truly termed 'artificial climbing'. It still calls for superb fitness, nerve and judgment, and a determination to get to the top. It was a great performance even if it was not exactly a communing with nature.

Leader

Room for one more at the top

❈ JULY 14 1965 (APPEARED JULY 15) ❈

The Matterhorn was climbed again today on the 100th anniversary of Edward Whymper's first ascent, and it would be nice to report that a *Guardian* placard had been left to canvass all comers on the summit. The record insists, however, that our one-man team was turned back at 11,000ft by a combination of ill wind, failure of nerve, and absent friend.

What the *Guardian* needed most of all on the Matterhorn was a good guide. It didn't get one and so a height equivalent to Snowdon's was left still to be desired.

The man in charge of Zermatt's centennial jamboree this week had shrugged in astonishment when we applied for a passage to the top. Conditions on the mountain, he said, were terrible: what's more, every guide in Zermatt had given his parole d'honneur that he would accompany no one on such an escapade but the crack climbers hired for the occasion by the television corporations of two countries.

He was quite wrong about the conditions: they weren't at all terrible, they were just difficult. But he was never more correct in his assumption about the guides. There wasn't a one to be begged, borrowed, or stolen.

Effortless

The guides not being the only people with a parole d'honneur prodding them in the small of their backs, the *Guardian* parted company with Old Cold Shower amidst mutual expressions of esteem and suspicion, and began its assault yesterday. It took the cable car to Schwarzee, and so got up to 7,000-odd feet with effortless expertise, and as all the best climbers do it this way, too, it felt that it wasn't really dishonouring its parole. After that it was all on its own.

The climb from there up to the Hornli hut is something that anybody's granny could do given lungs like a farrier's bellows, legs like Spring-heeled Jack's and a convenient weekend. It took the *Guardian* a couple of hot and aching hours, as the ridge grew steeper, the glacier began to fall away on either side, and the slush started to seep into the top of its boots.

And when it got to the hut it found something that was not so much a mountain refuge as cubby hole transplanted from Lime Grove. There were climbers to be sure, but they were altogether different from the breed you meet at Pen-y-Gwryd. They seemed to be obsessed with talk of time signals and fadeouts. There wasn't a mention of 'v diff' or 'severe' all evening. They kept tripping over camera cables and barging into batteries, which showed how much they were losing their grip.

Early start

They remembered themselves enough to be up at four o'clock this morning, just before the sun hauled itself over the tip of the Taschorn, while Zermatt was still enjoying the night of a mile nearer sea level. Slowly a faint flush came to the cheek of the Matterhorn but at 10,000ft it was cold enough to make your goggled eyes run and your gloved fingers nip. One of the loveliest mountains in the world stood mockingly at ease, daring anyone to have a go at it.

The caravan moved off, a harlequin column of white helmets, scarlet balaclavas, ultra marine sweaters, and breeches. They moved stealthily up the ridge probing the ice with their axes, aerials whipping to and fro in their packs. They became a line of dots, the technicians at the hut trudging in for breakfast, and the *Guardian* plucking itself from a reverie, struck out along the line of new steps in the snow.

For a little while you can get up that ridge if you watch your step and don't think too much about the drop on either side. After a time your temples start to pound, but you comfort yourself with the thought that the north face, careering away to your right, is a death-trap by comparison. A painstaking fingerhold here and you are getting along fine, while 3,000ft above a cloud circles the summit like a merry-go-round, hiding the place where Whymper's four companions fell, 100 years ago today.

But there comes a point where the ridge is punctuated by a sheer face of rock. It is not a very big face and you can see exactly how to overcome it. Handhold here, big stretch up there, and with a steadying hand on the rope you're on the way up. Only today there isn't a steadying hand on the rope and you aren't yet silly enough to try without.

So the *Guardian* swallowed its pride and beat a retreat. It crawled back to the hut, trying not to look too sheepish about it and then jogged down to the Schwarzee. It reduced its uphill record by a warm 20 minutes. And it was just in time to watch the director of

BBC Television, Mr Kenneth Adam, posing for his picture (four times) with a helicopter as foreground and the Matterhorn as a backdrop. This almost made up for not climbing the mountain.

Crisp comments

As for the hard news of the day, this will by now be no news at all to anyone with a television set. The BBC team, led by Mr Ian McNaught-Davis, got to the top of Whymper's route and made a few crisp comments at the summit. The Swiss team did likewise and played *Auf Wiedersehen* on the mouth organ. Mme Yvette Vaucher climbed the north face with her husband and became the first woman to get up the hardest way.

There was only one accident. It befell the Matterhorn. A number of peaks have had some queer things done to them at times: the Jungfrau has been subjected to a cable car from top to bottom. Snowdon has been crowned with a cafe. The Matterhorn has now taken the biggest tumble of the lot. Today it was just a prop in a TV spectacular.

Geoffrey Moorhouse

Obituary of a climbing ground

❋ OCTOBER 10 1963 ❋

Obituary notices are, regrettably, not uncommon. Obituaries of climbs are rare. But there is an example, composed by Mr Showell Styles, in the current issue of the *Climber* – and to add an edge to it, the deceased did not die a natural death. It was blown down.

Tremadoc Rocks are not among the great crags of Wales. But climbers began to turn to them as the better known rock faces were fully explored, and found that their dolerite yielded climbs of great difficulty, though not of great length. The first climb was done there in 1951; by 1955 there were enough routes to fill a guidebook.

Conspicuous on the face was a massive block 200ft high known as the Hound's Head Buttress (or Pen Ci).

Climbing on Tremadoc Rocks flourished, in spite of some local opposition. But last year came an ominous report that a jammed rock, used as a hold on the buttress, had altered its position. This was not taken very seriously; but later a larger movement was detected. Cracks were found to have opened in the lower part of the pinnacle; and the insertion of wedges made it possible to prove that cracks were widening. A jury of 15 men (climbers, naturalists and local councilors) tried Pen Ci, found that its base was unsound and condemned it to destruction. In July it was blown down with gelignite.

This is a very minor incident in the history of mountaineering. But it suggests a sinister possible development. Pen Ci was destroyed because it was unsafe. What has it left behind it? Presumably a new rock face, which will weather in time and (if it seems sound) be climbed. Other new climbs may lie behind other removable protuberances. There are sometimes complaints that old and well-known rock faces have been worked out. Civil engineering could put a new face on them. For the forseeable future, orthodox mountaineering opinion would frown on such treatment of old and valued friends, even though acknowledging that they had had their day. But might not iconoclasts arise who would risk destruction of the old face of the crag – the quarryman can tell them how – with the object of opening up a new face for exploration? Almost everybody would condemn them – but some would sneak off to see whether there were not good first ascents to be found there. And the process could even be repeated as a second generation of climbs became too familiar. No, it won't bear thinking of.

Leader

CHAPTER SEVEN

EVEREST FEVER

The decision by the Nepalese government to allow climbing expeditions back into the country in 1968 was to usher in a new era of Himalayan mountaineering. Most of the 8,000m peaks had been conquered by their 'easiest' routes, so the prize now lay with getting to the summit via harder, direct routes. The new age started in earnest in 1970 with the first ascent of the south face of Annapurna by Don Whillans and Dougal Haston as part of a British team. This showed that hard climbing could be done at high altitude. It also saw the emergence of Chris Bonington as an impressive leader of large expeditions. After a number of years as an adventure journalist, he had returned to elite mountaineering and one of his many skills was the ability to raise the large amounts of sponsorship that Himalayan adventures required. This was demonstrated in 1975 when he convinced Barclays Bank to back an attempt at Everest's unclimbed south-west face, 'the hard way', to the tune of £100,000.

Against all the odds, the expedition managed to get four people on the top, becoming one of the major feats of Himalayan mountaineering history. With its huge army of climbers and porters it was also 'one of the last great imperial experiences' as Peter Boardman, a member of the team, joked. Following the success, a new, streamlined way of mountaineering began to be adopted and Bonington was to go on to lead many more expeditions in this 'Alpine' style – setting off with everything in the rucksack and without fixed ropes or high-altitude support.

Grades of rock climbing routes were also to increase in the 1970s, with lines going up apparently blank walls or up sections of rock that had formerly only been possible with aid. This was extremely physical climbing that was only possible by adopting the training methods used by serious athletes. The undoubted star of the time was Pete Livesey, an outdoor education lecturer who had trained on a climbing wall in a school in Scunthorpe. At first climbers were shocked by these dynamic routes appearing all over the country, but Livesey injected vitality into the scene and others began to follow in his wake. Rather than 'training' in the pub and then climbing in a pair of jeans, sessions in the gym and on a wall followed by a day on the crags wearing tracksuit bottoms gradually became the norm.

Methods of protecting the climber were also to change radically during these years. In 1976 a Californian climber called Ray Jardine invented the 'Friend', a spring-loaded camming device that expands under tension in cracks. Along with new types of chocks (small metal shapes with tapered faces also jammed into cracks), these meant that a fall by the lead climber, in most cases, no longer meant serious injury.

This seemed a very long way from a debate at the beginning of the decade over pitons and artificial aid. In 1971, Simon Winchester headed to North Wales to write about the use of Rurps (Realisation of the Ultimate Reality Piton), tiny, postage-stamp sized pitons. A few years later and climbers were getting worked up by an attempt by the Russians to get rock climbing against the clock accepted as an

Olympic games event in 1976. It was said at the time that in Britain people climbed for the hell of it, not money. How things were to change in the 1980s.

The Everest fever

❈ MAY 22 1971 ❈

If Don Whillans and Dougal Haston had climbed the monumental south-west face of Everest it would have been the greatest achievement in mountaineering history. In the event, with the Japanese climbers Naomi Uemura and Reizo Ito in support, they came within little more than 1,500ft of the 29,028ft summit of the highest mountain in the world – by the route that is the most formidable and daunting ever attempted at high altitude.

There is no shame in their failure to become the first Britons to climb Everest. Almost from the outset, the 1971 International Himalaya Expedition was beset by difficulties that would have dissuaded many from even contemplating the summit attempt.

Painfully, the moving spirit of the exhibition, 52-year-old Swiss-American Norman Dyhrenfurth, was not even in base camp when the summit climbers decided to return, having been evacuated to Kathmandu two weeks ago suffering from glandular fever. 'There can be no doubt that the south-west face offers the greatest challenge possible,' said Dyhrenfurth, with some prescience, before the expedition left for the Himalaya in February. It was a challenge that was to prove too great even after 18 months of rigorous preparation and a six-week assault. The multinational expedition was defeated by bad weather, bad luck, and internal dissension – a devastating combination, which even the superb Whillans-Haston partnership could not overcome.

Dyhrenfurth was not alone in dreaming of a face climb – a 'direct' route, in the modern manner – to the summit of Everest. The British army officer Lt Col Jimmy Roberts, who was transport officer to the 1953 expeditions, had already begun to lay plans for his own expedition when Dyhrenfurth suggested a joining of forces early in 1969. And Dougal Haston, now 29, had discussed climbing the face while still at grips with the north face of the Eiger in March 1966, when a storm pinned him and the American John Harlin in a snowhole for five days.

Shortly after that conversation, Harlin was killed in a 5,000ft fall. It was then that Haston displayed the streak of tenacity that has since taken him up some of the hardest routes in the world. Initially the talk was of abandoning the attempt – but Haston was for continuing, and three days later he and four German climbers reached the summit in the teeth of a 100mph winter storm. Yet afterwards Haston, the son of a baker from Currie, said he had already experienced such conditions in winter in Scotland – and there is no doubt that his apprenticeship on Ben Nevis had prepared him well for survival problems on the world's highest peaks. His first Himalayan expedition was to the south face of Annapurna last year, when he and Whillans completed what is still the hardest climb ever made at high altitude.

Haston's partner on Annapurna and Everest, 37-year-old Don Whillans, was already, as the saying goes, 'a legend in his own lifetime' 10 years ago. He and Joe Brown (both Lancastrians, both plumbers by trade) put up a series of rock routes on the gritstone and in Wales in the 1950s that were a dramatic advance on previous climbing standards. Then Whillans, unlike Brown, decided that climbing in the greater ranges could bring him the kind of reflective satisfaction he sought from mountaineering. But he had not reached a major Himalayan summit until Annapurna, having been balked by last-minute mischance on several expeditions.

This week's failure does nothing to affect his reputation among climbers. 'If you want to survive, when the chips are right down, Don's your man,' said one; and it is probable on Everest, with the four climbers operating longer at high altitude than anyone before, the final decision to retreat was his.

There were many points of similarity between the final assaults on Annapurna and Everest. With the monsoon imminent, time was short – and the summit team faced dwindling food and an ever-weakening supply line. Haston and Whillans snatched the summit of Annapurna, 26,545ft, with nothing to spare. On Everest, although they reached 27,500ft, the extra height was crucial.

There is little doubt that the 1971 expedition's chances were seriously affected by the most bitter and certainly the most public row to have befallen a major expedition in progress. There were arguments on Annapurna, but the expedition was able to overcome them by virtue of its members' previously shared experience. No such binding factor held the Everest expedition through misfortune and adversity, which began with appalling weather conditions and the unnecessary death of Indian Major Harsh Bahuguna. When a group of climbers walked out it only confirmed the gloomiest fore-casts of dissension made before the expedition set out – Dyhrenfurth himself conceding that the team had been dubbed 'a tower of Babel'.

In some ways Dyhrenfurth was a victim of the sheer logistical effort needed to get such an expedition off the ground. He had posed three objectives: the south-west face, unclimbed; the west ridge, climbed in part by his 1963 expedition; and, if the first two routes were completed ('a very big if', he admitted), a double traverse of the mountain, with the face climbers descending the ridge, and the ridge team going down the face.

To mount such a venture, Dyhrenfurth needed almost £100,000. To raise such a sum, he needed, as well as donations and discounts, to sell media rights throughout the world. And his best chance of doing so lay in having climbers from a number of differ-ent countries – although this is not to doubt the spirit of interna-tionalism behind Dyhrenfurth's view that 'the days of extreme nationalism in mountaineering are over – we are conducting coop-eration among nations on a high level.'

Climbers had raised other objections related to the size of the expedition too: was it right that one giant expedition should use up resources that could have financed half a dozen or more smaller teams? It was partly with this argument in mind that the Mount Everest Foundation, the body which dishes out the proceeds from the 1953 British triumph, declined to back the 1971 attempt – though it did add that Dyhrenfurth seemed to have done very well at raising money himself anyway.

It is unlikely that Whillans and Haston, members of the elite handful of British climbers who make enough from the sport to live on, allowed such considerations to trouble them as they made their summit bid. 'Everest has always been an ambition of mine,' Whillans said before he left.

The ambition remained unfulfilled. Yet climbers have a way of dwelling on near-misses, on thwarted hopes. Nepalese government permits to attempt Everest have been taken up for several years to come – and Dyhrenfurth has said that this attempt on Everest will be his last. But it will be surprising if Whillans and Haston do not find their way back.

Peter Gillman

The drills are alive

❄ JULY 24 1971 ❄

Three months after the Everest fiasco, the climbing fraternity is riven again. Editorials in the glossier mountaineering journals are urging a Return to the Panache and Boldness of the Great Mountaineers of the Past.

Letter writers continually complain of the development of a device known as the Rurp, an acronym derived, it is said, from the

Realisation of the Ultimate Reality Piton. (It looks rather like an ordinary picture hook.)

The climbers are undergoing another of those periodic spells of self-examination that afflict them from time to time. But the neurosis seemed pretty remote yesterday morning out in the sunshine as we took our first beer of the day on the back lawn of the Pen-y-Gwryd Hotel, watching the late risers strolling off for their day on the hills.

'Of course, when I first came here you knew where every single peg was in North Wales. Mind you, there were only three, and we pulled those out when we got to them. We didn't think it good sport at all,' David Cox, senior lecturer in medieval history at Oxford and the new president of the Alpine Club, had brought us all back to earth.

Of course, climbing has changed. Snowdonia may look as timeless as ever, but those young men clumping along the road are surely all very different from the young bloods, all Oxford and Cambridge one might suppose, who came here in the Long Vacs between the wars to leap from Adam to Eve on Tryfan, or make the first tentative ascents on Cloggy. David Cox, climber of Machha Puchhare, the famous 'Fish Tail' of the Himalaya, and the man who first led Sunset Crack to the Sheaf on Cloggy, comes back to Pen-y-Gwryd every year about now. His companion is a venerable Irishman, Kevin Fitzgerald, who began his love affair with the cliffs on the great Eckenstein Boulder 30 years ago, and led an Amphitheatre Buttress when he was 60. Sitting there in the sunshine yesterday, their years insulated by Viyella and Veldtschoens, they were chatting, as every time they meet, about the Present State of the Art.

'There was a time when you would put the word "climber" on your application for a job. You wouldn't need any references – for most decent employers that was enough.' Fitzgerald moans gently on about the decadence of the modern climber. 'In the old days you never had to lock your doors because all the other chaps were absolutely scrupulously honest.'

Cox is more concerned with the standing of his haughty old club among modern climbers. 'They tend to think we at the Alpine Club are all fuddyduddies, and it's true there are a lot of fairly old chaps in the club. But to get elected you have to show you've done three good Alpine seasons – the subs are only four guineas a year and we've the best library in London. I can't really understand why they don't like us.' There are only 700 members of the Alpine Club these days; there were probably more than 700 climbers around Llanberis yesterday.

The pair shake their heads sadly when they talk of the natural beauty of the mountains. 'These people nowadays, they're just engineers, no regard at all for the birds or the plants. It's all so very aggressive and competitive.' And with his last point, it seems, climbers are beginning to agree – hence the self-examination which has gripped the literary end of the climbing business.

In *Mountain*, the hard man's monthly, a dashing young alpinist named Reinhold Messner is sowing the seeds of discontent: 'Who has polluted the pure springs of mountaineering?' he asks. 'The decisive factor now is no longer courage, but technique. Rock faces are no longer overcome by climbing skill but are humbled, pitch by pitch, by methodical manual labour. Today's climber,' – he concludes with an avalanche of profundity that still rumbles down the valleys, 'carries his courage in his rucksack.'

Messner's ideas run counter to the very principles that journals like *Mountain* have exploited. The magazine rings with the aggressive, deadly serious, mechanistic approach to climbing. The information columns read like a Jennifer's Diary of the climbing elite, with Chuck and Joe solving new problems in Yosemite and Don walking up Wall of Morning Light where, the writer states blandly, no less than 330 holes have been drilled – with electric power drills carried by this new breed of climber – into the face.

But Rurps and power drills and expansion bolts are pretty much out of fashion in Llanberis these days. Joe Brown sells them (and 57 types of nuts, 47 types of pitons, and 31 types of boot), but demand is mercifully low. He finds his best business selling fancy sweaters to day trippers: climbers spend as little as possible, and only the bar-room mountaineer will spend hundreds of pounds to swathe himself in the latest, brightest gear.

The hard school will continue on its way, Joe supposes, Messner or no. The present trend is for climbers to solo all the traditionally hard routes and he assumes that they will all be killed off in the months and years to come. 'It's the only logical end of this trend. But it's not for me – I'd be frightened to bloody death.'

On the hills, three lads from Wolverhampton were scaling a nameless area on a face across the road from Dinas Cromlech, going up time and again until their movements became panther-smooth, their precision and their confidence impeccable. Their leader reck-oned he was there for the beauty, the grand feeling of being really fit, and the sheer joy of bringing schoolkids out from the Midland grime and on to the hills. The change that comes over them is unfor-gettable, he says.

And back at the top of the Pass, Cox and Fitzgerald, stiff and tired after a long trek across Carnedd Dafydd, were hiking back for tea and scones. No rope, no Rurps, and certainly no power drills for them: just a well-filled pipe, a long summer evening and hours of memories of Climbing As It Used To Be.

Simon Winchester

Accidents on the mountains

❄ FEBRUARY 22 1971 ❄

English city dwellers have found it a mild winter so far, but it is seldom mild in Britain above 2,000ft. That is one reason why deaths on British hills are not infrequent. By the international standards to which everyone has become accustomed, our mountains are absurdly low – 'an easy walk for a lady'. Expeditions to the Himalaya or the

Andes are expected to equip themselves in advance with rich sponsors, climbing cameramen, and ironmongery by the ton. But there are still, apparently, schoolmasters who are prepared to walk a party of children up Snowdon or Scafell in winter without acquainting themselves with the use of an ice axe. According to a speaker at the recent conference on mountain safety, held in the University of Salford, 10 out of the 16 deaths in Snowdonia over the past three years were winter accidents that took place in areas considered safe enough in summer.

By comparison with road casualty figures, the number may seem acceptably small. But the scale is rising rapidly. Sixteen deaths in three years is twice as many as there were in the previous four, and the problem is naturally not confined to Snowdonia. About a third of the mountain accidents in Britain occur in Scotland, where weather changes can be particularly drastic and sudden. Every new motorway leading to a mountain district imposes a fresh burden on the local rescue team, for it puts hills that were formerly summer holiday playgrounds within the reach of determined winter weekenders.

Both from the climber's and the walker's point of view, this is all to the good. There are other ways of enjoying mountains in winter besides sliding down them on skis, and the man, woman, or child who climbs them all the year round is both fitter and wiser than the occasional visitor. Hotels and other services in out-of-the-way areas will be glad to see the use of the hills intensify without the gross overcrowding that summer brings to their narrow roads. The greater intensity with which mountaineering as a sport is approached has also brought with it notable contributions to the safety of life and limb: crash helmets, sneered at a decade or two ago, are commonplace on rock faces today, and cheap, light plastic or plasticised 'survival bags' can be bought for a few shillings.

Ultimately at stake is the voluntary character of the mountain rescue service. The services provide a few excellent teams, but in most cases the man who turns out late in the evening to look for a party which may or may not have told anyone where it was going is surrendering his own time, and hence often his own money, with every step he takes. Like the blood transfusion service, mountain rescue in Britain is a 'gift relationship'. Most people will be sorry if British climbers or their relatives have to be presented with realistic bills for services rendered, as often happens in the Alps. But failing Exchequer subsidy, it may be inevitable.

Leader

The social climber

❄ MARCH 10 1973 ❄

The man who led the expedition to climb Annapurna's south face in 1970 is now a household name, not so much because householders really care about Annapurna but because a certain brand of margarine spread well up there and he went to the nation telling them so. The name of Chris Bonington, after Hunt and Hillary (but even that was another era), and probably even before Joe Brown, is the one people think of when they see men suspended from their waists on an overhang of granite – simply because Bonington is the one climber who has entered that fourth dimension, the communications world. His is the name that will hardly have stopped ringing in your ears from the recent failure on Everest – and attempt at the south face. And now, he's back in the public eye, with the second volume of his autobiography, *The Next Horizon*.

Bonington is not a hard person to get to know. For a start, his autobiographical books (the first volume was *I Chose to Climb*) tell you not only about climbing but a lot about himself; and then he's naturally gregarious and an easy person to talk to. He's 38, lives with his wife, Wendy, and sons Daniel and Rupert in a neat medium-sized, average-looking Edwardian house in Rowdon, outside Manchester.

Bonington himself wouldn't immediately impress you as being a climber – no hirsute mountaineer here. But his face does bear the lines of long weathering, and his voice, toned down for domestic usage, sounds as if it could span a few valleys and maybe has done.

Talking to him in his office, very steely grey and white, and surrounded by the latest in audio-visual equipment (lecturing is no lantern-slide show any more, but a sophisticated super-production), you are of course talking to a man who had made climbing his means, and way of life. As for household name, well, because he has spoken out loud about climbing, he tends to be taken as climbing's spokesman, which of course he's not. He's Bonington and a climber. He went into freelance writing for the freedom, rather than continue as a management trainee with Unilever. He can't possibly speak for all climbers. Others have put their ideas on paper too. Of his own peer group, there are notably Dougal Haston and Don Whillans, but neither exposes his personal motives so thoroughly.

'I try to write factually. In fact I get obsessed with the truth and being true to one's own emotions. It's terribly easy in this adventure game to write yourself into the adventurous image that perhaps you would like to see yourself in. But the main difficulty is when you come to the actual experience of climbing and why you climb ...

'The joys of climbing are partly of going into an unknown situation; the challenge of making a dangerous and very airy situation safe, the feeling of elation when you're climbing well, and the danger element is then an extra thrown in. Which is maybe why climbing is so gripping on the people who do it. A footballer, for example, isn't playing in an inspiring environment and there's no risk.'

Except for the adulating crowd. And Bonington admits that climbing is a very private sport. But people like to watch a climb on television. That's partly because of the danger, he says. They think that a man will kill himself if he falls (actually he probably wouldn't if he was well protected on the route). And what the viewer doesn't see is the pure hedonism of the sport. Climbing on a hot day, says Bonington, when the rock is warm to touch and you're climbing well, feeling confident, is really a very sensual experience.

To go further into 'why climb' we talked about why so few women climb. One of the climbs booked for Everest (and Everest is booked for the next six years) is an all-female team of Japanese climbers. 'I think women have a much stronger sense of life preservation and a much higher sense of responsibility that the average man. There are some very good women climbers but even the best lack the pushiness of men, necessary to get among the elite of climbers. A man will say "Right so far and to go any further there's a bloody good chance of my being killed, but I'll go on and get to the top." And he will and probably won't be killed.'

Climbing began as a gentleman's sport, but now someone like Bonington is almost an anachronism. His background, although not rich as a fatherless child, was not penniless either. He went to both Cranwell and Sandhurst, and from his spell in the services emerged with an aptitude for organising large parties of men and equipment. His very London-Sandhurst ways and seemingly easy affiliation with the press and media have led to a certain section of the tight climbing community eyeing him with distrust. He says that as a public figure he has to learn to take the brickbats.

'I started earning a living from climbing in 1962. I sold the Eiger story to the *Daily Express*. They gave it the treatment. I felt it was cheap sensationalism and now I'm very careful with reporters. Then we were like babes in arms. But I've been the big bad bogeyman in some climbing circles because I have been a spokesman and I've taken an in sport and shown it to a wider audience, and have been quite successful too. Many climbers fear that popularisation will mean more will come and we've only got a few hills. Yet, as I see it, people need this form of expression and I'd rather have the hills overcrowded and less vandalism on the streets.'

His own turning points are now as a writer. He feels he's reached saturation point in writing about climbing. He is working on another book on the Everest expedition, which will be his third book in four years, and each one is an effort to write.

'There may not be the need for my kind of books in the future. I enjoy my own style of complicated existence, my wheeler-dealing, rushing around lecturing, writing articles, books and organising expeditions. But then I see it that I filled a niche in my particular generation of climbers. The younger ones now want to do new things, and produce a fresher approach. They're going more and more for solo climbing.

'They're also going to farther places as more and more climbers can put their hands on, say £250–£300 and go off abroad, there's not so much need for major expensive expeditions. I think you'll find climbing will go back to being more private again and people will go off in small groups, just to climb abroad, without the fanfare of publicity.'

Carol Dix

Fresh storm over chip off old block

❊ DECEMBER 29 1977 ❊

The Cromlech boulders have little in the way of intrinsic beauty. They are two irregular lumps of rock, each as big as a house, which have lain alongside the Llanberis Pass since the retreating glacier plucked them from the steep hills.

They stand, moreover, inconveniently in the way of a road-widening scheme.

But to rock climbers and mountaineers the Cromlechs are the 'stepping stones to the Himalaya'. Over the decades thousands of climbers have used the ice age boulders beside the road at Pen-y-Pass as their training ground. Mountaineers, from Lord Hunt to Joe Brown, have practised their climbing techniques on the boulders by day and slept beneath them by night.

*Chris Bonington, Britain's most famous moutaineer
and the public face of climbing for over three decades*

Snowdonia, however, is not the sole preserve of climbers, It is visited by hikers, caravanners and motorists who arrive in ever greater numbers each year and clog the 17ft road running beneath the Cromlechs. Gwynedd county council wants to relieve the congestion by widening the road, which will entail blasting a 4ft slice off one of the boulders.

The outcry has been so great that the Welsh Office has ordered a public inquiry, which is likely to be one of the most strongly contested ever to be held in the national parks. Petitions are being organised in many parts of the country and climbing and conservation interests will gather in strength for the hearing on January 10 at a chapel in Llanberis.

The old Caernarvonshire county council tried to blow up the Cromlechs in 1973 without telling anyone. But climbers on the nearby cliffs saw workmen drilling holes for the explosive and, in no time at all, the boulders were 'occupied' and the whole project was abandoned.

According to Thomas Pennant, who wrote about them in 1773, the Cromlechs were inhabited by witches and giants who demanded proper respect from ordinary mortals. Any attempt to interfere with the boulders can still have powerful repercussions, as the planners have now found.

Although January 10 is still the official date for the public inquiry, the hearing will have to be delayed if a Welsh-speaking inspector cannot be found. The county authority insists on a bilingual hearing, but a suitable inspector has yet to be discovered.

James Lewis

Everest beaten – the hard way

❄ SEPTEMBER 26 1975 ❄

Against all the odds, Chris Bonington's team has climbed the south-west face of Everest – 'the ultimate challenge', as he called it. It is one of the major feats of Himalayan mountaineering history.

The team had faced an extremely demanding test because of the severe conditions on Everest in the autumn. Nobody was more acutely aware of the problems than Bonington himself, because his expedition was beaten back from 27,000ft up in 1972 by fierce winds and bitter cold.

The men who went to the top were two of Britain's most experienced mountaineers, Doug Scott, a schoolteacher aged 33, from Nottingham, who is married with two children, and Dougal Haston, a Scotsman of 32, who runs a climbing school in Switzerland.

They reached the top after a 10-hour climb and then, incredibly, survived a bivouac on the descent. This is the highest bivouac ever accomplished by climbers. It would have been like spending the night in a sheet sleeping-bag in a deep freeze, with the oxygen cut by two-thirds. This in itself is a physiological achievement of tremendous significance. Nevertheless, despite the dangers of this final climb and descent, few mountaineers would have missed the chance to make it and to bivouac high on the world's highest peak.

The success of the climb stemmed from the strategy that Bonington and this team adopted. They knew they had to push up the route extremely rapidly to be able to tackle the difficult section high in the mountain before the winter storms gathered. No period of good weather seems to have been wasted, and they reached the rock band at 26,500ft in record time. The huge cliff that spans the face is the major obstacle of the route. Six expeditions have failed at this point.

Bonington's men were determined to try and climb it by a new line, a steep and impressive gully on the left-hand side. In the event, this proved to be the key to success.

Climbers throughout the world are hailing this climb as one of the most important ever achieved in the Himalaya. Yet the feeling in the mountaineering world is mixed. On the one hand all climbers will be elated that the south-west face has at last been climbed and will warmly congratulate Chris Bonington and his team for their fully deserved success. On the other hand there is growing distaste for this type of old-style blockbusting expedition with its hundreds of porters, tons of supplies and thousands of feet of fixed ropes.

Already there is a growing trend to lightweight expeditions with small teams of climbers making fast, exciting climbs to gain summits rather than engaging in weeks of tedious build-up. This type of ascent was not possible on the south-west face, though Haston's and Scott's summit climb contains many of the undertones of such an approach. Thus this magnificent success may also signal the decline of an era, when massive national teams laid siege to the highest peaks of the world.

Ken Wilson

The Maoist way up Everest

❄ OCTOBER 4 1975 ❄

The British Everest expedition has found a Chinese surveying pole on top of Mount Everest and regard it as proof that the Chinese did reach the summit in May. The original Chinese claim was so embroidered by Communist propaganda and the sayings of Chairman Mao that the mountaineering world disbelieved it.

Not only did the Chinese reach the summit, but they did it with only one oxygen bottle. Mountaineers, including Sir Edmund Hillary, originally dismissed this claim as unbelievable and Sir Edmund said: 'I know that the Chinese, with Chairman Mao on their side, may be tougher than the rest of us, and I am sure they have got some very good climbers. I only wish they would make it a little easier to believe them.'

Now, because of photographs taken on the summit by the British team, the world's mountaineers are having to eat their words and accept those of Mao. On the way up, the Chinese said they had spent their time at 20,000ft holding Communist party meetings and criticising Lin Piao and Confucius.

They reached the summit by the north ridge route, which defeated a number of British expeditions before the last war. Though it is technically nothing like as difficult as the new south-west face just conquered by the Britons, the Chinese ascent tops this as a physiological achievement. Most medical experts had discounted any possibility of carrying out strenuous activity above 28,000ft without succumbing to hypoxin (oxygen starvation).

The Chinese climb forced medical opinion in London yesterday to revise its ideas, though the fact that eight of the Chinese team were Tibetans, used to living at around 10,000ft, would have helped.

Ken Wilson, the British mountaineer who went up Everest in 1972, said yesterday: 'Many mountaineers have always disagreed with the medical men and have placed higher value on good acclimatisation and a determined state of mind. This proves them right.'

Alpine Club to fight off women

❄ APRIL 26 1974 ❄

Members of the Alpine Club, one of the most exclusive mountaineering bodies in the country, are fighting a determined rearguard action to ward off the admission of women into their company. Although no rule debars women from applying, none has been accepted for membership since the club was formed in 1858, in the pioneering age of British alpinism.

The secretary, Mr Michael Baker, said yesterday that membership was in the hands of the committee, which would always 'uphold the traditions of the club' unless instructed to do otherwise. Strenuous opposition to the issuing of such an instruction is expected when the issue is raised at a special meeting on May 7, although the committee itself is in favour of women members.

Since 1907 there has been a separate Ladies' Alpine Club, and in recent years many British visitors to the Alps have been allowed to join the Austrian Alpine Club instead of the British one, since the qualifications are few and membership is open to both sexes.

Paradoxically, women are also allowed to join the Alpine Climbing Group, an offshoot of the Alpine Club, which comprises the true elite of British climbers currently tackling difficult Alpine routes. There are three women members at present, and supporters of the open-door policy argue that they are being denied privileges for which they are obviously qualified.

Peter Hildrew

Obituary: Rock of the north – Peter Livesey

❄ FEBRUARY 17 1998 ❄

British rock climbing at the beginning of the 1970s was bitterly factional, moribund and directionless, and had not progressed since the early 1950s heyday of Joe Brown and Don Whillans. That its development did get under way again, and that it was transformed into the modern mode of eclecticism and extreme physicality allied to the effective and sophisticated exclusion of risk, is due in the main to the influence of Peter Livesey, who has died from cancer aged 54.

Livesey was born in Huddersfield and began climbing at the age of 12 in local quarries hewn out of the surrounding gritstone moorland. His first sporting love, however, was not rock but the track: he was *victor ludorum* of his grammar school, as a junior ran the mile in close to four minutes, was twice Northern Counties junior steeplechase champion, was coached and ran in the same club as Derek Ibbotson, and came third in the Amateur Athletics Association Steeplechase at White City – effectively the British championship race.

It was failure to win that event, he once wryly admitted to me, that caused him to turn away from athletics. Climbing was still only a subsidiary interest to him. Most of his leisure time he spent in the hazardous activity of cave diving. He took part in several expeditions, and even spent a year in Jamaica employed by a millionaire to chart unexplored river caves.

Even in caving, however, his competitive instinct failed to find ultimate satisfaction. His closest companion, Michael Boone, was short and slight; Livesey was rangy, muscular and tall. The one could get to places the other could not. Livesey moved on again. He had, after leaving school, gone into electrical engineering (even there the quest for excellence asserted itself and he was voted Electrical Engineering Apprentice of the Year), but this palled, and he enrolled for a teacher training course at Bingley College.

Outdoor activities featured on the curriculum, the college had boats and transport, there were suitable rivers nearby and within a couple of years he was a first division slalom canoeist and was winning white water races. He went from college to an instructing job at Bewerley Park, an outdoor centre in the old West Riding, moved from there to teach PE in Scunthorpe, and in the flatlands of Lincolnshire, in the most inconceivably unsuitable environment for rock climbing, he laid the seeds for its next revolution.

He had in fact kept up his rock climbing, making early ascents of most of the top climbs of the 1960s in Wales and the Lake District. He had even managed a second ascent of the forbidding Rimmon Route on Norway's 5,000ft-high Trolltinder Wall. So the ability was there, if latent.

What he did in Scunthorpe was to harness it to the ruthless standards of training that obtained in athletics. He practised daily on the school's climbing wall, carrying weights, lengthening the sessions, building up stamina – dedicated modes that were anathema in a sport that prided itself on anarchic, wild-living unprofessionalism. When he came to apply the results to rock itself, in 1972, it was to produce a series of climbs on the limestone cliffs of the Yorkshire Dales that marked a clear advance in standards and brought his activities under the sharp critical scrutiny of climbing's old guard.

His tactics of cleaning and pre-inspection before climbing a line provoked outrage. Stories were circulated about other more underhand methods supposedly employed. Livesey answered his critics with yet more climbs that now number amongst the established classics of the region: Jenny Wren, Face Route and Deliverance at Gordale Scar; Central Wall, Diedre, and Claws on Kilnsey Crag; Wellington Crack on the gritstone of Ilkley. Nor did he confine his activities to Yorkshire.

He made new climbs in Derbyshire, Wales and the Lake District that marked substantial advances in each of those regions: Downhill Racer on Froggatt Edge; Right Wall on Dinas Cromlech; Fingerlicker on Craig Pant Ifan; Footless Crow on Goat Crag, and many others.

Routes like these brought standards of rock climbing in Britain in line with those on the continent and in America, in both of which places Livesey himself climbed extensively, at the same period. The techniques they relied on underpinned the next 20 years of the sport's development in Britain. It was a development in which Livesey himself, after the mid-1970s, played little active part.

In the wake of his example, younger climbers came through and began to operate at a standard he himself could not reach. He retreated into orienteering, at which, as usual, he excelled, though he did maintain his contact with the sport through a long-running and popular column in the magazine *Climber*.

He even retained much of his climbing ability. In the television series *Lakeland Rock* he led Chris Bonington up his benchmark climb, Footless Crow, 10 years after its first ascent. In a humorous moment that passed straight into climbing folklore, he lowered a £5 note on a line down to a point just out of reach of the notoriously commercially minded Bonington as incitement, while the latter dangled helpless and in extremis on a taut rope from the climb's crux.

Professionally, he directed an outdoor pursuits course of enviable reputation from Bingley College for many years. Personally, with his Sri Lankan wife, Soma, he ran a cafe in Malham that became one of the social hubs of the climbing world. He had a caustic wit, a gruffly amused manner, and a steadfast refusal to take life too seriously. In his climbing, where his fame must ultimately rest, he was effective rather than stylish – a fast and economical mover whose fitness made up for any lack of innate awareness of the medium.

His method, too, was not beyond reproach. Climbs such as Downhill Racer and Claws undoubtedly relied on 'improved' holds – and this in a sport where defacing the rock is the most heinous crime. But the man was so good-natured, unpompous and funny, and his recognised contribution so huge, that he was generally forgiven for these anomalies. His climbs are his memorial, half a dozen or so from among them surely as fine as any that have ever been pioneered in this country.

He is survived by Soma and their daughter Tai.

Peter Livesey, climber, born September 12 1943, died February 26 1998

Jim Perrin

Climbers knock rock against the clock

❄ OCTOBER 29 1976 ❄

An attempt by the Russians to get rock climbing against the clock accepted as an Olympic games event has united British climbers in furious opposition.

According to Denis Gray, secretary of the British Mountaineering Council, the issue strikes deep at the philosophy of climbing and could split the international mountaineering body, the UIAA (Union of International Alpine Associations) – with Russia and the eastern block on one side and Britain and America on the other.

Mr Gray, as British representative on the UIAA executive, argued long and acrimoniously against competitive climbing at the UIAA's annual meeting in Barcelona this month, but he and his allies – the

United States, Holland and Yugoslavia – were outvoted and the executive decided to set up a subcommittee to consider possible developments of the sport.

British climbers seem unanimous in supporting Mr Gray and the BMC. Competitive rock climbing as developed in Russia, Poland, Czechoslovakia and East Germany, consists of selecting a demanding rock face (probably 'extreme' by British gradings) and sending every competitor up it in turn, protected by a harness clipped on to a wire cable that is winched in from the top as he climbs.

Competitors are marked for time, skill, and grace. They are graded by several judges, as in ice skating or diving.

The Russians made a determined attempt to win the interest of western climbers at Munich in 1972 and a demonstration event was arranged by the German Alpine Club.

Since then invitations have been coming from the Russians to observe or take part in their national championships in the Crimea. 'Invitations are flying out to western climbers but we try to ignore them,' said one climber.

Mr Gray says that the rooted opposition of British and American climbers stems from a very different attitude to mountains. 'The thing is that in Russia you can only get money to develop your sport if in the end the paymasters can see competition results and medals. In climbing there are no medals. We climb for the hell of it. It's a very subtle sort of competition against yourself and against the mountain.'

Walt Unsworth, editor of *Climber and Rambler*, was astonished at the response to the idea of competitive climbing. 'We got more letters about that than we've ever had about anything – over 60, which is pretty good when you consider that climbers never put pen to paper if they can help it – and the amazing thing is that every single one of them was against it.'

Both Mr Gray and Mr Unsworth are worried that competition climbing with all the publicity and ballyhoo involved could ruin the sport by commercialising it. 'Look what happened to skiing,' says Mr Gray. He has a horror picture of what might come about if climbing sponsorship developed.

'You can imagine ICI or something buying up half the quarries in Derbyshire for sponsorship meets with stadia built at the bottom for the Manchester v Leeds climbing match.'

The Alpine nations in general share the British and American dislike of the idea. On the other hand, some of them – Italy in particular – are very anxious to get ski mountaineering accepted as a winter Olympic sport.

There are suspicions among the British contingent of unpublicised deals, with the Communist block supporting ski mountaineering in return for Italian support of Olympic rock climbing.

According to Mr Unsworth, if Olympic mountaineering is introduced it will be impossible for British climbers to remain uncontaminated by it, however hard they try. He said, 'The power of television is too strong, and if it gets world recognition it will be very hard for young climbers in this country to resist it.'

Gillian Linscott

CHAPTER EIGHT

EXTREME SEVERITY, AND MORE

It was the decade when climbers began to wear Lycra tights, sticky-soled rock shoes and when standards rose to unimagined, extreme levels. The 1980s were also to see a *Guardian*-sponsored expedition reach the summit of Jitchu Drake, an unclimbed Himalayan peak in Bhutan.

In June 1988, three climbers, including the veteran mountaineer Doug Scott, made it to the top of the 7,000m mountain while not far below at camp 4 was the *Guardian*'s reporter, David Rose.

The sponsoring of a serious Himalayan expedition stemmed from the fact that Jim Markwick, the *Guardian*'s managing director at the time, was a keen mountaineer. Markwick knew Scott and through various conversations it came to light that the explorer had a permit to climb in Bhutan but was finding it hard to raise sponsorship. Bhutan severely restricted the number of climbing expeditions it allowed into the country and the canny managing director spotted the marketing possibilities, as well as the challenge of such a venture.

Once the expedition was up and running, an elaborate system involving mail runners and aircraft pilots was devised to get David Rose's copy and pictures back to London. Despite the potential for disaster, it worked, and four days after bashing out a story on a manual typewriter in the sub-zero temperatures of base camp, it was with the newsdesk.

A couple of years later, and with the gradual opening up of the Soviet Union to visitors from the west, Markwick instigated another *Guardian* trip, this time to the Caucasus to climb Mount Elbrus, the highest peak in Europe. The mission was accomplished and as the team were relaxing in the sauna of a palatial dacha much favoured by the former Soviet president Leonid Brezhnev, Markwick, a one-time Tory candidate, observed: 'Well, if this is communism, I'll have to revise my opinion.'

Talking of Tories, it could be said that Margaret Thatcher had an indirect affect on the raising of climbing standards during this time. Because of high youth unemployment in the 1980s, some climbers had opted to live off the dole, and any other crumbs of money they could come by, and dedicate their lives to getting up rock faces. This produced yet another wave of extreme climbs, often in new areas such as the slate quarries of Llanberis, North Wales. Ultra-bold traditional climbers such as Johnny Dawes and Paul Pritchard were making daring climbs that required both athletic prowess and supreme confidence in their ability. The least consequence of a fall from some of their routes was serious injury, the probability was death.

Just as the *Guardian* had reported the exploits of rock climbing pioneers around the turn of the century, so in the latter part of the 1980s it recorded the achievements of this new generation. This was down in part to the presence of two members of staff who climbed: David Rose and Roger Alton. Rose had joined the paper in 1984 as a general reporter, later to become crime correspondent; Alton, arts editor in the late 1980s, was to go on to become features editor and play an important role in raising the profile of mountain-related articles into the paper. Both were members of the London Mountaineering Club and climbed together every few weekends in North Wales. Here they met many of the leading climbers of the day and being plugged into this scene meant they were often the first to report new climbs in the national press. In October 1986, they wrote about the first ascent of the Indian Face, a route on the north flank of Snowdon and then Britain's hardest climb, by the 22-year old Dawes. That a newspaper would give coverage to this ascent had a big impact on the climbing world.

Of course not all climbers were ready to take such calculated risks as the new elite. The 1980s also saw the appearance of the bolted climb, where pre-placed metal anchors were permanently fixed to the rock. This reduced the element of danger so the climber could concentrate on the actual climbing and not have to worry about placing protection such as chocks or other aids. Many continental crags were equipped with bolts and 'sport climbing' in Mediterranean sunshine began to gain in popularity. In Britain, the bolting of routes was resisted apart from in a few quarried areas and steep and overhanging limestone. For some, however, there was a feeling that once the danger had been removed from the sport, all that was left was gymnastics.

And rock gymnastics was precisely what climbing competitions were all about. These had been scoffed at and resisted in the mid-1970s, but in the late 1980s competition climbing for large cash prizes was established.

Back in the real world of mountains, experiencing the Himalaya was more popular than ever. Organised trekking groups were exploring the trails up to base camps and, while bringing in much-needed money to the Sherpas, they generated heaps of rubbish. So much so that in 1983 the Nepalese government announced that in future groups had to take extra porters to bring back their waste. For a number of years mountaineers had been opting for low-key expeditions to often unclimbed routes in remote corners of the world. The danger of this lightweight approach, though, was that if something went wrong, there was little chance of rescue, as Joe Simpson and Simon Yates were to find on Siula Grande, a mountain in the Peruvian Andes.

A Country Diary: Keswick

❄ JANUARY 21 1980 ❄

I have lately received a number of old stereoscopic glass slides and their elegant French viewer. These slides were taken by my family mainly between 1890 and 1902 and most of them are of rock climbing in Britain, the Alps and the Dolomites, especially around Arolla. The ones of snow and ice have an almost uncanny reality and though the gear of those early climbers was very different, the mountains have changed only in varying degrees. The local valley views are perhaps unremarkable but some of the high mountain ones have surprises – for instance, Napes Needle with a figure suitably on top has a thick, shrubby growth near its base. There is nothing like that now. My father, in old age, used to complain that a lot of interest had gone from the more popular routes with ledges and holds cleared of debris and the rocks near-polished by nailed boots. He should see, say, the ground above Ashness Bridge (a too popular beauty spot) now for not only is the grass gone but the earth itself is going fast and the rocks are bare. It is, it seems, the actual skin of the land that suffers worst, and while the National Trust does its best to nurture the land it holds, it must be a discouraging battle at times. Not only are there more people; there are more animals too.

Yesterday a neighbouring farmer told me, as we talked over his yard gate, pushed and rattled by young cows, that there are four times as many animals on that farm as there were in his fore-elders' time. That afternoon I met another farmer on the hill road, a small ageing man in an elderly car carrying fodder for his beasts in the valley. The car boot was open and piled high with blocks of hay until it seemed astonishing that the front wheels of the car were still on the road at all, and as I got home in the gathering dusk a helicopter crossed High Lodore, its lights winking, to leave more blocks for the sheep on the fell tops before the real winter sets in – as it will.

Enid J Wilson

Trash trail

❄ JANUARY 31 1983 ❄

In the mid-70s, I joined a party of Swiss climbers en route to the Everest base camp. Their leader had climbed there two years before, and he was horrified at the change: 'Look at the garbage. There'll be road cleaners on Everest in 10 years' time.'

It hasn't taken that long: the Nepalese government has just announced that any future group on the Everest trail must take with them 10 extra porters to bring back their rubbish.

It must be very bad by now: then, there was only an 18-month queue to climb the world's top mountain. It was very odd, on the way to the ultimate outpost of human life, to trip over beer cans and boxes, and to see azaleas flowering at 15,000ft – only they turned out to be face tissues and plastic bags.

Unfortunately, a diet of yak and potatoes and tea with melted butter instead of milk does not keep you regular, and what is biodegradable at 5,000ft is preserved for posterity at 15,000 ft. Even for the Swiss, who responded morning and evening to some communal inner call and rushed out together into the freezing dark to queue at a tented hole in the ground, there are only a limited number of flat places to dig holes.

The Sherpas had made good use of some of the detritus left behind by western civilised industrial culture. The 60-degree landing strip at Lukla was marked out for the pilots of incoming aircraft with the shells of broken planes, frozen for all time.

Disconcerting though, to stand like stout Cortez ... and look down on the back of some huge hawk hovering thousands of feet above its prey, and hear Frank Zappa throbbing from above as a young Sherpa walks by with his pocket radio at full blast.

There are more far-reaching pollutions too. VD, unknown three years before, had become a problem since large numbers of American tourists had passed through. Colds and flu can kill the locals – antibiotics, apparently, are not as effective over 10,000ft.

There were, of course, the commercial effects of hundreds of thousands of tourists en route to the experience of treading where so few had trod before. Most monasteries, even then, had the authentic Yeti head or hand, reddish and bristling; smiling Sherpa women moved ahead of you along the path and spread their curios and souvenirs; Beer like Back Home in the Everest View Cafe.

As we all queued at Lukla for the tiny plane back to Kathmandu, a man tried to flog the petrified body of a bear, the size of a child, as a souvenir of the trip of a lifetime.

What was already becoming clear in the mid-70s, when trekking was in its infancy, was that the young Sherpas wanted no more of the hard, high life. They wanted the bright lights of Kathmandu, rather than the struggle to clear the stones from terraces of earth snatched from the mountainsides to grow potatoes.

There was an old man there who had translated the whole of *Paradise Lost* into Nepalese. He was full of memories, nostalgic for the past, hating change. 'Nothing good will ever come of them,' he said, of a group of young and eager visitors photographing Everest for future reference.

All that garbage clogging the path to the unknown proves him right. It's ironic that when civilised man tries to escape his civilisation, he pollutes everything he touches.

Jane McLoughlin

Joe Brown & Jim Perrin on Suicide Wall, Cwm Idwal, Wales, 1990

Extreme severity, and more

❄ OCTOBER 25 1986 ❄

One hundred and twenty feet above the rocky screes at the foot of Clogwyn d'ur Arddu, a towering cliff on the north flank of Snowdon in Wales, the rock climber Johnny Dawes moved up and onto a ledge just four inches long and two inches wide.

This minute resting place was smaller than a bar of chocolate. But it was the key to Dawes' historic ascent earlier this month of a new climb on the cliff's featureless Great Wall. The climb was so difficult and dangerous that it marked a turning point in climbing, as significant for this high-risk sport as the first four-minute mile was for athletics.

Reaching the ledge, Dawes was at the outer limits of his physical and mental capabilities, was able at last to rest the screaming muscles in his arms and legs. Any mistake as he inched his way up the vertically below the ledge would have meant death or serious injury. The rock was virtually bereft of cracks or niches in which he could have slotted metal wedges, attached to his ropes, to limit any fall. Above lay more of the same.

'I stayed on the ledge for half an hour,' recalls Dawes, 22, the former public schoolboy who is now indisputably the bravest and most gifted rock climber in Britain. 'I was literally too "gripped" to move. I thought, I don't have to be doing this. Then I saw a friend away over on the left. We looked at each other, but we didn't smile. Any break in my concentration would have been too dangerous and I could have fallen off.'

Dawes had been psyching himself up for months, waiting for the fine autumn to dry out the high and sunless crag. But even then, he says: 'as I walked up to the cliff, I knew I might not be coming back.' Yet he felt it might be his last chance, 'By next year I might have been too old. I don't think I'd be prepared to accept that level of risk again.'

Even experienced climbers find it difficult to comprehend the technical demands and the risks involved in Dawes' 150ft-high new route, which he has called Indian Face. None of the holds had positive edges on which to pull up. Dawes had to use tiny ripples in the rock to lever and balance his body in a gymnastic sequence of moves, using subtle shifts of weight from to limb to limb. Tiny flakes on the rock face on which side pulls could be made also allowed upward progress.

'It was as if the rock was wired up,' say Dawes. 'If you touched holds in the wrong sequence, it was like a short-circuit through my body, and I quickly had to think again – otherwise I'd have been electrocuted and fallen.'

He gave the climb the ninth grade of Extreme Severity, E9, the first ever of that standard. Dawes was also responsible for the country's first E8, a blank groove he climbed earlier this year on a gritstone outcrop in Derbyshire. Few climbers, even those of the highest skill and ability, can manage E3 or E4. A small elite in British climbing goes on to E5 and E6, and occasionally E7. Only Dawes has gone beyond that.

Dawes is obsessed by climbing, which has dominated his life for the past few years. He is a small, wiry, affable man whose climbing makes up for the lack of inches with supreme technique. Supported by wealthy, and indulgent parents, since leaving Uppingham School he has led a peripatetic existence, moving from crag to crag.

Of the many new climbs he has established in Britain, the central line up the Great Wall of Clogwyn d'ur Arddu (or Cloggy, as it is known) has haunted him – just as it has every other top climber over the years. For Cloggy has been, since its first routes in the 1920s, the spiritual heartland and forcing ground for aspiring hard men of the hills. Great climbers of the past such as Jack Longland, Joe Brown and Don Whillans have all made their mark on its awesome, rearing bastions.

But it was not until 1962 that Pete Crew, a college lecturer, made the first impression on the Great Wall. His line – still a magnificent route, but now graded a mere E3 – only skirted the edge of the huge triangular buttress that is the focus of the cliffs.

In recent years other top climbers, such as Jerry Moffatt and John Redhead, have made attempts on the blank central line, knowing that once climbed it would be the hardest route in Britain. Each had either to retreat or move away at half height. The difficulties were too much.

Only a man with a unique combination of boldness and skill could hope to succeed. Says Steve Haston, a Llanberis climber and himself responsible for several ferocious E7s up the overhanging sea cliffs of Anglesey: 'Johnny's like a fighter pilot in the war – it's all or nothing.'

How good is Dawes? Where does he stand in the great tradition of British rock climbing? One who is in no doubt is Trevor Jones, author of the definitive history, *Welsh Rock* (Pic, £16.95), and a leading activist of the 50s and 60s; 'I rate him the best in the country,' he says, 'Dawes is a diminutive King Kong; small, powerful and very brave. And of course, he's a purist. He won't use any artificial aids. With Johnny's ascent, the great challenge of Wales has now been met. A 30-year dream has been realised.'

Dawes himself feels that, in spite of the danger, climbing such a route was a creative act. He compares it to music and poetry, and he talks of climbing as a means to achieve a unique and harmonious relationship with Nature.

'When you look at the great climbs of the past, they seem to have the personalities of the men who climbed them,' he says. With Indian Face, Dawes has not only pushed British climbing into a new era, he has stamped his name indelibly on the sport.

David Rose and Roger Alton

How to get to the top and stay honest

❊ APRIL 5 1983 ❊

At 32 you can easily be over the hill, for rock climbing is generally a young person's passion. But Jill Lawrence, the best woman rock climber in the country, is still improving.

The sport's image blurs in with that of mountaineering – a host of Boningtons waving ice axes aloft as they grit their teeth behind ice-encrusted beards and straddle the summit of Terror Peak. Rock climbing isn't like that. It is practised as a distinct sport in its own right – sunny days on rocks in shorts and a T-shirt, free-form gymnastics. It is attracting ever-greater numbers of women into its ranks.

There is no organised competition in rock climbing – that takes place within the individual and almost objectively graded scales of difficulty. Lawrence's particular skill is at leading – going first on the rope – the core experience of rock climbing. The leader is the one who takes the risks, perhaps even the falls, who faces up to the weaknesses in her or his own character and whose personality wins through. To go second on the rope is very much second-best – a more secure, circumscribed, and safeguarded experience. Many women who come to climbing are attracted or dragged into it by a bullying or pleading male who wishes to impress on her through the sport his own manliness. Thus the recurrent syndrome of the eternal female second, time and again taken onto climbs beyond her experience and developed capabilities.

Lawrence came to climbing in 1973. As a student at Bingley College of Education, she was taken up a severe climb on the Yorkshire gritstone outcrop of Almscliff. 'At the top I nearly bounced off the edge of the crag, I was so excited,' she recalls. At Bingley she came into contact with Peter Livesey, then the leading British rock-climber and a lecturer at the college. She was soon following him up the hardest climbs.

Although in many ways this was a good entree into the sport, it fostered in her technical ability rather than independence of approach. Although the prestige and intrinsic interest of taking part in the first ascents of some of the country's hardest climbs held her for a while, she quickly realised the direction in which she wanted to go, and more and more she started to lead on less difficult climbs with people, drawn from the supportive community into which she had been introduced, of her own standard. Her climbing improved and her ideas on it clarified. 'I became much calmer about it, and instead of rushing at a series of moves, knowing I'd be all right if I fell off, I would consider them, work out how to use my body, conserve my strength, and stay relaxed. It became a much more complete and interesting experience.'

College over, she instructed for two years at an outdoor centre until 1979, when she took up a post in Barnsley teaching ESN children. She travelled widely to different climbing areas – the French and Swiss Alps, the Dolomites, Baffin Island, the Yosemite Valley. This summer she resigned her teaching job to become 'a full-time rock climber, till I run out of money'. She plans to organise courses based in North Wales, with female instruction for women who would like to climb. But she hopes that these will not merely develop the obvious and relatively easily acquired skills. She believes that through the activity of climbing women can acquire self-confidence, resourcefulness, aggression, honesty, and insight, which will help them in other social situations.

The particular quality of excellence Lawrence's climbing displays is in her style. 'Style' in climbing has two senses. 'Good style' is a code term for climbing without recourse to any of the little tricks that many climbers use to lower a route to their own standard – artificial aids, tension from the rope, and so on. In this sense, Lawrence is a very honest climber – she does not cheat against the sport's unwritten and unenforceable rules.

The other aspect of style is an aesthetic one, and it is here that women possess some advantages over men. There is something akin to dance in the actions of supremely good rock climber.

The moves are rhythmical, perfectly balanced; their stretch and flow, gather and release are, at the best, a joy to watch. At present there are probably no women capable of leading routes of the very highest standards of difficulty, where strength of fingers and arms becomes paramount. Come down just a little, put a good woman and a good man on the same route, and the woman will generally give the appearances of greater ease and awareness.

I was out on Stanage Edge, one of the brutishly steep gritstone outcrops in Derbyshire, with Lawrence a few weeks ago. In the course of a full day's climbing I did not see her make a single false move. The delicacy and poise, the easy swing of movement with which she overcame climbs that, for a previous generation, had been the hardest of their time, was a continual delight. Climbers such as Joe Brown and Chris Bonington, even in their prime, could never have approached its studied perfection. When questioned about her style, she simply says, 'I'm not as strong as the men, so I have to be more careful in the way I use my body to get up climbs.'

The point holds even among absolute beginners. Girls are generally more precise, economical, and considered in their movements, and in consequence are often able to get up technically more difficult climbs than boys.

Rock climbing is perhaps a unique activity in the dialectic it mounts between self-analysis and controlled action. Independence, resourcefulness in the face of hardship and physical danger, consideration for others and an ability to cope with your own fears are useful traits to acquire. Jill Lawrence possesses them all; there can be few better climbers to emulate.

Jim Perrin

The conquest of Jitchu Drake
Through blinding snows to the summit

❄ JUNE 10 1988 ❄

The *Guardian* expedition to Bhutan has made the first ascent of Jitchu Drake, having reached the summit by a new route in a gruelling Alpine-style assault, which lasted eight days.

Jitchu Drake, in north-west Bhutan, had repulsed five earlier expeditions; it is the first important Bhutanese summit to be climbed since 1937, when H Spencer Chapman reached the top of the neighbouring 24,000ft Chomolhari.

The expedition had hoped to use altimeters to fix the height of the mountain, which had never been surveyed properly. But the appalling weather, and consequent fluctuations in atmospheric pressure, meant that a precise evaluation was impossible. Jitchu Drake's altitude, therefore, can be stated to be only somewhere between 22,500 and 23,000 ft.

The expedition leader, Mr Doug Scott, aged 47, Mr Victor Saunders, aged 38, and Ms Sharu Prabhu, aged 29, the only woman member of the team, left camp 4 at about 31,500ft and arrived on the summit nine and a half hours later.

They returned to the camp shortly before dusk, rejoining the two other members of the expedition, Mr Lindsay Griffin, aged 39, and myself. We all descended safely to advance base camp, just below the snowline at 16,000ft, the following day.

Until the summit day, the climb had been marked by severe snowstorms, which doubled the number of bivouacs and the time we thought necessary for the ascent.

Climbing in Alpine style means setting off from the bottom with everything in the rucksack, without fixed ropes, established camps or high-altitude porters. Blinding streams of snow and enveloping mist made route-finding and the location of ledges large enough to pitch a tent extremely difficult.

The team was forced to stretch the three days' food taken above camp 1 at 19,000ft to six days' supplies.

Leaving base camp, we reached camp 1, which we had explored the previous week, two days later. From there, we struggled with heavy loads, gasping in the rarefied air, through a maze of crevasses in the glacier to pitch camp 2 below the icy slopes of Jitchu Drake's south face, not far below the 20,000ft mark.

After one abortive foray on to the face in the teeth of an advancing storm, we left camp 2. By mid-morning, driving snow and wind had turned the climb into a desperate battle against the elements. The weather forced us rightwards from our intended line in the middle of the face towards the south-east ridge, where lay the only hope of camp sites.

It was not until well after dark that all the members of the expedition reached the ridge, to find a ledge big enough for only two, and a draughty, freezing snow-cave, which we enlarged with our ice axes long into the night.

Next day we made only a few hundred feet of progress up the ridge before establishing camp 4 amid another storm. It lasted for most of the following night, forcing us repeatedly to dig the tents from the weight of snow that threatened to crush them. It snowed again for much of the next day.

But after so much evil weather, the following day was perfect. Climbing steadily up the icy ridge, the summit trio attained Jitchu Drake's south peak. This point had been reached by previous expeditions from Austria and Japan, but both were defeated by the 900ft-long ridge linking it with the mountain's main north summit, some 300ft higher.

Moving gingerly on the lee side of huge, cream-roll cornices of unstable snow, the *Guardian* team took only an hour to negotiate the ridge, so completing the first ascent of Jitchu Drake. They were rewarded by 200-mile views far into Tibet.

The following day was equally fine, and the ground made with so much effort was speedily descended. On the steep ice face between camps 2 and 3, we abseiled from ice screws driven into the mountain.

Back at base camp at last next day, there were gales and snow-storms all afternoon. We had escaped a further ordeal by the skin of our teeth.

'The bad weather we've had for virtually our entire stay here had more or less resigned me to the fact that we were unlikely to reach the summit,' Mr Scott said. 'But Himalayan climbing is always a waiting game.

'Right at the 11th hour it all came together and we were allowed our opportunity. To have been in Bhutan has been a fascinating experience and a great privilege. To have climbed the mountain as well, and to have seen so far across the eastern Himalaya, has made it truly memorable.'

David Rose

Climber achieves first free ascent of Kilnsey Crag's 20ft overhang

❄ SEPTEMBER 22 1988 ❄

One of Britain's fiercest rock climbing challenges has been overcome by a 23-year-old former engineering student who spent most of last year unemployed.

Mr Mark Leach, from Rossendale, Lancashire, has made the first free-climbing ascent of the main overhang at Kilnsey Crag, jutting over Wharfedale, North Yorkshire.

The climb was described as 'staggering' and the 'coup of the decade' by the Yorkshire Mountaineering Club, which has set new technical standards on Dales limestone cliffs. Kilnsey's 20ft 'lip', running out horizontally above 90ft of vertical rock, has long been a target for free climbers, who rely on their hands and feet, using ropes and pitons only for emergency protection.

'I climbed Kilnsey artificially, with pegs, in the 60s and I reckoned then it would be 50 years before we saw a free ascent,' said Mr Frank Wilkinson, an author of the YMC's *Yorkshire Limestone Guide*. 'This puts Mark among the very best climbers in the world.'

Mr Leach, now a climbing instructor, spent 10 days roped to bolts on the crag, practising each move before making the free climb. After scaling the vertical pitch, pioneered artificially by Joe

Brown in 1953, he clung by his hands and feet to a flake line running diagonally across the overhang for 35ft.

'It was pretty wild – the holds got smaller and smaller as I reached the edge,' he said.

Martin Wainwright

Room at the top

❄ NOVEMBER 17 1984 ❄

'Has anybody here seen my old friend John? I just looked around, and he was gone.'

Marvin Gaye's mournful tribute to President Kennedy should be adopted as an anthem by the climbing fraternity. The mountain gods have feasted well these past few years: Dougal Haston, Nick Estcourt, Joe Tasker, Pete Boardman, all 'gifted' climbers, have been their fodder.

To a non-climber trying to make sense of their deaths, one cruel irony stands out. Mountaineers may miss their footing, but seldom their copy deadlines. Their thoughts on life, death and each other are safely lodged with publishers before they 'peel off'. Their books are served up as memorials to dead heroes, inspiration to a new generation of climbers, for whom the death rate creates more room at the top.

No book better encapsulates this *danse macabre* than *The Shishapangma Expedition* by Doug Scott and Alex MacIntyre, and not just because of its superb reportage. This unconventional expedition in 1982 by a team of six to a virgin peak in Tibet had succeeded without tragic incident, when they learned that two other climbers, Joe Tasker and Pete Boardman, had disappeared on the north-east ridge of Everest.

The news, compounded by tensions within the group, had an explosive effect. In Peking, nearly legless, Scott whirled MacIntyre around a disco floor then dropped him. Suddenly they were locked in a furious scuffle. 'Is this where I put the nut in?' wondered Scott, lining up for a head-butt.

Back in England and friends again, they completed their manuscript. Less than five months later, MacIntyre was descending from the south face of Annapurna when a solitary stone struck him dead and hurled him 800ft below.

The awful saga was crowned earlier this month when MacIntyre and Scott were awarded the Boardman/Tasker prize for mountain literature. Both Boardman and Tasker had books published only months before their deaths.

At 43, Scott is a legend in his charmed lifetime. His only serious mishap was breaking both ankles on the Ogre in Pakistan in 1977. In the darkness he had slipped, swung 100ft across a gorge and smashed into a rock wall. For five days he crawled down the mountains on his hands and knees. Then the helicopter bearing him to safety crash-landed.

He reckons that on aggregate he has sustained more serious injuries while playing rugby. To an extent he is fatalistic, citing Mrs Gandhi's remarks about death shortly before her assassination. 'She could no more stop being the prime minister of India than a committed climber can stop going high.'

He mentioned that Alex MacIntyre's colleagues had felt his obsession with the danger of stonefalls signalled a kind of premonition. 'Dougal Haston was even stranger. He wrote a novel, *Calculated Risk*, in which the hero goes down this couloir, triggers an avalanche and manages to outrun it. A few days after writing the book he did that very thing, except that the avalanche overwhelmed him.'

Scott learned of his co-author's death while climbing in South America. 'When I got the phone call I wanted to climb harder, not less. I've never thought of packing it in.'

Their painfully honest book reveals Scott as a complicated man, a former secondary-school teacher whose unfathomable strength and tetchiness at being thought 'an old fart' contrast with his interest in Tibetan culture and a more measured approach to mountaineering.

'I am more into exploring ways to keep alive,' he said. 'It's a question of what is success? There may be other criteria. A successful expedition could be one that is not so attached to the gung-ho idea of getting to the top, where people are at ease with each other and in touch with their own intuitive feelings. If you wait for the time that you feel right, and the weather's right, there's nothing can stop you.'

To this end, although still committed to the Alpine style of quick, lightweight dashes, he has lately encouraged wives and girlfriends to join his base camps. Relaxation, contentment and good food are essential prerequisites to success and safety, he believes.

Failure is no longer unthinkable. 'I have backed off loads of climbs. I've had three goes at K2 and three at Macalu [in the Himalaya] and we still haven't got up.' Stacked against these attempts are innumerable successes, notably his conquest, with Dougal Haston, of Everest's south-west face in 1975, when they bivouacked without oxygen or sleeping bags just below the summit.

He admits that the death rate among his friends is forcing him to climb with increasingly young companions whose ambitions are hard to tame. 'When you have a big one under your belt you can rest on your laurels.'

He is most at ease with French climbers, and particularly feels the loss of Georges Bettembourg, who was killed during a stonefall on Mont Blanc. 'He and I had plans to do all sorts of things. So did Alex and I. People like Nick Estcourt ... all those lads who looked like they would be around for a long time.'

Stuart Wavell

Miracle, miracle on the wall, GB is the best of all

❄ NOVEMBER 20 1989 ❄

After Everest, Lyons. In a stunning climax to the first world cup for climbing, Britain's Simon Nadin yesterday snatched first place from his glitter-pants French rival, Didier Raboutou. The distance, as they say, was 1.4m. Eight thousand pairs of French hands in the Palais des Sports applauded politely.

In sporting terms this was roughly equivalent to Mike Tyson being knocked out by an eskimo at Madison Square Garden. Raboutou is a hero in a country where mountaineers rank somewhere between soap stars and Sorbonne professors in the public estimation. Nadin, 24 years old and a professional for only six months, would have trouble being recognised in his native Buxton.

Yet in yesterday's final round of the Lyons Grand Prix – the seventh and last stage of the world cup – it was Nadin whose nerve and muscle held.

Going third in a final group of eight competitors, which had been whittled down from 82, Raboutou reached 18.6m on the 20m wall before falling on to his tether. Nadin, next to go, reached the top faultlessly.

As both men had been tied on 98 points in the world cup rankings – 25 points for first place, 20 for second and so on – and their nearest rival, England's Jerry Moffat, had 65, this confirmed Nadin as champion.

To rub more salt into French wounds, Nadin and Moffat took first and second places (worth £3,000 and £2,000) in yesterday's contest after a timed super-final climb-off with the West German star Stefan Glowacz and another Frenchman, Jean-Baptiste Tribout. The women's final was won by the American Lynn Hill.

There can now be no doubting climbing's legitimacy as a spectator sport. The excitement in the Palais des Sports was extraordinary: watching Nadin slither his way beyond the chalk fingerprints that marked the point where his rival had spun off was a stupefyingly exhilarating moment.

The intellectual and physical effort required to manoeuvre the human body up what is effectively a cliff of crumpled sandpaper is immediately apparent and awe-inspiring: it is chess and all-in wrestling and *Where Eagles Dare* rolled into one, with the added complication for the competitors yesterday that they had only two minutes to study the problems before starting an assault that had to take 16 minutes at most.

Once someone has cracked the code and made it to the summit, the spectators are put in the exquisite position of the *Twenty Questions* audience who know the answer before the experts begin. Add spotlit entries, the music of Jean-Michel Jarre and lots of live bodies prancing around in post-Impressionist leotards and you have a grand sporting circus.

It was good, too, to see the proprieties observed. The spectators cheered on everybody when they started and, if they failed, when they fell – regardless of nationality. The French officials were scrupulous in applying the rules, critically penalising the national pin-up (and home-town girl) Isabelle Patissier on Friday night for actually over-reaching the target. British fears that the final route would be riddled with short reaches, thus favouring the dumpy Raboutou over the lanky Nadin, were unfounded.

Of course, the Union des Associations d'Alpinisme, organisers of this event, have to be on their best behaviour. Their long-term ambition is to win Olympic status for competition climbing. The sport will be 'exhibited' at Barelona and Albertville just before the next summer and winter Games.

All this, plus Nadin's achievement last night, sets a poser for the organising body of British climbing, the British Mountaineering Council. Many among its 40,000 members are suspicious of competition climbing's razzmatazz, and fear that it could consume resources that might be better spent in the Cairngorms or the Himalaya. Competition success, however, brings prestige and the promise of Sports Council funding for climbing walls – which is many young people's introduction to the sport.

Certainly the six-strong official British team in Lyons, looking ruefully at the managers and PR staff that cocoon the opposition, feel that if the BMC nominates climbers for these events then their grant should do more than cover the £10 entry fee.

Watching Nadin on the podium last night, it was sobering to think that he had twice come within seconds of being disqualified for late arrival. It was only through luck and perseverance on the part of a team supporter that crucial instructions posted at the official (expensive) hotel were relayed to the UK team's official youth hostel.

Ereland Clouston

To the brink and back

❄ SEPTEMBER 2 1988 ❄

Most of those with the experience of having looked death in the face, who survive in the mountains or at sea against huge odds, are not particularly good at writing about it afterwards, and if their stories reach a wider public, they tend to be told secondhand. This quite extraordinary and moving book is the terrifying exception that proves the rule.

It is quite clear that Joe Simpson ought not to be alive. Descending with Simon Yates, his mountaineering partner, from the summit of Siula Grande in the Peruvian Andes, he fell and sustained a hideous fracture of the leg. Lashed by storms, still high above base camp, and without support Yates began to effect a one-man rescue: lowering him painstakingly on a rope down a precipitous face made of unstable powder snow.

Less than 150ft from the bottom, Simpson found himself dangling uncontrollably in space: he had gone over the lip of a huge overhanging cliff that the mist had concealed. The storm prevented any communication, and the knot joining the two lengths of rope had jammed in Yates's lowering device. He too was now in mortal peril: frostbitten and slowly freezing to death, he was being slowly dragged by Simpson's weight from his fragile 'bucket seat' of snow, which was his only protection against the abyss.

So Yates cut the rope – paradoxically saving both their lives. Simon survived the night and climbed down to safety. Joe plunged into the black crevasse at the foot of the face, landing on a tiny snow bridge 50ft below its lip, many times that distance from its icy bottom. But he sustained no further injury.

Yates, and their sole other companion at base camp, thought him dead. But having climbed from the crevasse, constantly risking a further, final fall into the depths, he crawled down the glacier, weaving his way through further crevasses, onto the bouldery moraine beyond and finally, after two nights in the open without food or water, back to camp, arriving a few hours before the others had decided to begin their return to civilisation.

His account begins like a lot of climbing books, with colourful prose about the fine scenery and some enjoyable training climbs before Siula Grande. Gradually, it builds an effect of looming menace, as the descent of the peak, before the accident, becomes unexpectedly difficult and dangerous.

But in Simpson's description of the fall, his hours in the crevasse and escape, the tale has found a teller equipped for the challenge. Transcending the increasingly arid genre of mountaineering literature, *Touching the Void* touches the Great Questions in an understated, yet utterly compelling way.

A note in the acknowledgements almost conceals an additional literary feat: Simpson's telling of Yates's story, based, one assumes, on lengthy conversation after the event: itself a convincing version of

Simon's agony at cutting the rope, and of his despair – how would he tell Joe's parents what had happened, no one would believe him. It supplies the other side of a unique relationship: the friendship between a man who saved another's life by an action he thought would kill him.

Touching the Void, by Joe Simpson (Cape, £10.95)

David Rose

Ascent of the rock stars

❄ SEPTEMBER 10 1988 ❄

I first started rock climbing some time in the middle of the last century when I was fresh out of college and at my first job in Liverpool. I was introduced to it by my uncle, a very small, very successful engineer who drove very powerful cars very fast.

He wanted to show me the mountains of Snowdonia, so I went. Now, umpteen years, lots of money, hundred of routes, and several climbing partners later, I'm a hopeless addict, and, let's face it, a pretty hopeless climber.

But I try, and I wouldn't swap it for the world. Through climbing I've made some of my closest friends, had some of my wildest times, and seen some of the most beautiful places in Britain and Europe. I've also been wet, cold, miserable, and frightened. But what the hell …

For starters, it's completely pointless. That's the beauty. It's not for anything. You don't win anything, you don't beat anyone (forget competition climbing for the moment, that's a total side issue). It's like reading books: you do it purely for fun … and maybe you find out something about yourself as well.

I can remember climbing a route called Hardd (and bloody hard it was too) on Carreg Hylldrem in North Wales and coming to a point where I was clinging on to a sharply overhanging wall, not only unable to make the next move but also quite incapable of seeing what I was supposed to do.

I thought then that it was the worst moment of my life and nothing, literally nothing, would ever be that bad. And that's what's happened: no broken love affair, wrathful editor, vengeful bank manager – not even Liverpool losing at home – has ever made me feel quite so bad. And in the end I made the move ...

Until about the middle of the 18th century, of course, mountains were generally regarded as nasty, dangerous, pointed things that served only to make it harder for people to have wars with each other. And cliffs were to be avoided at all costs.

But then the Romantic Imagination took over and in 1786, amid a level of media hype that would be familiar now, Jacques Balmat, a wily Chamonix guide, and Michel-Gabriel Paccard, a self-effacing doctor, made the first ascent of Mont Blanc. Afterwards Balmat went off to claim the quite considerable reward and allowed it to be thought (falsely) that he had done all the climbing and Paccard was something of a dead weight.

So the sport of mountaineering was born. So also were born two recognisably recent developments: the almost comic level of bitchiness practised by some leading climbers, and a distinct fondness for money.

The modern sport of rock climbing in this country maybe began with Coleridge, who in 1802 wrote a graphic account, complete with leg trembles, histrionics, and exhaustion, of a descent down Broad Stand on Scafell in the Lake District. And towards the end of that century the great pioneers, men such as Jones, Haskett-Smith, the Abraham brothers, Archer Thomson, were braving the gullies and chimneys of most of the main Lakeland and Welsh crags, setting in motion the developments of the last 70 years or so.

And that, broadly, was the state of the art when I came upon it a few years ago: there was mountaineering and there was rock climbing, not necessarily exclusive of each other, and the best – people such as Joe Brown and Chris Bonington, Dougal Haston and Doug Scott – dominated both.

Not any more. The sport is fragmenting and recreating itself like a crazed atom. For a start, climbers have become very trendy. Once shabby men in filthy jumpers and breeches, now they are lean young athletes in high-tech Lycra. They are also big business (well, biggish).

Ron Fawcett, a Yorkshire climber who did as much as anyone to accelerate climbing standards over the last 15 years, can be seen, thinly disguised as someone called Jack, on TV and in newspapers advertising a building society; Ben Moon modelled climbing tights in the first issue of the ultra-trendy *Arena* magazine; rocks are seen as suitable places for stylish Reed Employment girls to spend their spare time; speed climbing is thought of as a sufficiently groovy subject for Network 7 (and Breakfast TV) to devote air time to it; in France rock stars such as Patrick Edlinger are as popular as Rock stars, with a public image and an income to match.

Now, horror of horrors, rock climbing has been named as the No 1 chic sport in *Time Out*, the weekly handbook for Home Counties yuppies. It's all a far cry from Brown and Whillans roughing it in Llanberis in the early 50s and climbing on a washing line.

And there's not just rock climbing any more. There's bolt climbing (using drilled bolts as protection to limit the distance of a fall), commonplace in France and much favoured by Yorkshire limestone hotshots; there's pink-pointing and red-pointing (obscure subdivisions indicating how much protection is left in place on an ascent); there's flashing (doing an ascent first time) and yoyoing (effectively bouncing up and down off your top runner); there's rigid training and dieting; and there's even Christian Griffith, a superb American climber, filing away the skin on his finger-tips so they can fit into the tiniest of pockets on the hardest of the European super-routes. Absurd? Well, maybe. But these are athletes at the top of their chosen sport.

Mercifully there are still elite climbers doing things that Mallory and Irvine – and probably even old Coleridge – would have recognised as climbing. In Wales and the Lakes, men such as John Dawes, Andy

Pollitt, Steve Haston, Pat Littlejohn, and in Yorkshire, Craig Smith and Fawcett himself, are starting at the bottom of ferocious climbs and simply, desperately, getting to the top. They're at the top of the sport; me, I'm quite happily trying to get off the bottom because the beauty of climbing is that your horizons continually expand.

When I started, there were about five levels of difficulty. You began with a 'diff' (a climb graded, not fantastically imaginatively perhaps, as Difficult), and progressed through Severes and Very Severes, with your distant goal an Extreme (a climb graded Extremely Severe). Now there are nine grades of Extreme, E1 up to E9. And, in the way of all things, the recent explosion of climbing standards at the highest level has brought everything else up behind. Lots and lots of people now climb, and climb damn well.

At its best, in fact for most of the time, climbing is the most purifying activity I know. Physical chess. Your mind and your body are utterly engaged in the route, the pitch, the next move. After a weekend's climbing you feel totally cleansed; though maybe not totally clean; it does tend to rain all the time.

How do you start? Well, you've got to get a partner: so one person can lead the pitch while the second belays the leader, removes the protection (gear to insert in the rock, which stops you hurting yourself if you fall off, which is not recommended), shouts encouraging remarks (as a thoroughgoing coward I'm one of the world's natural seconds).

You don't have to like your partners very much (after all, you're going to meet only for a few moments at the belays on a climb) but you should trust them: a lot could depend on it. You will need a rope and some climbing protection.

You'll need a guide book to the cliffs, listing and grading the routes so that you can pick a climb to suit your ability. Then, if you feel like it, you can squeeze yourself into a pair of exotically flowered Lycra tights. Oh well, here we go again. 'Climb when you're ready ... '

Glossary

Abseil: Quite terrifying. A method of descending a cliff by sliding down a rope using an aluminium brake. Often the only way to approach inaccessible routes (eg, sea cliffs) and essential for retreating in the event of bad weather, or loss of nerve. Make sure that when you do it the first time your partner knows his business.

Belay: Essential to have a good one. This is the anchor the leader will use during or at the top of a climb to hold himself onto the rock while bringing up his second.

Bolts: Drilled placements on a cliff. By definition, you hope, they will not come out. Some people hate them, claiming they desecrate the rock – and they're right of course; I love them because I'm a coward and they are dead safe. But don't start hammering them in unless you are very good, and have a lot of friends.

Lycra: Essential for the modern hotshot. Squeeze beefy thighs into Lycra tights and then pose at the foot of the crag. It's best to be pretty good before you splash out, though, otherwise you will look a total wally.

Protection: Don't climb without it. Assorted metal wedges of varying sizes, and tape slings, to plant in natural cracks in the rock. You then clip your rope through and so make sure your falls won't be terminal.

Pete's Eats: The cradle of Welsh climbing, and probably the best cafe in the world. This Llanberis caff has fed every good climber in Britain and most of the bad ones.

Rope: Now for the basics. If you're starting, climb on one good 11mm 50-metre rope. As you get better, climb on two 9mm 50-metre ropes. If you are approached by someone offering to sell you a good secondhand one, run a mile.

Winter Trilogy: The three classic Alpine north faces (Eiger, Matterhorn, and Dru) climbed in winter, in 24 hours, by the French master climber Christophe Profit. Another classic Winter Trilogy on a wet Welsh day is breakfast in Pete's Eats (qv), lunch in the South

Stack cafe on Anglesey, after the long and fruitless drive in a forlorn search for dry rock, and tea in Eric Jones's Tremadog cafe after another 50-odd miles trying to get away from the rain. Total journey: well over 100 miles; total climbing: nil.

Roger Alton

Reaching the tragic heights of obsession

❄ AUGUST 19 1986 ❄

On the Savoia glacier at the bottom of K2, a three-week trek from anything that resembles civilisation, there is a small cairn bearing a cross and a series of aluminium plaques with the names of those who have died on the mountain's slopes.

The British climbers Alan Rouse and Julie Tullis, who perished from cold, exhaustion and hunger with four others sometime last week, must now be added to a bleak roll-call. K2, the world's second highest peak, deserves its epithet 'the savage mountain' only too well: it has now claimed 20 lives.

Since 1978, when Nick Estcourt disappeared under tons of falling snow on another expedition to K2, the tiny elite of British Himalayan climbers prepared to attempt the 14 mountains more than 8,000 metres high has lost many of its brightest and best.

In 1982, Joe Tasker and Peter Boardman – arguably the two most gifted writers of mountain literature this country has produced – disappeared high on the still-unclimbed Everest north-east ridge. Two years later, Alex MacIntyre, a Scot with a string of high-altitude successes to his name at the age of 28, was killed by a falling stone on the south face of Annapurna. Last year Roger Baxter-Jones, another mountaineer of vast competence and experience, was killed in the Alps.

The poignancy of the deaths of Rouse – on his last expedition, two weeks before the birth of his first child – and Tullis, who did not begin Himalayan climbing until her 40s but went higher than any British woman, is almost unbearable.

But as the news of their disappearance began to break among the climbing community at the weekend, the enthusiasm of those who remain seemed undimmed. Sandy Allen, a veteran of Everest, Lhotse and other Himalayan ventures, said: 'I never encourage anyone to take up climbing. If they really want to do it: fine, I'll give them every support. But otherwise, no. It takes over your life.'

Since Mallory's celebrated, if enigmatic comment that he wanted to climb Everest 'because it's there' both climbers and non-climbers have attempted to explain the fatal attraction, mostly without success. But the all-consuming nature of the obsession is not in doubt.

Most of the highest peaks have been scaled, usually many times: the emphasis now is on new, hard routes, done in 'Alpine style' – without porters, oxygen, chains of fixed rope and well-stocked camps, in a single push.

To achieve the fitness and acclimatisation necessary for such ascents, it is no longer possible, as in the days of Mallory, to do much but climb.

The theory behind Alpine-style ascents is that they minimise danger: by spending less time on slopes prone to avalanche and storms the chances of individual climbers falling victim to these 'objective' risks over which they can have no control are reduced.

The theory has statistical backing: according to a survey in the latest issue of *Mountain* magazine, 60 per cent of the 280 deaths on 8,000-metre peaks up to the end of February 1986 were caused by objective events.

To those bereaved by the deaths of Alan Rouse and Julie Tullis, it is small comfort: but the same survey also found the odds of dying are rather better than was once thought. The fatality rate among those setting off for 8,000-metre peaks is not the often-quoted figure of one in ten but 3.4 per cent, although as the survey noted, 'for those who return again and again the risk is obviously higher.'

In recent years, parties climbing in Alpine style have succeeded on routes in the Himalaya that would once have seemed inconceivable. Perhaps the most remarkable was the ascent last year of the west face of Gasherbrum 4, a 26,000ft peak a few miles from K2. The two-week climb by a single pair involved unprotected rope lengths of nearly 300ft between ledges on crumbling, technically difficult rock, followed by a descent of an unclimbed ridge: besides such an achievement, Reinhold Messner's solo, oxygen-less ascent of Everest in 1980 begins to seem almost easy.

New routes have been climbed Alpine-style by British parties on Shishapangma and Kangchenjunga. Alpine-style, according to Messner, means climbing by 'fair means': for those who succeeded, the personal reward and satisfaction appears to be much greater.

But the margin for coping with the unforeseen must be pared almost to nothing. Speed is essential, and speed means reducing weight. When a storm breaks, as it did on K2, the climber has only the contents of a rucksack and the will to live.

Expressing another aspect of the climbing obsession described by Messner and Sandy Allen in their different ways, Rob Collister, a mountain guide and instructor and a close friend of Boardman, Tasker and Rouse, said that as he had become more capable as a mountaineer, he had found it necessary to do harder and harder routes to derive the same 'peak experience' and heady euphoria, to climb in smaller teams in increasingly dangerous and remote locations.

Then there came a point where he, like many climbers, stood back: he began to wonder if striving to attain such an experience was any longer worthwhile.

David Rose

CHAPTER NINE

LOOKING DOWN AT THE WORLD

It was business as usual on Everest, one day in May 2006, with climbers including a double amputee, grandparents and a *Playboy* model all queuing up near the summit of this once-unattainable peak. Now it seemed that anybody who was reasonably fit, determined and, most importantly, could afford the thousands of dollars charged by mountain-guiding companies, could get to the top.

For much of the 20th century, climbing Everest and the highest Himalayan peaks had been the preserve of a small elite of experienced mountaineers. However, in 1985, Dick Bass, a wealthy Texan with limited climbing ability, got to the top of Everest with the help of David Breashears, a professional climber and filmmaker. Thus began the commercial expedition and by the mid-1990s there were numerous outfits offering clients the chance to attempt Everest and fulfil their mountain dreams. It seemed that just about anyone could get up the South Col 'yak route', the line taken by Hillary and Tenzing in 1953, and stories circulated about people turning up at base camp who had little idea how to don crampons or what was involved in climbing a mountain.

The majority of companies were professionally run and hundreds of people were guided to the top. But with the handing over of money, there was more of an expectation of getting to the top and a feeling developed that the danger could be managed. However, with so many people climbing the highest mountain in the world and entering the 'death zone', the area above 26,000ft of thin air and sub-zero temperatures, it was inevitable that disaster was going to strike. This happened on May 9 1996, when, with five expeditions on the mountain, a ferocious storm resulted in eight people dying, including two vastly experienced leaders, Rob Hall and Scott Fischer.

Someone who had made it to the top the year before was Alison Hargreaves, one of Britain's top female climbers. After years of trying to make it as a professional mountaineer, she was finally being noticed by the media, not least because she had two small children. Keen to capitalise on this attention, both to cement her reputation and secure her family's financial future, Hargreaves almost immediately embarked on another expedition, this time to K2, the world's second highest peak. When the news broke in August 1995 that she had died in a violent storm near the top of the mountain, she was savaged by the media, who were outraged that a mother would take such risks but ignored the fact that fathers had been doing this for more than a century.

Writing about this for the *Guardian* was Ed Douglas, the founder of the climbing magazine *On the Edge*, who had started contributing to the paper in 1991, and eventually became the paper's de facto mountaineering writer (although still writing for other publications). This was at a period when broadsheets expanded their obituary sections and mountaineers with their adventurous lives, coupled with dramatic pictures, were perfect material. Jim Perrin, probably Britain's foremost climbing writer, covered many of these deaths, bringing a literary sophistication and depth of knowledge to the paper's obituary pages.

Rock climbing became even more popular in the 1990s. Sheffield, with its proximity to the Peak District, was the British capital of the sport with many students opting to study there purely for the climbing. Throughout the country, the climbing wall in the corner of the local leisure gym had been replaced by huge, dedicated climbing centres with all manner of artificial rock faces. These attracted a much wider range of people into the sport and even if many of them rarely ventured out of doors and into real mountains, it contributed to the growth in the climbing retail market. This in turn led to the growth in sponsored climbers displaying logos. However, there remained plenty of young recruits who disdained the sponsored side of the sport, having for their sole motivation the spirit of adventure.

Climbing grades continue to rise, although new routes are as likely to be found on large boulders as high cliff faces. Here the climber attempts short, extremely hard climbs without a rope above a thick padded mat. Similarly, in Britain at least, low-key indoor bouldering leagues at climbing walls have caught on more than the big prize international competitions.

It is Everest, though, that continues to dominate the reporting of mountaineering, no doubt reflecting an obsession with the highest place on earth. In 2007, more than 500 people made it to the summit and the media covered everything from the tonnes of rubbish generated by expeditions and stories of climbers being abandoned in the death zone to the success of a team using 1920s equipment in an attempt to show that Mallory and Irvine could have made it to the top in 1924. Then, the expedition took five weeks just to reach the bottom of the mountain but in June 2007 it was announced that China intended to build a 67-mile tarmacked road to Everest, partly to enable the base camp in Tibet to be developed as a resort. The effect on the area's fragile eco-system did not seem to have been considered.

As people who spend a lot of time amongst the world's highest peaks, climbers and mountaineers are often the first to witness the effects of global warming, particularly the shrinking of glaciers. It is to be hoped that in the future they will continue to be vocal in alerting the world to the changes they see.

A Country Diary:Wharncliffe

❈ JANUARY 12 1991 ❈

It's exactly a century ago that those two gritstone pioneers, Puttrell and Watson, put up the first rock climbs on Kinder Scout. The promontory on Upper Tor and Primitive on neighbouring Nether Tor may seem tame these days but were a real pioneering effort in 'forbidden' territory on the Peak District's best-known upland, overlooking Grindsbrook. Kinder Scout is not, though, where outcrop climbing began: that honour seems to belong to the long-overlooked but once mightily popular Wharncliffe Crags high above the Don Valley. Puttrell, Watson and Co came here in the early 1880s and put up several interesting routes on what is actually coal measure sandstone, not gritstone. It has a good supply of positive, incut holds so the techniques required are more akin to those of our volcanically derived mountains than the friction methods of most gritstone crags of the area. Wharncliffe became notorious as Britain's dirtiest climbing ground on account of the copious deposits of soot – the edge lies immediately down-wind of the former Samuel Fox's steelworks at Stocksbridge and high above the Sheffield–Manchester 'Woodhead' railway. Though the elements have cleaned the rocks in the years since the steel works and railway went electric, few climbers come here now. Looking north along the crest of Wharncliffe the other day as the soft, winter sunlight slanted through the silver birches, no living soul came into view. What a contrast to the early postwar days, when cragsmen came by bus to Deepcar, or by train to Wortley station, and climbed through those birch woods to the foot of the rocks, Others came 'via devious leafy glades' from Grenoside and Chapeltown in the east. As I went along the sunlit crest, jackdaws shouted to one another in the trees below, a Swaledale ewe watched me from a rock pillar. The stage was set for Puttrell's ghost to come swinging up from Deepcar, a hemp cart rope slung across his shoulders.

Roger A Redfern

Rocks in the head

❄ DECEMBER 27 1997 ❄

Last year, Paul Pritchard broke his back in four places. He was ice climbing on Creag Meagaidh in Scotland and the ice gave way. He fell 200ft onto his back, and then had to be lowered a further 1,000ft to a flat area before somebody could be sent to get rescue. The back was painful – he knew it was broken as soon as it happened – but not as painful as the broken sternum. Or the fractured skull.

Still, the accident was nothing to the occasion in 1993 when he fell while climbing the Gogarth seacliffs near Holyhead on Anglesey. It was raining that day, the rock was wet and loose and the protection he put into it just exploded out. He thought the climb was easier than it was. He fell 90ft and bounced off some rocks into the sea and was in the icy water for 10 minutes. The friend he was climbing with managed to drag him on to a ledge and resuscitate him, but he kept losing consciousness, the tide was still a factor and it was five hours before someone walked past on the cliff above them and went to find help. He was carried up with two broken shoulders, a broken arm, a broken ankle, a broken rib ... and a fractured skull.

Pritchard, who is 30, has been a full-time climber for 12 years and in that time has known 20 people, some of them very good friends, die on the mountains. This year alone, four people he knows have been killed, 'which is quite a lot really'. He's just been on a lecture tour, with his first book, which has won the Boardman/Tasker award, the mountaineering Booker. He's been talking not just in shops but at universities and to climbing clubs, to people whose passion is climbing, who know their belays from their rappels, their portaledges from their pitons, who know rocks.

227

In his talk he doesn't dwell on his injuries – he may live his life on the edge, but he's a quiet, modest man and they have to be coaxed out of him. But there are questions afterwards. And the most commonly repeated question is: 'Do you think you're mentally stable?' To meet Pritchard, to find out, you should really go to Llanberis in North Wales, Britain's largest climbing community, which grew up in the 1980s around the deserted slate quarries in the shadow of Snowdonia, where he lives in a farmhouse, surrounded by other climbers. You should meet him on a ledge halfway up a seacliff with seabirds wheeling, above a wrinkled sea. Or on a rock spire, vertical on every side, fixed to a rope, above a rainforest (which is where he chose to spend Christmas Day). Or dangling in a hammock in a snowstorm on a glacier slab above a frozen fjord. But bugger that. I met him in a 'coaching inn' in Surrey off the M25. (He was in between lectures in Bristol and Brighton.) Pritchard, who lives while vertical on dried porridge, brings a new meaning to the word lean. His face looks like it has been hammered out of granite, the nose a prominent outcrop of bone between sunken cheeks. He has a fuzz of beard over an angular, lopsided jaw and when he talks his mouth opens only a slit to reveal a crenellated ridge of wonky teeth.

His body is gaunt: arched shoulders in a therma-jacket, skinny legs in chinos above red suede shoes (the one touch of frivolity in his whole demeanour). Even his hourglass thumbs are thin. 'I'm a bit creaky now, after the injuries,' he says in a gentle, soft Lancashire accent, sipping a half of bitter in the hotel coffee lounge where the manageress is busy preparing for a function, and radiators pump out heat to the piped strains of Elton John's *Song For Guy*. 'I'm still trying to get myself back on my feet.' It was after the 1993 injury that Pritchard first began to write. He couldn't do much because of the smashed bones and the concussion and he started writing as a form of exorcism. 'Climbing had been so destructive to me physically and to my relationships – the lad who pulled me out of the water hated me for a while ... It's very complicated, one minute it's mates having a load of fun and another minute it's fatal.' Writing the experience down helped him clarify matters, see sense at last. 'I went from thinking I was never going to climb again to within three and a half months I was in the Himalaya.' The essay he wrote then formed the basis of *Deep Play*, which has just beaten highly rated books by Joe Simpson and Jon Krakauer, the latter a US bestseller, to the Boardman/Tasker award. It is a remarkable book.

Some passages can leave the non-climber baffled: 'I belayed Steve on the double groove pitch. Easy nutting up the first groove led to a pendulum for a massive expanding flake.' But for the most part it is wonderfully textured and inventive, a poetic description of 'slate days', 'sagging skies', cliffs like 'a crimson headboard to the seabed', hills like 'velvet cushions' or like 'the underside of some great beer gut'.

It's a love letter to the mountain, an obituary for lost friends, a Joycean study of a community. Most of all, in its roughshod description of thrills and achievement, adventure and comradeship, of trips to India, Patagonia, Yosemite, of cerebral oedema and amoebic dysentery and dropped boots, it's an explanation of a way of life: 'I don't have a job or anything. I just go climbing,' he says.

Pritchard has been up and down a rope since he was a kid, growing up and wagging off school – bit of arson, bit of nicking – in the gritstone quarries of Bolton. One of the lads he hung out with killed himself drunk while joyriding. Two others are in prison. Two are in the army. Pritchard could have gone the way of any of them, but instead he fetched up in North Wales and became one of the dole climbers of the 1980s, tracing out routes in the disused slate mines.

'It was the punk era, a time of revolt,' he says. 'It's not conspiracy theory, but we're expected to conform within various parameters in society and by saying, "No I'm not going to get a job down the Hoover factory – I'm going to find new ways to climb up this cliff because that's where my heart lies," that's a small form of rebellion.' He stops. We listen to a bit of *Goodbye Yellow Brick Road* and watch the bar staff arrange napkins on the tables. 'The Thatcher years were really special to British climbing,' he continues ruefully. 'It was made so incredibly easy to sign on. I used to be abroad all the time ... I've even been to the Himalaya on sickness benefit.' He doesn't have to sign on any longer, he doesn't have to abseil down high buildings cleaning windows or rappel down the chimneys of nuclear processing plants to sweep out the dust in the chambers ('there's quite a lot of high-access, well-paid work') as he once did. He can eke out a living with grants and a little bit of sponsorship and money from writing (largely for *On the Edge* magazine).

The £2,000 prize for the award has bought two round-the-world tickets for him and his girlfriend. First stop: Kinabalu in Borneo, 'a couple of big granite walls in the middle of the jungle, where the British army got lost a few years back'. Pritchard is a purist: he won't use artificial aids such as cordless electric drills or oxygen. He holds the new type of poseur climber – driving to the base of mountains in their sports cars and posh gear, heading for Everest with their canisters of gas, their prepackaged meals – in contempt.

'One of the main aspects of climbing for me is experimenting with danger – and that's not a macho thing. I know there are some terrible risks taken and I feel sorry for my parents, for people who are left behind, but for you it doesn't matter. The paradox of climbing is that the draw of the mountains and cliffs is so great that if you are a climber it's hard to stop doing it.

'I think it goes deeper than being an adrenalin junkie. To cope and to perform and to keep your brain working rationally in dangerous situations, making moves upwards that you could never climb down again, going further and further into the unknown, knowing that if you fall off you're going to hit the ground ... ' Pritchard, it becomes clear, is a bundle of paradoxes. He's the bravest of athletes, pushing at the limits of human physicality, who turns philosopher at one glimpse of a breathtaking view ('suddenly you're looking down at the world instead of up') and describes what he does in the same terms as an art form.

'The most creative part of it is reading a cliff or a mountain that nobody's ever climbed and using your imagination – it's all about imagination, to find a new way up it. You're trying to piece together a line of features up a cliff, the cracks and flakes and edges and ledges, in order to perform. Some people call it vertical ballet. The French do, anyway.' He's a self-confessed egocentric, who likes to see his name alongside routes in guidebooks, who says he has come to terms with his own insignificance ('conquering is a bad word – it's about working with the mountain, not against it') a member of a community ('it's quite obvious that the rope is a really strong metaphor') who knows that at any point that community can be reduced by one.

Here he is, for example, on his best expedition ever: 'It was a climb called The Devil's Horse, El Caballo di Diablo, in Patagonia. I climbed it with a South African called Philip Lloyd in one day, completely free style. We moved so fast and fluidly together – we were at the same standard as each other, it was just so fluid, great company, a special friend. We climbed in this little window between two huge storms and we just managed to nip in there. The best climb I've ever done.' Philip Lloyd died on the same mountain, shortly afterwards. 'He was retreating in the storm. He was abseiling. His weight pulled off the rock.' Before Pritchard gets up and walks away to a beaten-up old car in the middle of a field, en route to Brighton, to North Wales and on to a mountain at the other side of the world, I ask how he answers those who ask whether he's mentally stable. 'I say, "Yes, I think I am." I think I am mentally stable. Much more sane than a lot of people who fritter their lives away in some meaningless way.' He pauses in a silence disturbed only by Bing Crosby crooning 'May all your Christmasses be white'. 'Perhaps,' he adds.

Deep Play is published by Baton Wicks at £16.99

Sabine Durrant

Climbers honour sensitive Villain

❄ JANUARY 25 1993 ❄

With steam billowing from 100 champagne-soaked anoraks, the great and gruff of British mountaineering squeezed into a Staffordshire cave at the weekend to honour one of the outstanding buccaneers of their trade.

Eight years after his death at 52, improbably in his sleep, the Don Whillans memorial hut was opened by his widow, Audrey, at a ceremony 20ft inside a gritstone cliff called The Roaches.

Restored at a cost of £100,000, the Victorian mock-gothic fortified villa with a neolithic kitchen cave attached will offer climbers bunks, showers, a heater and toaster – luxuries generally denied the legendary hard-bitten Mr Whillans, who once survived five days above 23,000ft with no food.

'Don would have had a few dry comments,' said stone mason Steve Read, who once almost pulled himself and Britain's greatest postwar mountaineer off a Dolomite.

'I was hanging on the rope for five minutes and Don, who hadn't been able to belay properly, was sliding towards the edge,' he recalled.

The timely discovery of a crack to take a man-supporting peg had saved the day. Mr Whillans, a 5ft 3in Salford plumber nicknamed 'The Villain' because of his mordant wit, perpetual flat cap and occasional tendency to punch his enemies on the nose, went on to make many world-class climbs, including the first ascent of Annapurna's south face in 1970.

Later, over sandwiches and pints, veteran mountain men recalled with awe other Whillans climbs – and the night it took six Lancashire policemen to subdue him after a heavy session in the pub.

'He did not like the law inhibiting his freedom to drink,' acknowledged Doug Scott, aged 51, his partner on three Himalayan trips. 'But he had a sensitive side and the kids used to love him.'

Funds to refurbish the 'hut', a listed building originally called

Rockhall Cottage, were raised from climbers, the Sports Council, the Rural Development Commission and the Peak Park. The custodian, Mr Whillans would no doubt be disappointed to learn, is the local policeman.

Erlend Clouston

Between a rock and a hard face

❄ AUGUST 5 1994 ❄

Would you like to climb Everest? Me neither. It's much too cold and frightening and probably boring as hell. But press coverage of last winter's tragic accidents in Scotland [14 people died] has left the impression that climbers spend their lives on the edge of oblivion in a freezing maelstrom and, what's more, get a kick out of it. Truth is that most climbers are content hauling themselves up steep cliffs in the sunshine with no intention of ever going near a mountain. It can be spectacular but it's usually safe.

Being a top rock climber used to be a laid-back, hippyish existence, but those now at the cutting edge spend their lives turning tendons to wire and honing down their weight to survivable minimums. They train obsessively, practising on tiny boulders where each move up is impossibly hard. Danger is no longer in the equation, just difficulty.

The climbing capital of Britain – to those who live there at least – is Sheffield. Drawn by the proximity of the Peak District and a feeling of zeitgeist, young hopefuls come to join the galaxy of resident stars. In the dim cellars of rented terraced houses throughout the Nether Edge area, plywood walls with tiny fingerholds have been built. Here, with a Zen-like simplicity, the rock geniuses of tomorrow, aka the cellar dwellers, train for fame, sustained by a diet of bananas and broccoli.

Those who graduate may be allowed to go to school. Or The School, as it is known, constructed in an arts centre called The Circle not far from the heart of the city. Here leading lights such as

Ben Moon and Jerry Moffatt train on an overhanging board of fiendish difficulty. One particular sequence of holds is known to cognoscenti as one of the hardest in the world. The School's exact location is kept secret, as if you're good enough to train there, you'll know where it is.

Many of the UK's top rock climbers now spend more and more time climbing indoors on artificial structures, where the rain of winter is kept out and the heat of summer does not make the finger-holds too sweaty. When they do emerge into the sunlight, it is often as not to travel to crags in the south of France or Spain, where the vagaries of the weather won't interfere with their climbing.

The ultimate indoor arena is The Foundry, across town on Mowbray Street. The walls here are big enough to require a rope and no matter what time of day, there are always a few remarkably lean young people effortlessly pulling their way up. It has become, more or less, a community centre for the city's climbers, with a noticeboard advertising cheap accommodation, events and second-hand climbing gear. Upstairs, a group dressed in clothes that would look right at a roads demo relax still further over mugs of tea.

To make ends meet when they're not training, the dedicated have joined the enterprise culture, creating what local climber Paul Evans calls 'a hive of scatty entrepreneurialism'. Evans is a cartoonist and artist, works for an offbeat clothing company called Rock Designs, and edits an alternative climbing magazine called *The Thing*.

Climbers, like many compulsive obsessives, have always had a reputation for playing hard. The Victorian pioneers who formed the Alpine Club weren't averse to a tipple on the mountain if it lifted the spirits and, by the 1950s, the dance hall on a Saturday night was almost as important as the climbing. When the summer of love rolled along, these adrenalin surfers didn't need much encouragement to join in.

The scene centred around the sleepy village of Llanberis in the shadow of Snowdon. There are legends of JCB jousts, of racing towards the edge of flooded slate quarries in 'borrowed' vehicles and escaping at the last moment before they soared into oblivion. There were those who climbed without the safety of a rope while their consciousness expanded. And it was all accompanied by loud music and often managed in the dead of night.

Then came Thatcher's decade and the work ethic even permeated climbing while, paradoxically, many of those doing it were released from the rigours of labour on a permanent basis. The emphasis turned from big, expensive-to-reach mountains, to small and accessible cliffs. The excesses of the 80s came instead in training.

But when the fit young things of Sheffield do abandon their diets to party, what do they do? Dancing has become a big scene among the city's more happening climbers and, as Paul Evans explains, it's easy to see why. 'Climbing is a very sculptural thing, relating to natural forms. There's an obvious correlation to dance and choreography.'

But what of the debauched excesses of the 60s and 70s, does any of that survive? Waiting at traffic lights, a car screeches to a halt opposite mine. The driver, pink-eyed and demonic, barks out an address and disappears, tyres squealing.

When the house is traced, inevitably located in Nether Edge, I find an old friend considerably straighter and hard at work renovating. John was a stalwart of the renascent Llanberis scene in the late 1980s that went a long way to recreating those halcyon days. Despite a lifestyle that could be termed colourful, he is still one of the best rock climbers in Britain and his flamboyance is in obvious contrast to the dietary obsessions of the new generation.

'Ah, parties,' he sighs. 'There are only two kinds of parties these days. Dinner parties and raves.'

Ed Douglas

A dot on the landscape

❈ MAY 31 1995 ❈

Alison Hargreaves beams out of the shots she took of herself on the summit of Everest, like a toddler with currant eyes, apple cheeks and new moon smile. One might expect a noble, middle-distance gaze of justified arrogance, but no: 'Look everybody,' her face seems to say, 'I've just climbed a whole flight of stairs.'

This childlike triumph adds to the 'Everest – so what?' feeling that such a climb increasingly provokes. Forty-two years on from Edmund Hillary and Tenzing Norgay's historic conquest, close to 500 people have topped the old jade, including a French teenage schoolboy and a 60-year-old Venezuelan man. The first woman to do it, Japanese Junko Tabei, celebrates the 20th anniversary of her ascent this summer. By 1993, when the inexperienced Rebecca Stephens became the first British woman to 'stand on top of the world', the activity was starting to look like a pastime for derring-doers with a flair for PR who needed to improve their CV.

Hargreaves, whom I met at the foot of Ben Nevis near her present home town, Fort William, is as unassuming in person as the summit pictures suggest. She is small, slight and not remotely craggy. You would never guess at her incredible physical strength and the only clue to her recent jaunt is a healthy apres ski glow. Hargreaves is polite about Stephens' climb – 'It inspired a lot of people and that has to be a good thing' – but makes it crystal clear that her own achievement is in an entirely different league. 'People don't realise she plugged into oxygen at 6,500 metres, so effectively reduced the height of the mountain to 7,000 metres.'

Everest is 8,848 metres high – 29,028 feet. Climbers refer to altitudes above 26,000ft as the 'death zone'. Oxygen here is so thin that the human body starts to perish, so without supplementary oxygen, Hargreaves had to take the summit as quickly as possible. 'This is an incredible thing to do,' says the climbing writer Ed Douglas. 'Hard work, painful and dangerous.' If Hargreaves needed reminding of that, the bodies of two climbers who died last year, within 200 yards of the peak, lay in her path. She had to get past their bodies on the way up.

This swift ascent was no lightning raid on the Mount Publicity Everest has come to represent. Hargreaves has been building up to this point since the age of 13, when she was first introduced to rock climbing at her state school in Belper, Derbyshire. Hooked from then on, by 14 she was travelling all over Britain with her best friend in search of challenging rock faces. At 18, she was expected to follow in her parents' and sisters' footsteps by going to read maths at Oxford, but she refused. She moved in with her fellow-climber and future husband, Jim Ballard (JB), 16 years her senior, and declared that she would make a living out of climbing. Her middle class parents were mortified.

Hargreaves has built up and maintained her stamina since her early teens. At 21, she started running uphill in the Derbyshire peaks for two hours a day. When she had children, Tom, now six, and Kate, aged four, she would get up and do it before her husband went out to work in the morning. Two years ago, the couple sold their house and outdoor equipment business and went to live in a Land Rover (for want of decent sponsorship) in the Alps for six months. During this period, Hargreaves climbed the six major Alpine north faces solo, becoming the first person to do so in a season.

While she geared up for Everest, JB looked after the children full-time. Paradoxically, nobody will take any notice of such a climb unless there is a gimmick – in her case, the fact that she is a woman and a mother has sufficed. These supposed disadvantages put her in a position to bag scarce sponsorship deals. A man doing the same climb would probably not have generated much interest – something Hargreaves and others say has engendered 'sour grapes' among fellow, predominantly male, climbers.

'It's Britain in general, but climbers in particular are terrible people. We're all terribly jealous of each other,' Hargreaves says, clearly stung by her detractors. 'A lot of climbers think climbing owes them a living, but unless they can appeal to the general public, there really isn't any money in it. Obviously part of it is the fact that I happen to be a woman in a man's world. Yeah, I am taking stick for that, but I have done right from the early days.'

How does she deal with that sort of hostility? 'I do not go around saying that I'm a feminist, because I'm not,' she says adamantly. 'I am a woman and I have had a rough ride, but that's understandable. I am in a male world. I've tackled it head-on, I've got on with the job, I've done the climbing and my routes always stick up for themselves. Nobody can ever take away the climbs I've done.'

Her status as a mother has also provoked criticism, including an attack from the journalist Nigella Lawson who, in a recent column, thundered against 'me-first mountaineering', describing Hargreaves' climbing as a neurosis that 'shows a reality-denying self-centredness'. Again Hargreaves is surprised that she should come under attack. She says the combination of motherhood and climbing career works well for her and declines to defend herself further. Her kids are there during our interview, playing happily around her. If someone finds a problem here, then it is theirs, she suggests. 'Maybe it's a British thing, we're supposed to be good sports, but not to win.'

She does admit, however, to being obsessed with her sport. 'Yes, it is an incredibly selfish thing to do and, like most climbers,' she laughs, 'I've got an ego as big as Mount Everest. We can't help it.'

She starts to explain, then falters. Hargreaves is not prone to introspection. When she stops to think about it, she seems as puzzled as others are as to why she does what she does. 'People say, wouldn't it be nice just to be a normal person, just to be at home and be satisfied? And I say, yes, it would be fantastic. But I'm not like that, there's something inside that is constantly going out and looking for the next challenge. It actually scares me to think I won't have a challenge in front of me. When I set off for Everest last autumn, I was desperately afraid that if I got to the top, I wouldn't know what to do next. I felt I'd have a big black hole afterwards and I was frightened. Very frightened.'

In the event, the weather was against her and she didn't make the summit on that first attempt. 'I was getting frostbite. I would have lost fingers and toes, and I wasn't prepared to risk that. But when I turned back, I felt like somebody had scraped away everything inside and just left me empty. The thing you have to understand is it wasn't me that failed, it was the weather that let me down.'

This time, Hargreaves wept during the final half hour of her historic ascent. Again, she's not sure why. 'I don't know, a sense of all sorts of things – relief, maybe, because I wanted to do it so much.'

While most climbers would take it easy for a while, Hargreaves is resting a strained tendon in her knee before setting off again, within a fortnight, for the world's second-highest and notoriously difficult mountain, K2. 'I've got K2, I've got my next challenge, and that's OK.'

Isn't she the teeniest bit apprehensive? 'No, not at all, I'm looking forward to it,' she says, indignation creeping into her voice. 'OK, so it's called K2, the killer mountain. Quite a few people have been killed on it, but that's because people have got caught in storms. The trick is not to be up high when a storm comes.'

She takes the suggestion that she might be afraid as a slight on her professionalism. 'If I was frightened, I wouldn't go. If I thought it was desperately dangerous, I wouldn't do it.' She frowns at the difficulty of making this point understood. 'Look, I drive on motorways at night, I consider that risky.

'I regard myself as a pretty safe climber. I've got friends who, the more frightening it is, the greater the buzz they get. A friend of mine really attacks mountains. He is a wild solo climber. His attitude is totally different from mine.'

By contrast, Hargreaves describes her approach as gentle. 'I'm so small, I'm such an insignificant little dot, that I can't start a battle against a mountain.' Hargreaves sounds as though she's thinking aloud, feeling her way around a subject which, being a pragmatic person, she doesn't care to dwell on. 'I have a great respect for the mountains, for the power that controls it all. When I'm totally on my own, I do feel that there's somebody looking after me. You get a really wild day and you feel everything's kind of angry. Whether it is Mother Nature, I don't know, but I can be on the mountain and I don't feel lonely. I feel more lonely walking down one of the big high streets in London with thousands of people around.'

Hargreaves is baffling because she is so straightforward. Her life is about climbing mountains. Everything else falls into place around that. She goes up a mountain, she comes down again, she moves on to the next. Her only worry is running out of them. It makes her a living and supports her family. If her ego is big, it is also simple. The child-faced figure in the summit pictures seems to know no mortal fear, has no concept of her own possible death. Perhaps that's why she can do it.

Emma Brooker

High anxiety

❄ AUGUST 21 1997 ❄

Two years ago, at a high camp on one of the most beautiful and technically difficult peaks in the Himalaya, I watched as a high-altitude porter employed by a Korean expedition packed up a tent and all its contents, added it to his already considerable load and, breathing scarcely harder than he would have done at sea level, ambled off sure-footedly down the route. He was a young Indian from one of the mountain villages of Himachal Pradesh. His aptitude brought home forcefully how flawed a project is much of what now passes for mountaineering in the world's greater ranges.

If I hadn't undergone that conversion to scepticism, then the events of last May on Everest, when the mountain reaped its worst-ever single-season death toll, might have left me aghast. They didn't. Like many other observers in the mountaineering community, I looked on it as the disaster that had been waiting to happen, the unavoidable concomitant to a fashion for nannying rich, acquisitive and driven non-climbers into one of the most dangerous places on Earth.

But this wasn't just a disaster, it was an ethical morass, as the American climber Jon Krakauer makes clear in his rigorous first-hand account. An ageing former activist, he was packed off by the magazine *Outside* to report on a commercial expedition to climb Everest by its easiest route. It was run by Rob Hall, whose firm, Adventure

Consultants, had established a reputation for this work. Krakauer's initial stance regarding this trip, for which each client paid $65,000, is detached. He notes: 'We were a team in name only ... linked to one another by neither rope nor any deep sense of loyalty. Each client was in it for himself or herself.' This latter statement – the opposite of the traditional ethos of mountain adventure – is the crux of Krakauer's book. Rob Hall dies, as does Scott Fischer, the leader of a rival commercial group, because they do not accede to the debasement of their code. But their exploitation of the mountain for personal gain had been the prime mover towards tragedy. Krakauer's account is masterly, with a glittering certainty of description and devastating insight.

A little storm, minor by Everest standards, in combination with a midden of small errors and unspoken rivalries, catches out guides and clients on the summit day. The rest is mayhem, heroism and loss, backlit by the nightmare image of Hall – oedemic and beyond help – speaking to his pregnant wife in New Zealand by radio link from his sketchy bivouac on the south summit. The morning after the storm, two clients, apparently dead, are found near the tents on the South Col. When the carapace of ice is chipped from their faces, they're found still to be breathing. 'There was only one choice,' Krakauer reports on the decision taken and its rationale. 'Let nature take its inevitable course ... and save the group's resources for those who could actually be helped. It was a classic act of triage.' *Into Thin Air* demonstrates with agonising clarity how the deadly conjunction of commerce, ego and competition has dissipated the morality of an activity where selflessness and responsibility were once commonplace.

Into Thin Air by Jon Krakauer, 293pp, Macmillan £16.99

Jim Perrin

Doomed climber's final call

❄ MAY 14 1996 ❄

Rob Hall knew he was probably going to die on Everest: he and his party were trapped at 25,200ft, frostbitten, without a tent or sleeping bag and almost no oxygen, fluids or food.

So on Saturday night, the New Zealander picked up the radio as bad weather closed in, called the radio operator and asked to be put through to his pregnant wife.

Only she knows exactly what he said, though friends later came on the line and encouraged him, telling him he was going to be OK. 'He said: "Hey, look, don't worry about me,"' said his assistant, Madeleine David, from New Zealand.

A climbing colleague painted a bleaker picture. 'A bivouac without equipment 150 metres below the summit in bad weather means at the very least you're going to get frostbite, and it could go right through to death,' said Peter Hillary, son of Sir Edmund, last night. 'He would have been aware of that.'

Now Hall, who had climbed the mountain five times, is assumed dead, along with eight other climbers from three separate expeditions. After one of the worst weekends in the history of climbing on the mountain, the recorded death toll stands at 67.

Those attempting Everest expect to face sheer rock faces and treacherous ice, but the mountain's fatal distraction is the weather, which can close in quickly and leave competent climbers stranded and helpless.

There is a two-week window of opportunity in May, when wind, temperature and snow are at their friendliest. But the 'season' carries no guarantees and when a blizzard struck the summit on Friday, Hall would have known that there was only a slim chance of escape. His wife, who had climbed Everest with him three years ago, would have known too.

John Duncan

Siberia diary

❄ NOVEMBER 10 1997 ❄

It was little more than a mile to the hut. It seemed further in the darkness and snow, picking our way through the trees, tripping over sinewy ice-greased roots, following the dancing pencil torch of the leader and the clinking of bottles in plastic bags.

Halfway up into the Stolby nature reserve, Alexander, a photographer, and his wife Yulia, an estate agent – she had driven us up to the edge of the hill at expert speed in a small Toyota on a wildly frozen road – stopped to point out the hulking rock formations.

Alexander and Yulia are *stolbisty*, rock climbers. The word comes from the Russian *stolb*, column. The 2,000 or so *stolbisty* in Krasnoyarsk in central Siberia have climbed in the Himalaya, the Pamirs and their own Altai mountains, but they argue that *stolbism* in the reserve on the edge of the city is not a sport. It's more like a religion, one which occasionally takes a human sacrifice. *Stolbisty* don't believe in safety helmets or, as a rule, ropes and pitons. 'It's not a sport for us. We just decided to climb for the sake of the soul,' said Alexander.

At 1am we reached the crowded hut, more of a chalet, where Russian soul food in liquid form had been going round the table for many hours. Vitaly, an Everest veteran, was playing guitar and screaming out a ballad in the rasping, throaty Vladimir Visotsky style. Alexander, suddenly violently angry, hurled a glass at the sullen Mikhail in the corner, luckily missing his head, and a murderousness smouldered. A young girl, one of the *stolbistys'* daughters, watched the adults from a bunk above the table where she was supposed to be sleeping, looking down in delight and scepticism, her face lit by the candles below.

In the morning, Alexander got up, dressed and went out to the granite pillars, scores of them rearing up red out of the pines, all with their own names – 'Grandfather', 'Little Elephant'. Flakes of ice flew across the rock faces in the breeze. 'I know I can climb after vodka,' said Alexander. 'I know the rocks. At night, drunk, whatever, I can climb up monkeywise and never fall.'

He put his rucksack down next to an ugly-looking *stolb* the height of a six-storey building, riven with two vertical clefts, one known as 'Skinflayer'. Without a helmet or any equipment, he began spidering upwards.

'You should use special shoes, of course. But what difference does it make?' he said as he disappeared into the rock chimney.

Just next to the cleft was a black marble slab embedded in the rock in memory of Volodya Tyoplykh, killed when he fell off in 1989. 'The cliff did not kill him,' says the inscription, 'She took him to herself.' Alexander shimmied down the other cleft. 'He fell from the top,' he said of Tyoplykh's fate. 'He taught everyone to climb. It was a shame.'

A particularly Russian zone of bravado, between the impossible and the impermissible, typifies *stolbism*.

It's the same place where the spirit dwells that kills hundreds of men each year when they get locked out of their flats in multi-storey blocks and try to climb in from the outside.

It's the same spirit that keeps space station Mir going and destruction-tested the Chernobyl reactor.

Alexander moved on to the squat mass of the Grandfather. He pointed out four black squares painted on the rock with names inside. 'The ones in the black squares are dead *stolbisty*,' he said. 'It doesn't show the ordinary day trippers who just fell off when it was frosty.

'A friend of mine fell. He fell the height of the trees but he managed to grab onto a branch as he was coming down. He broke his arm, but he survived.'

The day was clear. There were deer tracks in the snow, and empty vodka bottles. Alexander collected them to take to the rubbish bin at the reserve entrance.

We passed a cliff with a vicious-looking overhang. Alexander pointed out the limits of risk: this rock had metal fixtures embedded

in it for ropes. He knew there was no other way, but it still smacked
of heresy. 'It's just not *stolbism*,' he said.

James Meek

The only way is up: The dilemmas and the discrimination facing women who climb

❄ MAY 18 1998 ❄

Catherine Destivelle gives a slight shrug. 'If a man takes risks,
nobody gives a damn,' she says. 'But for a woman, it's different. A
woman should stay with her kid. It's the same the world over.'
Destivelle knows better than most the powerful emotions that can
be provoked by a woman, and especially a mother, taking risks. Over
the past two decades, her career as a professional climber has taken
her from a solo ascent of the grim north face of the Eiger to the sun-
drenched sandstone cliffs of Mali in West Africa. She is a celebrity in
her native France and even in the UK, where she has just finished a
series of lectures, she is better known than most male climbers.

Destivelle understands very well that sex and death sells. The
image of a beautiful woman hundreds of feet above the ground in
obvious peril is a sure-fire winner. In 1996, she broke her leg while
climbing a remote mountain in Antarctica with her partner of six
years, Eric Decamp. The year before, she attempted a peak in the
Himalaya on which one of their closest friends had been killed in a
fall. But if she ever thinks of quitting, she says, she simply remembers how stifled she felt working 9 to 5. 'I wasn't going to live the
rest of my life like that.' Full-scale mountaineering is one of the most
dangerous sports in the world and one increasing numbers of
women are choosing to do, partly inspired by the success of climbers
such as Destivelle. But in the same way that the role of women in the
armed forces has sparked debate, women taking risks in the mountains is proving controversial. The death of Alison Hargreaves in
1995 on K2, the world's second-highest mountain, provoked great

245

sympathy for her two young children and a feeling that it is somehow immoral for mothers to take risks.

Destivelle has a five-month-old son and confesses her motivation
for hard climbing has, for the time being, gone. 'I want to be at home
with Victor,' she says, 'but I won't criticise anyone who feels differ-
ently. I couldn't do what Alison Hargreaves did, but it was her choice.'
And what if her son wants to climb? 'We'll see. I don't want him to
take big risks. If he wants to climb, I'll make sure he's disciplined
about safety.' Someone who understands Destivelle's dilemma is Pam
Caswell, a 43-year-old science teaching adviser and mother of three.
In 1994, she was climbing in the Alps with Steve, her second husband,
and her son Simon when the snow she was walking across collapsed
and the three fell into a deep crevasse. Steve died from his injuries,
while Simon and his mother were finally rescued almost two days later.

Caswell was a few weeks pregnant at the time and she and Steve
were looking forward to having their first child together. Despite
now having a young baby she called Steven in memory of his dead
father, she hasn't stopped climbing.

When she left her child with Steve's parents to go climbing in
Peru last year, however, she hadn't anticipated the reaction her holiday would provoke in the media. After her local paper ran a story
about her plans, the national press returned to the tragedy she had
endured, to the distress of Steve's parents.

The *Times* columnist Nigella Lawson, who had condemned
Alison Hargreaves for 'me-first mountaineering', rounded on all
parents who take risks for 'brutally ignoring' their families. 'I just
don't understand people,' she continued. 'How could anyone, of
whatever sex, be so cruel, so aggressive?' While she made it plain that
she considered fathers who climb just as bad, her article was
prompted by a woman's actions and Destivelle believes that, had
Caswell been a man, Lawson's column and other articles condemn-
ing her wouldn't have been written.

Caswell herself is bewildered by such criticism. 'A lot of fathers do
climbs that are far more risky than anything I would contemplate,'

she says. 'But these choices are for individuals to make. I don't take as many risks as I did before the accident because of Steven. I am aware of my family, but I like climbing.' Her attitude is supported by Celia Bull, organiser of the international women's climbing festival held in Wales last weekend.

'I don't think there's a right way or a wrong way on this issue,' Bull says. 'Individuals have to make these decisions for themselves. Parents who are fulfilled in what they do are often better parents.' Catherine Destivelle did not attend the festival. 'Why have a women's meeting?' she says. 'What's the point? I think we should talk about all climbers, not just women.'

Ed Douglas

Mallory's mountain: Scaling Everest because it's there

❄ MAY 4 1999 ❄

Perhaps it's because mountaineering these days is so technically refined – technologically over-determined some might say, with its cell phones, satellite positioning and reliable air supplies – that the discovery of George Mallory's corpse 27,000ft up Everest has attracted such fascinated attention. Some 29 years before the ascent by Edmund Hillary and Tenzing Norgay, Mallory and Andrew Irvine set out for the top of the world. They were desperately ill-equipped by today's standards. If the Americans who discovered the body do go on to find written or photographic evidence that the two made it to the summit, it will be a triumph for the era of tweeds and hobnailed boots.

Pessimists might say the world is running out of this sort of challenge. Nowadays it's much more difficult to be unquestionably the first to conquer a physical barrier, mountain or sporting record; so capturing unalloyed and lasting fame becomes more difficult, too. Some might add there's something macho, overgrown, laddish about this kind of will to dominate – which could be why there are so few women mountaineers. Yet there's nobility of purpose here too.

Mallory acquired a kind of existence after death thanks to his bon mot about the reason for wanting to climb the peak in the first place. 'Because it's there' remains the best explanation, not just for climbing. It's the doggedness of just wanting to find out, to get to the top or the bottom for the sake of curiosity. British amateurism has a lot to answer for in industry and commerce but there remains something wonderful about the spirit of play that carries people into contests where there is no material reward, no point but the thing itself. The survival of George Mallory's physical remains, thanks to the cold, is an extraordinary breach in the fabric of time, a reminder of the constancy of heroic endeavour, come what may.

Leader

Irvine and Mallory

❄ MAY 4 1999 ❄

The frozen corpse of the English mountaineer George Mallory has been found on Mount Everest, almost 75 years after his attempt to conquer the mountain ended in tragedy.

The long-awaited discovery of the body – tweed coat and hobnail boots intact – could help to resolve a persistent uncertainty over who made it first to the summit of the world's highest mountain.

Mallory and Andrew Irvine disappeared on June 8 1924 and no one has ever established if they perished on the ascent or as they struggled to make their way down.

The discovery of the body brings the question of whether the pair managed to reach the summit 29 years before Sir Edmund Hillary and Tenzing Norgay conquered Everest in 1953 tantalisingly close to resolution.

The key to the mystery lies with a primitive Kodak camera, which Mallory was understood to be carrying. According to Kodak, the freezing conditions should have preserved the film and, if they made it to the top, the negatives could show the climbers at the summit.

The American Mallory and Irvine research expedition, who found the body on Saturday, have reported that the camera is still missing but they plan to continue their search until they find it, according to a report posted on their internet site, Mountainzone.com.

Mallory's son, John, now 80, had instructed the team to bury his father if they found him and the team laid the body to rest after they had conclusively identified him.

'My guess is they did make the summit, but probably not until very late in the day,' Mr Mallory told Radio 4's *The world at one*. 'Most people who don't make the summit until somewhere near sunset don't get down. To me the only way you achieve a summit is to come back alive; the job's half done if you don't get down again.'

News of the discovery was greeted with enthusiasm by Sir Edmund yesterday, despite its implications for his record-breaking claim. He said it would be 'very appropriate' if Mallory had reached the summit first, adding: 'He was really the initial pioneer of the whole idea of climbing Mount Everest.'

Sir Chris Bonington, the British mountaineer, said that whether they made it to the very summit or not, their achievement was 'absolutely huge … Their equipment was inadequate; their food was inadequate. It really was a fantastic feat,' he said.

Irvine, an Oxford undergraduate, and Mallory, a former teacher, are known to have made it to within 2,000ft of the top, but no one can prove whether they got any higher.

Eric Simonson, who is leading the expedition, was thrilled at the find. He said via the internet from Everest: 'This discovery is a huge achievement and beyond our wildest dreams … our job is not finished, however.'

The excitement would probably have left Mallory bemused. His approach to scaling mountains was phlegmatic; when asked why he wanted to climb Everest, he replied: 'Because it is there'.

Amelia Gentleman

Rock chick

❅ NOVEMBER 29 2002 ❅

Some people say Lynn Hill is one of the best female athletes in the world. Others merely that she is the best rock climber in the world.

Her skill is free climbing. That's climbing mountains using just her finger strength and balance, with no equipment to help her up. She has a rope to catch her if she falls (which in free climbing you do quite regularly) but other than that it's just her, dangling thousands of feet off perilously smooth walls of rock.

Back in 1993, Hill was the first person – male or female – to free-climb El Capitan, the 3,000ft 'nose' in Yosemite national park in California, considered unclimbable by most because of its steep, flat surfaces. Fellow climbers were slack-jawed, not least because the 41-year-old Californian is only 5ft tall and weighs 7st – a year later, however, she was back to do it again in just 23 hours, most of the time in darkness. Why?

'I wanted to do something that had meaning to me. I love being outside, I love natural rock, I love the whole experience. I chose the Nose route because it had never been done before, and it was one of the most beautiful things in the world that I had seen. When you see the valley, tears come to your eyes.'

Hill started climbing as a diminutive 14-year-old. Before that she had done a lot of gymnastics, but she hated the way 'the girls had to smile and do cutesy little routines on the floor. I had this reputation as this tomboy that rebelled against traditions anyway. I didn't like it, but I thought, if I'm different then I'll just be me and I'll do what I feel like doing. That gave me a certain freedom.'

Her sister Kathy's boyfriend, Chuck, was a keen climber and in 1975 he encouraged the Hill siblings to take up the sport. Kathy was never comfortable on the rocks but Lynn was a natural. The appeal lay in the freedom of climbing compared with the 'rigidity' of gymnastics. She also saw something rebellious in this unusual hobby.

Hill spent much of the 80s doing indoor and outdoor competition climbing, winning more than 30 international titles and enough cars and cash prizes to make climbing a lucrative career. With nothing left to prove, she spent the 90s challenging herself on bigger, riskier free climbs.

I ask her to show me her muscles and she pulls down her fleece, bends her elbow and makes her hand into a claw. Her forearm looks like a tennis ball is stuck under the skin. She looks older than her years, her face lined like a cliff face, weather-beaten and covered in cracks.

Her most distinctive feature, however, is her hands. She says they are less leathery than usual at present, and her fingers show a suggestion of nails and smooth skin, which she puts down to the fact that she has been doing more travelling than climbing of late. But the most striking thing is their tiny size.

'People said to me: "You were able to do the Nose because you have small fingers that fitted in the cracks." Well, OK, that's partly true. But think of all the other spots on that route where I had a more difficult time. I have much more difficult reaches, which is something taller people don't even realise they're doing. My message was the opposite of that: it was about adapting your body to the rock and looking for the solutions that work for you.'

Climbing is more like a chess game than like other adrenaline-fuelled, dangerous sports, she says.

But it is certainly more dangerous than chess. In 1989, while climbing at Buoux in France, Hill forgot to tie a knot in her safety rope and jumped backwards off a cliff completely unharnessed. She fell 72ft into a tree, which saved her life.

'The major lesson I took from it was to stop directing energy in the wrong way. On that occasion I was so busy looking at my partner's harness and not my own that I made a huge error. And when I stopped and thought about my life, I realised I was an accommodater, that I don't think first about whether something's good for me, when sometimes it's not. It's good to stand up for yourself, and women need to do that, too.'

But the fall neither put her off nor slowed her down. Today, she's four months pregnant and says she takes extra care on climbs – but still does them. Would having children earlier have made a difference to her career? 'I don't know if I would have done the Nose if I had a child,' she says. 'I wouldn't have had the time. I barely had the time to dedicate to a relationship. I was single when I trained for the Nose and I was very conscious that I was really just going to focus on this goal. I knew that when the time was right I would probably meet the right person, and then I could give myself to a child but only after I had done my best at that first.'

Many friends have died in the mountains ('a lot, I haven't counted'), including her original climbing mentor, Chuck, but Hill says the risks would never stop her.

'Everything you do is dangerous because we're all gonna die one day, right? One of my climbing friends died in a car accident. Another committed suicide. One got killed in an avalanche. Another froze to death on a mountain. Of course, it always makes you look at your own life. But you just hope it doesn't happen when you're young and that it's not a terrible death.'

Merope Mills

Obituary: Outstanding but publicity-shy young climber — Will Perrin

❄ SEPTEMBER 2 2004 ❄

Will Perrin, who has died aged 24, became one of the outstanding rock climbers of his generation without ever caring who outside his circle knew it. His great contributions came in his native Wales, particularly on the loose cliffs of the Lleyn peninsula and the slate quarries above Llanberis, where he earned a lasting reputation. He had a fluid, graceful style, more like dance than raw strength, and an intuitive understanding of the rock itself.

Lynn Hill, one of the greatest rock climbers of all time

Will was sometimes impish, had a wry, teasing smile and generous instincts. 'A bugger to know,' one friend told me, 'but everybody loved him.' He was six years old when I first met him, and he looked like an angel, albeit an angel who might call out the fire brigade because he liked seeing big red trucks. He was later branded delinquent at primary school after flicking a v-sign at a teacher.

His father, the writer and climber Jim Perrin, had been part of the mercurial and deeply anarchic climbing scene that existed in North Wales from the late 1960s until, more or less, the present. From a young age, Will found himself exposed to alternative ways of living and thinking. Even as a boy he found the promises of consumerist Britain dull, and set about exploring other options.

Given a pair of hiking boots by his dad, the young teenager took off for several days, walking the length of Snowdonia in a style that was more Patrick Leigh Fermor than Ramblers' Association. Wanting to impress a girl, and blushing at the mention of her name, he begged his dad to take him climbing. Anxious for his son's safety, Jim Perrin spent a year showing the 15-year-old around the magical other-world of Snowdonia's mountains and crags. By the end it was clear Will had a rare and special talent.

He usually attended Brynrefail school in the Gwynedd village of Llanrug, but they were not enamoured of each other. Instead, he spent his formative years with his friends roaming the world – from the small sandstone boulders at Fontainebleau to the oceans of granite in California's Yosemite Valley. Will disdained the sponsored puffery surrounding modern climbing and backed away from publicity. But he wanted the approval of his peers and earned it.

There were big risks in his chosen way of life, and not all of them were physical. Will could drop climbing for a while and pursue something else with equal intensity – he became deeply focused on yoga – before returning to it apparently as capable as ever. But somehow his feelings of dissatisfaction grew. Climbing was seductive but, as he entered his mid 20s, it was no longer enough.

Will earned cash as a roped-access worker and last winter he spent weeks in India on a docks construction project near Mumbai. He was deeply affected by the conditions his Indian co-workers endured. Soon afterwards he suffered a climbing accident that seemed minor but dropped him into a spiral of haphazard treatment and bouts of depression. Friends grew anxious for him, but Will was always fiercely independent and kept the core of himself apart. He wanted to mentally root out a place for himself in the world, but it became harder to see anywhere he might be content.

Committed to an expedition in Greenland, he drove his friends to the airport and told them he had decided not to join them. Then he returned to his house in North Wales and took his own life.

He is survived by his parents, Jim and Penny, and his extended family.

Will Perrin, climber, born May 5 1980 died July 26 2004

Ed Douglas

Obituary: Ray McHaffie

❄ JANUARY 5 2006 ❄

When Ray McHaffie, who has died aged 69, arrived in Keswick in 1965 from a Carlisle timber yard where he had worked for 14 years, he was the only employee with all his fingers and toes intact. They were to serve him well in his subsequent career as a rock climber and mountaineer, and as a builder of Lake District mountain paths.

His muscular frame, stoic disposition and 'eye for a line' (he had one eye, having lost the other in a teenage fight) brought him a total of 250 new climbs as recorded in the Fell & Rock Climbing Club's guidebook to Borrowdale. These included classic ascents of intimidating rock faces such as the Niche (with Adrian Liddell), the Coffin, Savage Messiah and the classic Lakeland Cragsman.

It was a regular sight to find 'Mac' studiously licking a stub of pencil as he entered details of this or that death-defying climb in the battered ledger that served as 'new routes' book in the Woolpack pub where Keswick 'crag rats' once congregated. One route on Shepherds Crag he even soloed in boxing gloves and roller skates for a wager.

Known for pithy utterances that earned him the sobriquet the Jaws of Borrowdale, his climbing achievements won wholehearted respect. This was mirrored in the acclamation for his conservation work.

'Ray McHaffie crafted footpaths that fit in with the landscape, using just the stones and rocks available, and turning them into what I believe are works of art,' Sir Chris Bonington said. When he retired in 1999 after 21 years as leader of the upland footpath repair team, McHaffie had been responsible for more than 100 miles of paved fells highway.

Born in Longtown, Cumbria, but brought up on the Raffles estate in Carlisle, McHaffie discovered climbing by taking a chance trip to Keswick on the fell walkers' bus. Although associated with Borrowdale, he also climbed the most recalcitrant faces, be it the Right Unconquerable on Stanage Edge or Kilnsey Crag Overhang in Wharfedale. Alpine ascents included the south face of the Marmolata and Vajolet Towers with his mentor, the spirit of the postwar Austrian climber Hermann Buhl (and pages torn from his autobiography).

Despite the onset of Parkinson's Disease, he continued to climb until a recent hip operation, happy to be among the climbers who meet at the cafe below Shepherds Crag, especially those finding a challenge in his routes – one sums up his achievement: Delight Maker.

He married Margaret Richardson in 1968 and is survived by her, two daughters and a son, also a climber.

Ray McHaffie, climber, born April 3 1936, died December 14 2005
Tony Greenbank

Mystery of Ben Nevis piano solved

❄ MAY 19 2006 ❄

The mystery surrounding a piano unearthed by litter pickers on Ben Nevis was solved yesterday when a Scots woodcutter revealed he had carried it up the mountain 35 years ago in aid of charity. Kenny Campbell, from Bonar Bridge, spent four days carting what was in fact a church organ to the 1,344m (4,408ft) summit near Fort William, mostly on his back. 'When I got there, I played *Scotland the brave*,' said Mr Campbell, who has also carried a beer barrel and a plough up the mountain. He plans another, so far unspecified, spectacular to mark his 65th birthday this year.

Martin Wainwright

A Country Diary: Orkney

❄ APRIL 7 2007 ❄

We walk across the moor from Rackwick with the sea soughing beneath. Beyond the cliff rim peers the upper section of the Old Man of Hoy. At 450ft, its Easter Island statue-shape is one of the great icons of British rock climbing. Even the easiest of the several ways up is graded extremely severe.

Some of my earliest memories are of my father showing me photographs he took when stationed here in the war. The sequence of events that led to my son's death began with a fall from one of its harder routes. I want to climb it on my 60th birthday, to honour them. So on a bright noon at the end of March, four of us scramble down steep slopes to its foot and rope up beneath the original route climbed by Baillie, Bonington and Patey in 1966.

For the next few hours we're immersed in the technicalities of jamming cracks, mantel shelves and overhangs. Fulmars peer at us with amiable interest. We feel grateful for being here before nesting, when their gambit of projectile-vomiting a stream of stinking, yellow, oily liquid can render your clothes evermore unwearable.

Ours is probably the first ascent this year. Every hand and foot hold is banked out with sandy mud washed down by winter rain and has to be excavated and cleaned as we climb, making our progress painstakingly slow.

A Stromness ferry passes toy-like below. The final 70ft block is riven right through. On the same latitude here as Cape Farewell in Greenland, we huddle briefly in a heathery hollow on top, our breath ghosting out, to shelter from an icy crystal wind, make phone calls to absent friends who declined invitations to the party, and prepare for the descent.

A bright moon near the full has risen. On the last 190ft abseil, hanging out in space spinning slowly on the slender thread of rope, it casts our shadows on the spire. Seals sing from the boulder beach beneath, serenading us up the cliff path, the Old Man withdrawing again into silvered, totemic mystery.

Jim Perrin

REFERENCES

Angell, Shirley *The Pinnacle Club* (Pinnacle Club, 1988)

Ayerst, David *Guardian: Biography of a newspaper* (Collins, 1971)

Baker, EA *Moors, Crags and Caves of the High Peak and the Neighbourhood* (Heywood, 1903)

Byne, Eric and Sutton, Graham *High Peak* (Secker & Warburg, 1966)

Elton, Oliver *CE Montague: A memoir* (Chatto & Windus, 1929)

Griffin, A Harry *The Coniston Tigers* (Sigma, 2000)

Hetherington, Alastair *Guardian Years* (Chatto & Windus, 1981)

Macfarlane, Robert *Mountains of the Mind* (Granta, 2003)

Montague, CE *Fiery Particles* (Chatto & Windus, 1923)

Monkhouse, Patrick *On Foot in North Wales and The Peak* (Diadem, 1988)

Monkhouse, Patrick 'Mountaineering and the Press' (Rucksack Club Journal, Vol.vii, no.3, 1933)

Morris, Jan *Conundrum* (Faber & Faber, 1974)

Perrin, Jim *The Villain: The life of Don Whillans* (Hutchinson, 2005)

Taylor, Geoffrey *Changing Faces: A history of the Guardian, 1956–88* (Fourth Estate, 1993)

Unsworth, Walt *Encyclopedia of Mountaineering* (Penguin, 1977)

Wainwright, Martin (ed) *A Lifetime of Mountains: The best of A Harry Griffin's Country Diary* (Aurum/Guardian, 2005)

Wainwright, Martin (ed) *A Gleaming Landscape: A hundred years of the Guardian's Country Diary* (Aurum/Guardian, 2006)

Wells, Colin *A Brief History of British Mountaineering* (The Mountain Heritage Trust, 2001)

Westaway, JH 'Fair-play Among Holiday Makers': CE Montague's editorial representations of mountaineering tourism in the Manchester Guardian, 1890–1925 (unpublished paper, University of Central Lancashire, Preston, 2003)

Wilson, Ken (ed) *The Games Climbers Play* (Diadem, 1978)

LIST OF CHAPTER ILLUSTRATIONS

INDEX